OXFORD HISTORICAL MONOGRAPHS

THE RE-ESTABLISHMENT OF THE CHURCH OF ENGLAND 1660–1663

by
I. M. GREEN

OXFORD UNIVERSITY PRESS
1978

Oxford University Press, Walton Street, Oxford OX2 6DP

OXFORD LONDON GLASGOW NEW YORK
TORONTO MELBOURNE WELLINGTON CAPE TOWN
IBADAN NAIROBI DAR ES SALAAM LUSAKA ADDIS ABABA
KUALA LUMPUR SINGAPORE JAKARTA HONG KONG TOKYO
DELHI BOMBAY CALCUTTA MADRAS KARACHI

British Library Cataloguing in Publication Data
Green, I.M.
The re-establishment of the Church of England, 1660-1663.—(Oxford historical monographs).
1. Church of England—History
I. Title II. Series
283'.42 BX5085

ISBN 0-19-821867-2

Phototypeset by Malvern Typesetting Services
Printed in Great Britain by
Billing & Sons Ltd, Guildford & Worcester

PREFACE

The thesis from which this book derives has been modified in a number of ways for publication. Two chapters have been added (the first and the last) and some of the supporting detail in chapter V and two of the longer appendices (listing the clergy discussed in chapter VIII) have had to be omitted. It is hoped that the new sections will compensate for the occasional footnote referring the reader to the original thesis (deposited in the Bodleian Library, Oxford).

As anyone who has heard him talk about the Restoration church will appreciate, my greatest debt is to my supervisor, Dr. G. V. Bennett. I am deeply grateful to him for his patient guidance and helpful criticism over a number of years. I should like to thank Dr. R. A. Beddard, Dr. A. Whiteman, Dr. D. M. Barratt, and Dr. G. F. Nuttall for the suggestions and information they offered at various stages, and librarians and archivists in Oxford, London, Winchester, Canterbury, Maidstone, York, and Belfast for many kindnesses. I should also like to thank Professor H. R. Trevor-Roper for his generous expenditure of time and effort in guiding this book through to publication. Finally, I must pay tribute to the patience of my wife in tolerating the intrusions of the 'merry monarch', his not so merry first minister, and hundreds of distinctly solemn clergymen for so long.

The Queen's University of Belfast
August 1977

CONTENTS

ABBREVIATIONS, SHORT TITLES, AND LOCATION OF MANUSCRIPTS

Abernathy, 'English Presbyterians'	G. R. Abernathy, 'English Presbyterians and the Stuart Restoration 1648–1663', *Transactions of the American Philosophical Society*, 55, pt. 2 (Philadelphia, 1965)
Addit. MSS.	Additional MSS., British Library
Alum. Cant.	*Alumni Cantabrigienses, Part 1 From the Earliest Times to 1751*, ed. J. and J. A. Venn (Cambridge, 4 vols., 1922–7)
Alum. Oxon.	*Alumni Oxonienses, Early Series 1500–1714*, ed. J. Foster (Oxford, 4 vols., 1891–2)
Barwick	P. Barwick, *The Life of the Rev. Dr. John Barwick* (London, 1724)
Bosher	R. S. Bosher, *The Making of the Restoration Settlement The Influence of the Laudians 1649–1662* (London, 1951)
Burnet	*Burnet's History of my own Time*, ed. O. Airy (Oxford, 2 vols., 1897, 1900)
Calamy, *Account*	E. Calamy, *An Account of the Ministers . . . who were Ejected . . . By, or before, the Act for Uniformity* (London, 1713)
Calamy, *Continuation*	E. Calamy, *A Continuation of the Account* (London, 2 vols., 1727)
Cal. Rev.	A. G. Matthews, *Calamy Revised* (Oxford, 1934)
Cal. St. Pap. Dom.	*Calendar of State Papers, Domestic Series*
Cant. Cath. Chap. Arch.	Canterbury Cathedral Chapter Archives
Carte MSS.	Bodleian Library, Oxford
Clarendon, *Life*	Clarendon, Edward Hyde, Earl of, *The Life of Edward Earl of Clarendon Containing I. An Account of the Chancellor's Life . . . to the Restoration in 1660 II. A Continuation of the same . . . to his banishment in 1667* (Oxford, 3 vols., 1759)

Clarendon MSS	Bodleian Library, Oxford
The Diary of Ralph Josselin	*The Diary of the Rev. Ralph Josselin,* ed. E. Hockliffe, Camden Society, 3rd series, xv (1908)
The Diary of Samuel Pepys	ed. R. Latham and W. Matthews (London, 8 vols., 1970–4)
'Diary of Seymour Bowman'	'Diary of the Proceedings of the House of Commons 18th June to 18th August, 1660', Bodleian Deposit f.9
Dict. Nat. Biog.	*Dictionary of National Biography*, ed. L. Stephen and S. Lee (London, 21 vols., 1908–9)
Duppa-Isham Correspondence	*The Correspondence of Bishop Brian Duppa and Sir Justinian Isham*, ed. Gyles Isham (Northants. Record Society Publications, xvii, 1955)
Egerton MSS.	British Library
English Historical Documents 1660–1714	ed. A. Browning (London, 1953)
46th Report	*The Forty-sixth Annual Report of the Deputy Keeper of the Public Records* (London, 1885), Appendix 1.
Hants Recd. Off.	Hampshire Record Office, Winchester
Harleian MSS.	British Library
Hasted	E. Hasted, *A History and Topographical Survey of the County of Kent* (Canterbury, 4 vols., 1778–99)
Hist. MSS. Comm.	*Historical Manuscripts Commission*
J.C.	*Journals of the House of Commons*
J.L.	*Journals of the House of Lords*
Kennett, *Register*	W. Kennett, *A Register and Chronicle Ecclesiastical and Civil* (London, 1728)
Kent Recd. Off.	Kent Record Office, Maidstone
Lambeth MSS.	Lambeth Palace Library, London
Lamb. Pal. Lib.	Lambeth Palace Library, London
Le Neve, *Fasti*	*Fasti Ecclesiae Anglicanae*, ed. J. Le Neve and T. D. Hardy (Oxford 3 vols., 1854)
Lib. Inst.	*Liber Institutionum*, Public Record Office, London

'Process of Re-establishment'	I. M. Green, 'The Process of the Re-establishment of the Church of England 1660–63' (Oxford D. Phil. thesis, 1973)
Rel. Baxt.	*Reliquiae Baxterianae: or Mr. Richard Baxter's Narrative of his Life and Times*, ed. M. Sylvester (London, 1696)
S.P.	State Papers, Public Record Office, London
Statutes	*Statutes of the Realm*
Tanner MSS.	Bodleian Library, Oxford
Till, 'Ecclesiastical Courts of York'	B. D. Till, 'The Administrative System of the Ecclesiastical Courts in the Diocese and Province of York. Part III. 1660–1883. A Study in Decline' (typescript in University of York, Borthwick Institute of Historical Research, 1963)
Traffles's 'Abstracte'	'An abstracte of the Accompts of the Cathedral church of Winton since . . . 1660', Winchester Cathedral Library
Tudor and Stuart Proclamations	cal. R. R. Steele (Oxford, 2 vols., 1910)
Walk. Rev.	A. G. Matthews, *Walker Revised* (Oxford, 1948)
Whiteman, 'The Episcopate of Seth Ward'	A. O. Whiteman, 'The Episcopate of Dr. Seth Ward, Bishop of Exeter (1662 to 1667) and Salisbury (1667 to 1688/9) with Special Reference to the Ecclesiastical Problems of his time' (Oxford D. Phil. thesis, 1951)
Whiteman, 'Re-establishment'	A. O. Whiteman, 'The Re-establishment of the Church of England, 1660–1663', *Trans. Roy. Hist. Soc.*, 5th ser., v (1955)
Whiteman, 'Restoration'	A. O. Whiteman, 'The Restoration of the Church of England', in *From Uniformity to Unity*, ed. G. F. Nuttall and O. Chadwick (London, 1962)
Winch. Cath. Lib.	Winchester Cathedral Library
Wodrow	R. Wodrow, *History of the Sufferings of the Church of Scotland from the Restoration to the Revolution* (Edinburgh, 2 vols., 1721–2)
Z. 26, Z. 27	Registers Z.26 (1660–61), Z.27 (1661–67), Canterbury Cathedral Chapter Archives

INTRODUCTION

Richard Baxter and the earl of Clarendon did not have a great deal in common; as lord chancellor, Clarendon presided over the passage and enforcement of that 'code' of laws which drove Baxter from the church and persecuted him for years. Historians have therefore been impressed by the close similarity between their accounts of the Restoration church settlement. In their autobiographies, both men implied that despite some early concessions to the Puritans, Charles and his ministers had aimed at a strict episcopalian settlement on traditional lines from the very outset.

Although this notion has been adopted in most subsequent accounts of the period, it does not stand up to very close examination. In the first place, it is contradicted by the behaviour of Baxter and Clarendon themselves in the early 1660s. Both of them then played a leading part in the attempt to bring about a moderate church settlement, Baxter as one of the leading divines of his day, and Clarendon as an experienced minister acting under orders from the king. It was only years later in the mood of bitterness engendered by persecution that Baxter began to think that there had been a plot to restore the bishops to their former powers. He then wrote that the concessions offered to the Puritans in 1660–1 had been 'for a present use', a ploy to keep them quiet until the government was strong enough to reimpose the old orthodoxy. Similarly, it was only after several years of disgrace in exile that Clarendon wrote his autobiography. In this, he sought to vindicate himself in the eyes of his staunchest supporters, the zealous Anglicans, by belittling the events of 1660–1 and pretending that the government had been intent on severity all along.

The writings of these eminent contemporaries have diverted attention away from the fact that in the first twelve months after his return to England, Charles II did all that he could to bring about a compromise settlement of the church. During the summer of 1660 he nurtured the spirit of reconciliation which brought Protestants of different persuasions closer than they had been for decades, and in October of that year he issued a crucial declaration on ecclesiastical affairs which proposed that the church be governed by a form of limited episcopacy. The purpose of this study is to show how this policy evolved, how it was implemented, and how after some initial success it was defeated by a combination of unforeseen difficulties and deliberate obstruction. First of all, it analyses the reasons for Charles's decision to attempt a compromise solution, and describes some of the means by which he sought to impose it upon his subjects. It then shows how the attempt to introduce modified episcopacy at diocesan level was fatally delayed for a few months by the need to repair the damage done to the administration and finances of the old church during the Great Rebellion. By the spring and summer of 1661, when the leaders of the church were in a position to implement the most important provisions of the king's declaration, the forces of reaction had gathered pace. The hostility of the most powerful members of the laity to Charles's scheme is studied at two levels, in the counties where the gentry adopted a variety of means to demonstrate their desire for a church on traditional lines, and at Westminster where the members of the Cavalier Parliament managed to force a series of intolerant measures upon the king. It will be seen, however, that in some respects the impact of this legislation was limited, and that Charles's efforts were not wholly in vain.

I

THE EVOLUTION OF ROYAL POLICY

On the morning of 12 May 1660, the mayor and aldermen of Winchester solemnly proclaimed Charles Stuart King of England, Scotland, France, and Ireland. Dressed in their scarlet robes and accompanied by a guard of 400 men, they set off from the market cross, paused awhile in the cathedral to hear a sermon by a local incumbent, and then advanced to the specially erected stage in the High Street. There the proclamation acknowledging Charles as king was read out, and after a salute had been fired by the attendant musketeers and a suitable anthem sung by surviving members of the cathedral choir, 'money was liberally threwn about the streets from the Scaffold and Windows, with several Volleys of shot and acclamations of the people, of whom there was a numerous appearance from all parts adjacent. Bells rung all day, and Bonfires were light most part of the night.'[1]

'Bells, Bonfires and Shooting' characterized many of the other ceremonies held in mid May. In London, the proclamation was followed by deafening shouts of 'God save King Charles the Second', three rounds from the cannon in the Tower, and the distribution of money at the bonfires. The hectic celebrations went on for several days.[2] A few places devised some variant. At Cambridge, the soldiers fired their volleys from the roof of King's College; at Sherborne, Bradshaw and Cromwell were tried and executed in effigy; at Ripon, a multitude of young maids dressed in white and bearing garlands were crowned 'in honour of their Virgin-King'![3] Nor was the day of proclamation the only occasion for loyal rejoicing, for there were official days of public thanksgiving on 24 May and 28 June, and a few privately

[1] *Tudor and Stuart Proclamations*, i, no. 3188: *Mercurius Publicus* (1660) no. 21, 17-24 May, pp. 323-4.

[2] *Parliamentary Intelligencer* (1660), no. 20, 7-14 May, p. 307; Clarendon MS. 72, ff.209, 323.

[3] *Mercurius Publicus* (1660), no. 21, pp. 324, 325, 332.

inspired gatherings on 29 May—the king's birthday—which from 1661 became an annual holiday.[4]

These celebrations were not without a deeper significance. It would perhaps be unwise to attach too much importance to the noisy acclamations of the people, even to those deafening shouts heard in London. England was experiencing one of its periodic cycles of dwindling harvests, and the price of bread was approaching its highest point ever.[5] When it is remembered that there was also a trade depression and consequently higher unemployment, it is hardly surprising that many artisans and labourers expressed such joy at the prospect of receiving large doles from dignitaries or from wealthy congregations who had been exhorted by their preachers to give generously.[6]

Of greater significance than the reaction of the people was the behaviour of the gentry and the clergy on these occasions. The county gentry were usually well represented at these essentially civic proclamation ceremonies, for example at Canterbury, Newport on the Isle of Wight, Sherborne, Warwick, and Southwark.[7] Not only did they attend in large numbers to show their active support for the new king, but they often appeared in military guise as well, as at Exeter where many of the Devon gentry 'for the more honor of so happy a work were pleased to traile a Pike to express their great and loyal affections'.[8] Such actions were more than symbolic gestures, for it is evident from the state papers and newspapers of the time that many of the gentry were very anxious to join the militia, in order to provide the king with an alternative force should the army or some other group of malcontents attempt to hinder his re-establishment.[9] Perhaps

[4] *Tudor and Stuart Proclamations,* i, nos. 3222, 3305; R. Feltwell, *Davids Recognition* (London, 1660); S. Brunsell, *Solomons Blessed Land* (London, 1660); W. Towers, *A Thanksgiving Sermon* (London, 1660).

[5] W. G. Hoskins, 'Harvest Fluctuations and English Economic History 1620–1759', *Agricultural History Review,* xvi (1968), 15–31.

[6] W. R. Scott, *The Constitution and Finance of English Joint-Stock Companies to 1720* (Cambridge, 3 vols., 1910–12), i, 259–62; *Parliamentary Intelligencer, loc. cit.*; *Mercurius Publicus* (1660), no. 21, p. 324; J.M., *Hosannah A Thanksgiving Sermon* (London, 1660), p. 32.

[7] *Parliamentary Intelligencer* (1660), no. 20, pp. 316–18; *Mercurius Publicus* (1660), no. 21, pp. 331–2, 322.

[8] *Parliamentary Intelligencer* (1660), no. 21, 14–21 May, p. 352.

[9] See below, chapter X.

the martial demonstrations on the days of thanksgiving provided an initial stimulus to this movement. These occasions may also have witnessed the framing of some of those loyal addresses and declarations of the nobility and gentry of various counties which were presented to the king in the early months of the Restoration. The earl of Winchelsea and many gentlemen of Kent were present both at the proclamation of the king at Canterbury in May and at the presentation of the Kentish address in June. The concourse of most of the gentry of Dorset for the proclamation at Sherborne in mid-May could well have provided the occasion for the drafting and signing of the address presented to the king in mid June; in it they urged a speedy return to the old order in church and state.[10]

By comparison, the behaviour of the clergy on the days of public thanksgiving was much more cautious. No instructions had been issued by Parliament on the form of service to be observed on these occasions, nor did the king issue any, so that the clergy who officiated at the proclamation or thanksgiving ceremonies were left very much to their own devices. It is true that one enterprising printer issued a suitable service for 28 June—pirated from the Book of Common Prayer and bearing the legend 'Set forth by Authority', but as it did not appear until the 27th of that month there was little time for ministers to be deluded into purchasing it.[11] The services probably consisted of extempore prayers, a sermon, and possibly a psalm, as at Northampton where the minister led the people in singing the eminently suitable twenty-first psalm immediately after the proclamation.[12] The use of the Book of Common Prayer, proscribed since 1644–5, was probably the exception rather than the rule. In only one place outside London do we hear of the Prayer Book being used in a thanksgiving service (at Lowestoft), and in London it was one of the most conservative elements in the country who insisted on its use—the House of Lords.[13] It should be remembered that

[10] *Parliamentary Intelligencer* (1660), no. 20, p. 318, and no. 26, 18–25 June, p. 416; *Mercurius Publicus* (1660), no. 21, pp. 322, 329–31; Brit. Lib. *669 f.25*, f.44.

[11] Thomason's date on the cover of *A Form of Prayer, with Thanksgiving*, Brit. Lib. *E. 1030* (9).

[12] *Parliamentary Intelligencer* (1660), no. 20, p. 320.

[13] *Mercurius Publicus* (1660), nos. 23, 31 May–7 June, p. 363, and 20, 10–17 May p. 310.

nearly all of the ministers who are known to have preached on these occasions had conformed to the religious practice of the Commonwealth—Complin in Hampshire, Barnes on the Isle of Wight, Bartholomew in Gloucestershire, and so on.[14] Furthermore, they were in most cases performing at the invitation of corporations nominated in Cromwellian times, which also militated against the use of the Prayer Book.

Over two dozen of the sermons preached on the proclamation or thanksgiving days have survived,[15] but while their authors yielded to none in their protestations of loyalty and their praise of the king's virtues, very few dared to touch upon the subject of the church settlement. Some urged the need to eject 'incorrigible Seducers and Blasphemers' from the clergy and to promote a pious, financially secure ministry,[16] but on the form of church government or the liturgy to be adopted they were much more reticent. Only two preachers—both of whom had suffered persecution in previous years—spoke openly of the need to restore bishops to the Church of England. Two others—who had also been harassed—slipped in a recommendation for episcopacy, one in the prayer at the end of his sermon, the other in the preface to the printed version of his sermon.[17] More representative of this body of sermons as a whole was that delivered in the Chapel Royal on 28 June by its new dean, Gilbert Sheldon. *Davids Deliverance and Thanksgiving* employs biblical rather than contemporary themes, is general in nature, and contains nothing controversial.

Some of these sermons were not only neutral but positively

[14] Complin had been rector of Avington since 1658, Barnes of Whippingham since 1650 at least; for Bartholomew, see *Walk. Rev.* p. 171. For their sermons see *Mercurius Publicus* (1660), no. 21, pp. 323, 331-2, 324.

[15] They are contained in the Thomason Collection, and can be traced in *Catalogue of Pamphlets . . . Collected by George Thomason, 1640-1661* (London, 2 vols., 1908), ii, 309-21. The authors are: J. Buck, J. Price, R. Baxter, R. Mossom, G. Ironside, W. Bartholomew, L. Womock, A. Short, C. Barksdale, W. Walwyn, F. Walsall, J. Douch, H. Jones, J. Warwell, R. Feltwell, S. Brunsell, W. Towers, A. Walker, T. Pierce, R. Eedes, G. Willington, G. Sheldon, T. Hodges, J. Whynnell, 'J.M.', W. Creed, S. Ford, E. Reynolds, J. Nelme.

[16] G. Willington, *The Thrice Welcome, and Happy Inauguration* (London, 1660), pp. 6-8.

[17] T. Pierce, *Englands Season for Reformation of Life* (London, 1660), pp. 15-16; W. Towers, op. cit. pp. 4, 10; C. Barksdale, *The Kings Return* (London, 1660); F. Walsall, *The Bowing the Heart of Subjects; Walk. Rev.* pp. 28, 285, 191-2, 67.

irenic in tone. Sheldon, for example, spoke of the need to 'strip ourselves of all unruly passions' in order that we should not be 'at enmity among our selves for trifles'.[18] The same sentiment was expressed by Simon Ford preaching at Northampton on the same day: the Presbyterians feared episcopacy and the Anglican liturgy, the episcopal party feared that its wings might be clipped or 'imped' with some feathers of Presbytery, while the Independents feared both the other parties. How much better it would be, he urges, if we would all help the king by 'abating voluntarily our mutual heights and heats'.[19] This mood is also caught in a pamphlet first published in May 1660 entitled *Eirenikon: or a Treatise of Peace between the two visible divided Parties*. The author was a minister calling himself Irenaus Philadelphus Philanthropus, perhaps the moderate conformist Robert Gell, rector of St. Mary Aldermary, London, from 1641 to 1665. It is for moderates to secure peace, he argues, for 'by such moderate men the Kingdom stands, and the Church also'. He raps the knuckles of both episcopalians and Presbyterians, the former for abusing their power in the past and for too great a reliance on the 'conceived prayers' in the Prayer Book, the latter for overturning the whole church in their efforts to reform it. The two sides must come together to fight 'the common enemy, even the Devil', and he offers practical advice on how to achieve such a reconciliation. One of his suggestions is that bishops should be restored, not the over-mighty prelates of the 1630s, but the overseers found in the primitive church. The Covenant, he points out to the Presbyterians, had not been aimed at the 'extirpation of Episcopacy itself', only at the removal of the 'tyrannical imperiousness and domineering of Bishops'. Even the Presbyterians, he adds, have a 'Yearly Moderator over the Presbyters'.[20]

These proposals were not original, for they owed much to the ideas expressed in the early 1640s by Archbishop Ussher in his *Reduction of Episcopacie unto the Form of Synodical Government Received in the Antient Church*. This had been

[18] *Davids Deliverance and Thanksgiving* (London, 1660), p. 47.

[19] S. Ford, *The Loyal Subjects Exultation* (London, 1660), pp. 45-6, 48.

[20] *Eirenikon* preface p. vii, pp. 98-9, 38, 54-60, 8-9, 13-18. For dating and authorship, see Kennett, *Register*, p. 170; cf. p. 267.

reprinted in 1656 and was to be reprinted again in June 1660 'to be considered by all . . . the Sons of Peace and Truth in the three Nations, for recovering the Peace of the Church'. The essence of the scheme was that bishops would exercise such powers as ordination and correction not from on high, but with the assistance of the senior parish clergy of their dioceses. Even before the king's return, many moderates had indicated their readiness to accept some form of modified episcopacy on the lines of Ussher's proposals, 'Primitive Episcopacy with Presbytery' as one of them termed it in a sermon preached before the lord mayor and aldermen of London in late February.[21] Moderate Presbyterians such as Reynolds and Baxter had probably come to support this form of episcopal government partly out of a genuine belief in its historical validity and in its suitability for the English church in 1660, and partly out of fear that intransigent support for a strict Presbyterian settlement might drive the king into restoring episcopacy to its former height. The scheme, however, also had support from the very beginning from moderate episcopalians such as Gauden and Gell who were alive to the faults of prelacy. Discussions on a settlement of church government began in April when George Morley was sent over to England by the exiled court to negotiate with the moderate Presbyterians, or 'Reconcilers' as Baxter once called them.[22] Discussions between episcopalians and moderate Presbyterians proceeded fitfully throughout the summer of 1660, and despite various alarms they were to bear fruit in the autumn.[23]

The path of reconciliation was not an easy one, for various obstacles stood in the way of a juncture of the moderates on the two sides. There was the problem of livings from which Royalist clergy had been sequestered in the 1640s or 1650s. Should these livings be restored to the ejected incumbents

[21] J. Gauden, *A Sermon Preached Before the Lord Mayor, Aldermen, etc. of London* (London, 1660), p. 79; see also p. 105.

[22] E. W. Kirby, 'The Reconcilers and the Restoration (1660–1662)' in *Essays in Modern English History in Honour of William Cortez Abbott* (Cambridge, Massachusetts, 1941), p. 49.

[23] The best account of the negotiations is in Abernathy, 'English Presbyterians', pp. 45–77.

where they were still alive and active, or should they remain in the hands of the ministers who held them at the Restoration? The episcopal party naturally supported the first solution, the Presbyterians insisted that only scandalous clergy had been removed and that it would be very wrong to reinstate them in their cures. Should those clergymen holding livings in 1660 who had never been ordained by a bishop be allowed to retain them, or should they receive episcopal re-ordination? The Presbyterians baulked at the suggestion that their own ordination was insufficient and had to be supplemented by episcopal re-ordination. What form of liturgy should be used—the Presbyterian Directory or the Anglican Prayer Book? The attachment of the one side to the forms contained in the Book of Common Prayer was as great as the aversion of the other to the many remnants of 'Popish' worship in that book. These and other difficulties represented deep-seated differences of opinion between the two sides, but there was at least some basis for agreement in the acceptance of the need for reconciliation and in the proposals for some form of modified episcopacy. This basis enabled the king to put pressure on both sides, so that in September and October the Presbyterians gave way on the problem of sequestered livings, the episcopal party did not insist on re-ordination, and the revision of the liturgy was deferred for a while.[24] One is left with the distinct impression that in the unprecedented circumstances of the summer and autumn of 1660 moderate episcopalians and moderate Presbyterians came closer to a rapprochement than at any time since their divergence in the middle decades of the reign of Elizabeth.

The prospect of a compromise settlement did not please everyone. There were those both to the right and the left of the moderates who scorned such a settlement. To the right there were the more extreme supporters of episcopacy who did not wish to see its powers reduced, and to the left the Independents and the covenanting Presbyterians who did not wish to see its re-appearance in any shape or form.

The first potential threat to a moderate solution came from the more zealous Cavaliers. It is noticeable that the first outspoken requests for the return of the old form of episcopacy

[24] See below chapter II.

are to be found in the declarations of the gentry presented to the king in June and July 1660. The nobility and gentry of Somerset expressed the hope that they would soon 'see once again the Church and State flourish, as in the days of your Royall Father and Grandfather'. Another address presented in June, by the gentry of Northamptonshire, suggested that one of the best means of securing the king's safety was the 'restitution of Religion, under the ancient apostolical Government by Bishops, according to the Undoubted Laws of this Kingdom' as asserted by the blessed martyr Charles I.[25] The nobility and gentry of North Wales delivered a rousing attack on those lately in power who 'under the pretence of propagating the Gospel, have for a long time shut up our Churches, converted the endowments of the Church to their own use, and sown the seeds of false Doctrine and Schism amongst us'. They felt it their duty to beseech the king to put into execution 'all those good and wholesome Laws' for the government of the church passed by Elizabeth and the first Stuarts.[26]

In addition to these statements from the gentry, there were one or two from zealous Anglican ministers who embarrassed the government by the warmth of their support for episcopacy. In March 1660, Matthew Griffith endangered the negotiations for the king's return by an intemperate attack on Presbyterianism; in late May, Thomas Pierce marked the king's return by a sermon in which he resurrected the controversial argument that episcopacy was of divine institution.[27] But either these men were not typical of the episcopalian ministry as a whole, at least not in England, or the most extreme Anglicans were too scattered or too old to organize a public expression of their opinion in 1660. If we examine the addresses presented by the clergy to the king in July and August, we find that they are much more prudent or ambiguous in their choice of words. Although the signatories include several sequestered clergy and many who had been ordained by bishops, not one of the addresses mentions

[25] Brit. Lib., *669 f.25*, ff.43, 49 (cf. also f.44).

[26] *Mercurius Publicus* (1660), no. 27, 28 June–5 July, pp. 417–18.

[27] M. Griffith, *Fear God and the King* (London, 1660); T. Pierce, op. cit.; Clarendon MS. 71, ff. 150–1, 156–7, 174, 233, 261–2.

episcopacy by name, or presumes to advise the king which laws affecting the church were then in force.[28]

The Cavalier gentry were much more explicit and vociferous, but in the summer of 1660 they were not yet in a position to exert much influence on the settlement of the church. They were riven by past quarrels dating from the failure of their plots against the usurpers, and they were vying with each other for preferment from the new king.[29] Those Cavaliers who issued 'cruel threats of revenge' were balanced by others—called 'Prudentialists' in one letter—who favoured moderate and healing counsels.[30] The likelihood of decisive intervention by the Cavaliers was further reduced by the irresponsible behaviour of many of them—their premature departure from the finely balanced House of Commons in the summer session of the Convention Parliament, and their prolonged carousals which were roundly condemned by churchmen of all standpoints.[31] Chancellor Hyde was particularly angry at the excessive drinking of toasts to the king, since he felt that the Cavaliers' negligence left the king exposed to the mercy of the army and the more militant Puritans.[32]

The submission of the Cromwellian army to the Restoration did not mean that it had suddenly become a strong supporter of the monarchy, let alone episcopacy. Nor did its ability to intervene in affairs of state disappear overnight, for the process of demobilization was not complete until early in 1661. It is perhaps true that this army was no longer the formidable weapon used by Cromwell in an attempt 'to invest religious aspirations with appropriate political forms'.[33] It is also true that two potential trouble-makers had been removed by the march of events or the march of General Monck—the ambitious but irresolute Fleetwood, and the restless, cynical Lambert. But the army still consisted for the most part of men

[28] Brit. Lib. *C. 112 h. 4*, ff. 37, 76; *669f. 25*, f. 76.

[29] D. Underdown, *Royalist Conspiracy in England 1649-60* (New Haven, 1960), chaps. 10, 13, 14.

[30] Carte MS. 213, f.683; cf. *Mercurius Publicus* (1660) no. 17, 19-26 April, p. 261.

[31] P.R.O., Transcripts 31/3/107, f.278; R. Mossom, *England's Gratulation for the King* (London, 1660); A. Walker, *God Save the King* (London, 1660).

[32] Clarendon, *Life*, ii, 18-22, 34-6.

[33] G. R. Cragg, 'The Collapse of Militant Puritanism', in *Essays in Modern English Church History*, ed. G. V. Bennett and J. D. Walsh (London, 1966), *passim*.

with Independent or Presbyterian views, and it was difficult to gauge the reactions of those officers and men outside Monck's immediate control to the apparent betrayal of the Good Old Cause and the godly reformation for which they had fought so long. The acquiescence of the lower ranks in the king's return seems to have been inspired by disillusionment with the factious and self-seeking behaviour of the officers and by a promise in the declaration from Breda that their arrears would be paid. There was no guarantee, however, that before their arrears were paid and their regiments disbanded they would not rise against some proposal which they deemed damaging to their interests—such as the confiscation of part of their Irish lands—or offensive to their principles—such as an end to religious toleration and the re-imposition of a state church and set liturgy.

In the spring of 1660 the army appeared to many observers to be in a volatile condition. Slingsby reported in early May that many soliders were grumbling and that some had been arrested for threatening to kill the king.[34] Morley confirmed that 'a mischievous and mallicious spirit' was still at work in the army of England.[35] From March to October, the king's friends in Ireland sent nervous reports on the unreliability of the garrisons there. In August a petition was circulating in the Irish army asking pointedly that the 'learned Orthodox and pious Ministers of the Gospell who have . . . borne the heate and burden of the day with us . . . may be continued and countenanced',[36] that is, guaranteed a place in the church when it was finally settled. Even after they had been demobilized, Cromwellian soldiers were regarded as a dissident element, and they were repeatedly ordered to leave the capital in a series of proclamations running from December 1660 to June 1670.[37] The hare-brained schemes of Thomas Venner and his Fifth Monarchist supporters for replacing King Charles by King Jesus were put down in January 1661, though not without some initial difficulty. But Venner's rising only increased the tendency of informers to

[34] Clarendon MS. 72, f.360 (and cf. ff.234, 387).

[35] Carte MS. 214, f.127.

[36] Carte MSS. 213, f.676; 31, ff.3, 22, 24; 44, f.230.

[37] *Tudor and Stuart Proclamations,* i, nos. 3270, 3296, 3339, 3362, 3397, 3403, 3425, 3533.

link plots with the suspicious movements of militant sectarians and ex-Roundhead troops.[38] With hindsight, it can be seen that the army was in fact disbanded peacefully, and that those with the most radical religious and political views—both in the army and in the civilian population—succumbed almost without a struggle to the re-imposition of many of the old forms in church and state. But this could not have been anticipated with any confidence, and in the first months after the Restoration the government was bound to avoid any move towards a religious settlement which might provoke opposition from an army which it would find difficult to resist.

The third and certainly the most serious challenge to a compromise church settlement came from the covenanting Presbyterians who had significant support in all three kingdoms and who were actively co-operating to achieve their goal—'the Extirpation of Prelacy' and the firm establishment of 'Presbytery, the Ordinance of Jesus Christ' throughout the British Isles. In the early months of 1660, Presbyterians of various hues had established links which were designed to secure the king's return 'not . . . upon any Terms, but upon the Terms of the League and Covenant' by which he had bound himself in 1650.[39] In February, the Scottish Presbyterians sent an emissary to their brethren in London, on the assumption that 'Whatever Kirk-government be settled there it will have an influence upon this Kingdom'. Their choice of emissary, James Sharp, was to prove an unfortunate one, but the volume of correspondence which passed between Sharp in London and Douglas and other Presbyterian leaders in Edinburgh illustrates vividly how closely events in the south were followed in Scotland.[40] In early March, the Presbyterian ministers of Ulster wrote to their brethren in Scotland seeking 'a close Correspondence' in concerting measures for the settlement of 'Religion and Liberty, and Uniformity in the Three Nations' on solid and righteous foundations.[41] Mutual encouragement was given in further letters which passed between Ulster and Scotland from March to May.[42] The Ulster

[38] B. S. Capp, *The Fifth Monarchy Men* (London, 1972), pp. 199–200.
[39] Wodrow, i, Introduction, liv, viii.
[40] Ibid., Introduction, *passim*.
[41] Ibid., xiv. [42] Ibid., xxii.

ministers were also in correspondence with their fellows in London, so that the triangle of communication was complete.[43] Letters and addresses were sent to the king urging their case, though some of these may have been modified or even seized before they were presented. One of the more moderate letters, from five leading Presbyterian ministers in Scotland, informed Charles that he need never repent of having taken the Covenant, and that they had no doubt that the church would be settled according to God's word in all his dominions.[44]

The nature of the Presbyterian campaign, however, gradually began to alter. The English Presbyterians had never supported the ideals of the Covenant as enthusiastically as had those of Scotland or Ulster, and by the spring of 1660 it was clear that many of the more moderate Presbyterians in England were moving towards a compromise solution. Led by Reynolds, Baxter, and other 'Reconcilers', they began to see the best solution to the particular problems of their country in some form of modified episcopacy. There still remained a hard core of English support for the Covenant, as is demonstrated by the activities and writings of such ministers as Zachary Crofton, John Gailhard, and Giles Firmin.[45] In early June, these men inspired a petition to the Common Council of London urging them to remind the king that he had taken the Covenant. Although the move failed, another petition was organized two months later.[46] Furthermore, in a series of pamphlets published in the summer of 1660, these ministers waged a war of propaganda against episcopacy and those moderate brethren who were deserting the cause.[47]

Scottish Presbyterianism was also riven, into the more numerous Resolutioners in the centre and south-east and the determined Protestors in the south-west. The conflict was not the same as that in England, however, for in Scotland even the

[43] Ibid., xlvii.

[44] Ibid., xxiv, lvi; J. S. Reid, *History of the Presbyterian Church in Ireland* (Belfast, 3 vols., 1867), ii, 249–50; G. Donaldson, *Scotland James V to James VII* (Edinburgh, 1965), p. 361.

[45] Abernathy, 'English Presbyterians', chapter 5, e.g. pp. 69, 73, 74.

[46] *Hist. MSS. Comm. 12th Report, Pt. vii* (London, 1890), 26, and *5th Report* (London, 1876), Appendix, 168.

[47] Abernathy, 'English Presbyterians', pp. 69, 73–4; Bosher, p. 120.

more moderate party—the Resolutioners—believed firmly in the Covenant. Douglas and the other Resolutioner leaders bombarded Sharp in London with advice, instructions, and questions on the campaign to further the cause of the Covenant in the spring and early summer of 1660. But whereas the Protestors (and their near neighbours in Ulster) maintained an intense and determined stand against any compromise on the principle of strict Presbyterian government in all three kingdoms, the morale of the Resolutioners was gradually sapped by the stream of misleading and pessimistic reports which Sharp sent back to them. At the behest of his mentor, the duke of Lauderdale, Sharp successfully drove a wedge between the more moderate English Presbyterians and the Scottish Resolutioners, by encouraging the former to negotiate with Morley, while pretending to the latter that he was doing all in his power in the uphill struggle to further the cause of the Covenant in the British Isles. His insidiously gloomy reports gradually took effect, and the Resolutioners began to abandon hope of the Covenant being adopted in all three kingdoms, though not as yet of its being confirmed in the Northern kingdom alone.[48]

Thus there remained a few in each kingdom who stayed faithful to the idea of establishing the Covenant throughout Charles's dominions—the Ulster Presbyterians, the Protestors, and the covenanting ministers in London. Although there is no clear evidence of liaison between these groups in the summer and autumn of 1660, there are several indications that at the very least the example of one gave encouragement to the others. Thus, in early June it was reported in the English press that in Scotland the Covenant was 'very much pressed in all parts' and that there were great hopes of enjoying former freedom.[49] Shortly afterwards we find the English covenanters pressing the Common Council of London to remind the king of his obligations.[50] Soon after this, the Scots, probably the Protestors, sent over to Ulster several of the declarations which Charles had made in Scotland in 1650–1.[51] In mid-August it

[48] Abernathy's explanation of Sharp's behaviour ('English Presbyterians', pp. 45–7, 65) is more convincing than the apologia of J. Willcock, 'Sharp and the Restoration Policy in Scotland', *Trans. Roy. Hist. Soc.*, new ser., xx (1906), 149–69.

[49] *Mercurius Publicus* (1660), no. 24, 7-14 June, p. 375.

[50] *Hist. MSS. Comm. 12th Report, Pt. vii*, 26.

[51] Carte MS. 31, f.3.

was known in London that 'Scotland absolutely refused to admit of an Episcopacy & that England begins to speake the same language for London is drawing up a Petition to resettle the honour of Presbitery'.[52] Shortly afterwards, the Ulster Presbyterians made a solemn agreement to defy episcopacy, and began to disparage the royal government; 'they talke of resisting unto bloud, & stirre up the people to sedition', reported an Irish bishop-elect.[53] The chancellor himself was evidently aware of the inter-action between these groups. At a Privy Council meeting in December, Clarendon scribbled a note to the king urging him to give more attention to the situation in Scotland: 'Do you know how these rogues in this Citty and kingdome depende upon troubles ther. Downinge writes me worde . . . that ther are great stores of Armes of all kindes and ammunicion sent lately into Scotlande from Roterdam'.[54]

In practice, therefore, the English church could not be settled in complete isolation from the Scottish or Irish churches, for every move that the king made in one country was bound to be regarded as a foretaste of their own settlement by his subjects in the other two kingdoms. This placed Charles on the horns of a dilemma, for the kingdoms were so dissimilar that an absolutely uniform settlement for all three was out of the question. In England, the Presbyterian party was in a position of considerable influence in Parliament and to a lesser extent the church, but the basis of its power in popular support and grandee influence was being rapidly eroded by the defection of many leading laymen, by internal divisions between 'Reconcilers' and covenanters, by the hostility of the sectarians in Parliament, and by the threat of a Cavalier revival.[55] In Scotland the dominant Presbyterian party was also split, and many of its former supporters, especially among the nobility, were turning towards change, either a politically emasculated kirk or some form of episcopacy. As early as March, Douglas was bemoaning the fact that the new generation in Scotland which had never

[52] Clarendon MS. 73, f. 182. [53] Carte MS. 45, ff.38, 44.

[54] *Notes which passed at meetings of the Privy Council between Charles II and the Earl of Clarendon 1660–1667*, ed. W. D. Macray (London, 1896), p. 17.

[55] Abernathy, 'English Presbyterians', *passim*.

known the work of reformation had a deep hatred for the Covenant, and were 'feeding themselves with the Fancy of Episcopacy, or moderate Episcopacy' which he roundly condemned.[56] The all-pervading Catholicism of Ireland was traditionally ignored in favour of the Protestant minority there, but the situation was complicated by the presence of no fewer than three well-established Protestant groups. There were the militant Ulster Presbyterians, the Cromwellian soldiers and missionaries of Independent views, and the surviving members of the episcopal Church of Ireland who were actively re-grouping and proclaiming that their church had never been legally disestablished.[57]

Whatever settlement Charles introduced was bound to displease many of his subjects, and the memory of the dire consequences of his father's attempt to impose a moderately uniform settlement on all his territories in the 1630s underlined the need for caution. Charles was also faced by sharp disagreements among his councillors, differences which mirrored the political and ecclesiastical complexity of the situation at the Restoration.

As was to be expected, the councillors whom Charles inherited from his father—Chancellor Hyde, Lord Steward Ormonde, and Secretary Nicholas—were reluctant to make concessions to the Puritans, and in this they were supported by some of the new councillors, for example Treasurer Southampton.[58] Theirs was not a blind faith, in the sense that they wished to see every aspect of Archbishop Laud's discipline revived; one can detect an erastian, even an anti-clerical note in the attitudes of chancellor and treasurer on occasions.[59] But there can be no doubt of their conviction of the need for the re-imposition of vigorous episcopal government in 1660.

There were also influential advocates of a conservative

[56] Wodrow, i, Introduction, xv, xx, xi.

[57] J. C. Beckett, *The Making of Modern Ireland* (London, 1966), pp. 112-15, 123-6; cf. Carte MSS. 30, f.685; 31, ff.3, 30, 49, 56, 58; 45, ff.38, 44; 221, f.141; and *Rawdon Papers*, ed. E. Berwick (London, 1819), pp. 126-7.

[58] E. R. Turner, *The Privy Council of England in the 17th and 18th Centuries* (Baltimore, 2 vols., 1927-8), i. 372, 375; for Hyde, see chapter X below; Ormonde see next paragraph; Nicholas see Bosher, pp. 109-10, 174, 181, 238; Southampton was probably more moderate than Hyde, but was clearly nearer to the church party than the party of toleration, see Burnet i, 306, 401, and Clarendon, *Life,* ii, 468-73.

[59] Ibid., ii, 183-7; Bosher, pp. 97-9, 107, 125-6; *Rel. Baxt.* Lib. III, Pt. III, para. 7.

church settlement among those councillors who advised the king on Irish and Scottish affairs. The duke of Ormonde held no official post in the government of Ireland in 1660, but his influence behind the scenes (for example, in the choice of new bishops and deans for the Church of Ireland) was considerable. Ormonde had already shown his reluctance to compromise the position of the episcopal Church of Ireland during the 1640s,[60] and his continued distaste for compromise can be seen in the remark, made in 1661 when Charles was hesitating over the restoration of episcopacy in Scotland, that it would be very difficult to maintain episcopacy in Ireland while Presbyterianism continued in Scotland.[61] Less predictable than Ormonde's stand was the way in which two of the three Puritans with effective power in Ireland in the opening months of 1660, Sir Charles Coote and Roger Boyle, Lord Broghill, rapidly forgot their former religious allegiance and became notable supporters of episcopacy. We find Coote complaining about the third member of the executive, William Bury, that he was 'a grate obstruction to the setling of the church here being a grate presbeterian'. Equally Boyle was soon writing to Hyde that he hoped that the measures taken against the Puritans in Ireland had convinced the chancellor that he was 'no longer half a Presbyter'.[62] From October 1660, these two were harassing the 'fanatics' in Ireland, and pressing London to expedite the consecrations and translations of the bishops in order that the discomfiture of the Puritan zealots should be complete.[63]

In Scotland also, some of the new councillors had changed their religious allegiance. Middleton and Lauderdale had both once been ardent covenanters, though long before 1660 they had come to regard the Covenant with the particular hatred of the apostate. At the Restoration, they were in agreement that the kirk must not be allowed to exercise the power it had enjoyed during the revolutionary decades, but by

[60] Carte MSS. 41, ff.14–46; 45, ff.21, 78; 30, f.685; *Rawdon Papers*, op. cit., pp. 114–16; T. Carte, *The Life of James Duke of Ormonde* (London, 2 vols., 1736), i (Book 4); ii, 207–8, 211.

[61] Burnet, i, 235.

[62] Carte MS. 31, ff.49, 56; Clarendon MS. 74, f.98.

[63] Carte MS. 31, ff.30, 59 (cf. f.58 and Carte MS. 45, f.44); Clarendon MS. 74, ff.52, 98.

September 1661 a rift had appeared in the Privy Council for Scotland. On one side, Middleton and a majority favoured a return to episcopacy, while on the other Lauderdale and an influential minority argued that the restoration of bishops could provoke a rising, and that a better solution would be a presbyterian church deprived of all political influence.[64]

In the English Privy Council alone, it seems, could a majority in favour of a compromise rather than a conservative church settlement be found. Most of the men sworn onto the Privy Council in May and June 1660 had been servants of Parliament or the Commonwealth, and moderate Presbyterian or Independent in religious outlook. But despite their political change of front, they had not shed their religious beliefs as lightly as some of their Irish and Scottish counterparts. In the early months of the Restoration, men such as Monck, Manchester, Annesley and Holles acted as 'Reconcilers' between episcopalian and Presbyterian, while one or two councillors such as Ashley Cooper and Northumberland probably favoured toleration.[65] A few weeks before the king's return, for instance, General Monck had declared himself in favour of moderate not rigid Presbyterian government, with liberty for truly tender consciences.[66] With other leading members of the Presbyterian laity, he had drifted away from the extreme, covenanting clergy, and by the spring of 1660 their policy was one of 'condescentions': 'to bring Episcopal men and presbyterians to such a condescention in things which are not absolutely necessary, as that ther might be no iarrings, but all agree for publicke good and peace'.[67] Monck was also instrumental in introducing Sharp to the English Presbyterians with the results that have already been described. As the newly chosen lord chamberlain, Manchester arranged the appointment of several Presbyterian royal chaplains, and supervised their first ministrations in the royal chapel. Annesley acted in the Commons to calm the passions of religious debate on more than one occasion.[68] Manchester, Annesley, and Holles also

[64] Burnet i, 233-5; Clarendon, *Life*, ii, 101-7.

[65] Abernathy, 'English Presbyterians', *passim* and articles in *Dict. Nat. Biog.*

[66] Wodrow, i. Introduction, vii.

[67] Carte MS. 214, f.155.

[68] *Rel. Baxt.*, Lib. I, Pt. II, para. 88; Abernathy, 'English Presbyterians', p. 68; below chapters II, X.

helped to promote the negotiations between Presbyterians and episcopalians which took place in the summer of 1660. The fruit of these discussions was the royal declaration on ecclesiastical affairs of 25 October, usually known as the Worcester House declaration after the venue of the last debates. This declaration was a triumph for those 'Reconcilers' in the Privy Council and the moderate clergy who advocated mutual concessions, for it stated that bishops were to be advised and assisted by the 'most learned and pious presbyters of the diocese' in the exercise of certain episcopal functions, while other matters still in dispute were left to the discretion of the individual incumbent or to a future conference of 'an equal number of learned divines of both persuasions'.[69]

There is a revealing example of the part played by the moderate privy councillors in the genesis of this declaration. After the public debate at the penultimate meeting, a small group of six was named to settle one or two outstanding points at a final meeting. The six consisted of two Presbyterian divines, Reynolds and Calamy, two moderate episcopalians, Morley and Henchman, and two lay assessors, Holles and Annesley. This conclave clearly inserted some extra concessions to Presbyterian demands into the final declaration, for Baxter, who had been present at the penultimate meeting, was pleasantly surprised when he read the finished article.[70] The choice of two 'Reconcilers' to act as the only lay assessors at this meeting suggests that the king intended that the outstanding points of grievance should be decided in the Puritans' favour; Anglican Councillors who might have protested at this were excluded from the meeting. For no matter how much Hyde and the other ex-Royalists might disapprove, Charles was bound to listen to the views of the former Presbyterians, who constituted a powerful and sizable section of his English council.

What effect did the advice tendered by leading churchmen have upon the king? By contrast to that of his councillors, it

[69] Abernathy, 'English Presbyterians', pp. 45–77; *Rel. Baxt.*, Lib. I, Pt. II, paras. 105–11; *English Historical Documents 1660–1714*, pp. 365–70.

[70] *Rel. Baxt.*, Lib. 1, Pt. II, para. 121; T. H. Lister, *Life and Administration of Edward, First Earl of Clarendon* (London, 3 vols., 1838), iii, 110–11.

probably had none at all. An exception might be made for Sharp, who in early May spent an hour and a half closeted with the king alone; but Sharp's function was that of a politician rather than a theologian. A few English Presbyterians became royal chaplains and preached before the king, but none seems to have exerted direct influence over him. Edward Reynolds possibly came closest, through his friendship with Manchester and through his gentle but firm advocacy of limited episcopacy. Not surprisingly, Reynolds was the first Presbyterian to be offered a bishopric.[71] As for the episcopal clergy, none were close to the king in 1660. The surviving bishops were out of favour: on his return to London on 29 May, Charles failed to attend a service held by four of the old bishops in Westminster Abbey for him, and when he received a delegation of them in early June the audience was held publicly and the bishops were warned that the king throught it 'fit he should be advised by his Parliament' in the settlement of the church.[72] Nor is it likely that any of the younger episcopalian clergy had the king's ear. The new dean of the chapel royal, Gilbert Sheldon, was a stranger to Charles, and to judge from his thanksgiving sermon in June, Sheldon was moving cautiously until he knew the king's mind better. Sheldon was not prominent in the negotiations with the Presbyterians, or in any other capacity as far as can be seen. Some of the episcopal clergy who had gone into exile were better known to the king, John Earle and George Morley for instance; but it is doubtful whether Charles came under pressure from these men to favour a strict episcopal settlement, for both were relatively moderate. Earle had been Charles's personal chaplain during the Interregnum, but he was a mild man, averse to persecution, and very loath to become a bishop.[73] Morley had served the Hyde family in exile, and in 1660 at least may be regarded as a moderate churchman. Earlier in his career, he had been accounted a Calvinist, and had fallen foul of Archbishop Laud and other leading churchmen of the day for a *bon mot* at their expense:

[71] *Dict. Nat. Biog.*; Abernathy, 'English Presbyterians', pp. 62-4, 74-6; below chapter IV.

[72] Bosher, pp. 143-4, 150.

[73] Clarendon, *Life*, i, 51-2; *Dict. Nat. Biog.*; and chapter IV below.

when asked by a visitor what the Arminians held, Morley had replied 'all the best Bishopricks and Deaneries in England'.[74] There is a slight suspicion about his integrity in 1660; his letters to Hyde during the exploratory mission in the spring suggest a somewhat cynical campaign to lull the Presbyterians into a false sense of security, but on the other hand his behaviour during the autumn indicates a definite commitment to moderate episcopacy. We find Morley welcoming the offers of bishoprics to leading Presbyterians, acting as one of the episcopal representatives at the final conclave on the Worcester House declaration, and then writing off to Scotland to express his satisfaction with the final product and his belief that it would form the basis for a peaceful settlement of the church.[75] Although Sheldon, Earle, and Morley were regularly at court in their capacities as royal chaplains, it is unlikely that their advice carried much weight in matters of major importance, such as the selection of new bishops, a part of the royal prerogative which was too valuable to be delegated. There is clear evidence that the three of them were asked to approve the appointments of a few dozen cathedral and parish clergy, but they acted in a purely advisory capacity and never had cognisance of more than a very small proportion of royal ecclesiastical appointments.[76]

It has been suggested by Dr. Bosher in his *Making of the Restoration Settlement* that the chief architects of the church settlement were the Anglican clergymen of what he calls the 'Laudian' party. He suggests that there was a pre-arranged 'Laudian' strategy to restore the episcopal church to its former state, and that both Charles and Hyde were parties to this plan. Despite the necessity for one or two diversions from their intended path, the 'Laudians' were soon in such a strong position that they had virtually completed the re-establishment of the Church of England 'in all essentials' by May 1661.[77]

There are various difficulties in accepting this thesis. The term 'Laudian' is anachronistic in that it is reminiscent of the

[74] Clarendon, *Life*, i, 49-51; *Dict. Nat. Biog.*
[75] Bosher, pp. 113-14, 126-7, 134-5, 138-9, and chapters IV and X below.
[76] Chapters II to IV below.
[77] Bosher, pp. 278-82 and *passim*.

policies of Laud, some of which were quite impracticable in 1660 after fifteen years of Puritan supremacy. One or two of Laud's devices—the vigorous use of the Court of High Commission, for instance—were condemned even by the bishops' greatest allies in the Cavalier House of Commons. It is also difficult to identify the 'Laudian' clergy. Dr. Bosher calls them 'High Churchmen who shared the religious viewpoint of Laud', but weakens his own definition by applying it to men of more moderate opinions as well.[78] The term is applied to men who had fallen into disfavour under Laud and to the moderate bishops appointed in the early 1640s in an effort to assuage Puritan feeling; it is even applied to clergymen who had conformed during the Interregnum. Thus the term is stretched to cover churchmen as diverse as Wren (after Laud the most hated man in England in 1640), Frewen (described by his opponents as 'peaceable'), Cosin (a disciplinarian who succeeded in combining High- and Low-Church elements in his theology), Sanderson (whose sermons were admired by the Puritans), and Gauden (the Commonwealth conformist and self-appointed mediator at the Restoration).[79] One or two ministers labelled 'Laudian' in 1660 were not notably High-Church until later, after the religious legislation of the Cavalier Parliament had brought about a great change in atmosphere. Sheldon did not emerge clearly as an Anglican stalwart until the occasion in August 1662 when single-handed he thwarted the king's attempt to suspend the Act of Uniformity passed a few weeks earlier. Nor was Morley consistently in favour of an exclusively Anglican settlement until that Act had been finally passed. In March and April of the same year, Sheldon, Morley, and other bishops supported the royal provisos designed to obtain a measure of indulgence for nonconformists.[80]

It is equally difficult to detect the existence of a 'Laudian' programme or 'Laudian' activity after the Restoration.

[78] Ibid., p. xv; Bosher's list of about 150 exiled clergy (pp. 284–94) is of little value, since only a very small minority were actively engaged in ecclesiastical matters; the rest travelled, studied, and a few were converted to Catholicism. Of the active minority, very few received major offices in the early 1660s, though by the 1670s others had received a deanery or an Irish bishopric.

[79] These points are developed in chapter IV below.

[80] Abernathy, 'English Presbyterians', pp. 83, 85–6; Clarendon MS. 77, ff.307, 340.

Beyond the natural desire of many sequestered clergy for a return to the old order, of what did the 'Laudian' strategy consist? There survives a certain amount of correspondence between Royalist clergy during the Interregnum,[81] but there is no sign of a blue-print for a restoration of the episcopal church stage by stage circulating among a distinct group of dedicated clergymen. If Henry Hammond had not died within sight of the Restoration, or if the correspondence of Gilbert Sheldon had survived, it might have been possible to reconstruct the hopes and membership of a 'Laudian' party in 1660, but this is now out of the question.

It is not denied that there was a minority of churchmen in 1660 who were unswerving supporters of the form of church government they had known in the 1630s, Bishop Duppa in his ultra-cautious fashion, Thomas Pierce and Matthew Griffith in their noisy way, Peter Heylyn in his own pragmatic fashion.[82] Perhaps the most significant of these men was John Cosin, the only one of Laud's protégés to emerge with credit from the Restoration period, and the only episcopalian to object to the terms of the Worcester House declaration on the grounds that it would 'Unbishop' the bishops.[83] But these men were neither numerous enough to affect the settlement at parish level nor sufficiently well organized at court to bring pressure to bear there. The signs of 'Laudian' activity described by Dr. Bosher do not stand up to close examination: the evidence for a reaction in the parishes which drove out many Puritan clergy has been overstrained; far from royal church patronage being handed over to the 'Laudians' for them to select 'orthodox' ministers, church patronage remained firmly in the king's hands and was used to promote a broadly based ministry; episcopal government was not functioning fully in May 1661 but was only beginning to return to normal late in 1662 or 1663.[84] It is manifest that at no stage was the king submissive to 'Laudian' advice or committed to a 'Laudian' strategy.

[81] Bosher, chapters 1 to 3.

[82] *Duppa-Isham Correspondence,* xxv–xxvii, 52, and Tanner MS. 49, f.17; for Pierce and Griffith see above; P. Heylyn, *Ecclesia Restaurata* (ed. J. C. Robertson, Cambridge, 1849), i, clxxviii–clxxxii.

[83] W. Bates, *Works* (London, 1723), p. 725.

[84] Below chapters II to IV on appointments, VI to VIII on administrative recovery.

[illegible] Charles's position? What did he himself feel [illegible] us differences of his subjects? During his [illegible] maturity, Charles had encountered sufficient [illegible] transform even his sanguine nature into a [illegible]. During the years in exile, he had had to [illegible] ngs of his divided court; there had been the [illegible] his stay in Scotland when he had been [illegible] s friends and his private conduct had been [illegible] his hopes had been alternatively raised and [illegible] er of occasions, by the Scots, the Spanish, [illegible] ts, and others. Not surprisingly he had [illegible] mbler, offering promises, resolutions, and [illegible] Pope, to the Irish Catholics, the Scots [illegible] the exiled Anglicans—which were often [illegible].[85]

[illegible] owever, that some of these assurances were [illegible] an others. There is little doubt as to the [illegible] Charles viewed his treatment in Scotland [illegible] uncing his father's work which he was forced to take. [illegible] he commissioners who extracted Charles's assent to the Covenant in 1650 later wrote that they knew the king had sworn an oath which in his heart he hated.[86] By contrast, the assurances of fairer treatment for English and Irish Catholics were much more sincere.[87] Charles came under considerable pressure to adopt Catholicism during the several years he spent at Catholic courts, and it seems likely that he was flirting with the idea while in exile. If we may believe Burnet, Hyde suspected that the king had changed his religion before he left Paris, (though the chancellor 'would never suffer himself to believe it quite').[88] Ormonde is alleged to have seen Charles at mass in Brussels in 1659 and to have been assured of his conversion by two Catholic courtiers.[89] Their

[85] These transactions may be traced in *Calendar of Clarendon State Papers in the Bodleian Library*, ed. O. Ogle *et al.* (Oxford, 5 vols., 1869–1970), vols. ii–iv; cf. M. Ashley, *Charles II The Man and the Statesman* (London, 1971), chaps. 3–5, and Bosher, pp. 71–4.

[86] G. Davies, 'Charles II in 1660', *Huntingdon Library Quarterly*, xix (1955–6), 249–50.

[87] F. J. Routledge, 'Charles II and the Cardinal de Retz', *Trans. Roy. Hist. Soc.*, 5th ser., vi (1956), 49–68.

[88] Burnet, i, 133.

[89] T. Carte, *Life of Ormonde*, op. cit., ii, 254–5.

confidence may have been premature, for as Dr. Whiteman has said, though Charles was 'by temperament strongly attracted to Roman Catholicism, he accepted the political necessity of supporting the Church of England'.[90]

To pursue the vexed question of whether Charles was converted in the 1650s is really an unnecessary diversion. Charles realized that it was imperative that he should remain to all outward intents a member of 'the Church in which he had been bred';[91] his regular attendance at the Anglican chapel in exile, the foiling of the attempt to coerce his younger brother the duke of Gloucester into Catholicism, and the polite but firm refusal to abandon the Book of Common Prayer in his private devotions when requested to do so by a Puritan delegation in May 1660—all testify to his awareness of the fact.[92] That having been said, it should also be realized that his sympathy for his Catholic subjects was as strong as if he had in fact been a practising Catholic. He was grateful to them for their loyal support during the civil wars and in particular for helping him to escape after the battle of Worcester in 1651. His vivid remembrance of this escape led him to bore his companions with too many repetitions of the tale, and though not the most reliable of paymasters Charles kept his word to the poor Catholics who helped him escape by granting them life pensions after the Restoration.[93] There is also the record of an occasion in the 1650s when Charles first learnt (from Hyde) the harshness of the sanguinary laws against Catholics. He expressed his horror at 'Laws which caused Men to be put to Death for their Religion' and stated his determination to remedy this situation as soon as it lay within his power.[94]

There is strong evidence that from the earliest months of the Restoration Charles was trying to do just this. The liberty to tender consciences granted in Charles's declaration from Breda did not except the Catholics, and in August he was

[90] Whiteman, 'Restoration', p. 54.

[91] Clarendon, E. Hyde, Earl of, *History of the Rebellion and Civil Wars* (ed. W. D. Macray, Oxford, 6 vols., 1888), vi, 231-2.

[92] Ibid., and Bosher, pp. 74-8.

[93] R. Ollard, *The Escape of Charles II after the Battle of Worcester* (London, 1966), pp. 15, 140, 142, 150-4.

[94] Clarendon, *Life*, ii, 266-70.

party to the very revealing exchange of letters between the Abbé Montagu and 'Dick' Bellings.[95] Walter Montagu had begun his career in the service of the first duke of Buckingham, but after he became a Catholic he was imprisoned and then banished by the Long Parliament. In France he had taken orders and become abbot of St. Martin's near Pontoise, the house to which Henrietta Maria tried to commit the duke of Gloucester in 1654 in order to convert him to Catholicism. In 1660, Montagu was actively intriguing on behalf of the Catholic cause in England and Ireland, a role in which his many contacts proved invaluable. He was the Queen Mother's spiritual counsellor, a great favourite at the French court, the brother of the earl of Manchester (whom he visited secretly late in 1660) and cousin of the earl of Sandwich, as well as being in close correspondence with Richard Bellings.[96] Bellings was a Catholic also, a member of a minor Irish landed family and one of that loyal band of followers who had followed Charles on his travels round Europe during the Interregnum. He was later to be entrusted by Charles and Clarendon with secret negotiations such as the sale of Dunkirk, an embassy to the Pope in the winter of 1662-3, and the treaty of Dover. How completely Bellings was in the royal confidence in the early years of the Restoration may be gauged from the notes which passed between Charles and Clarendon and from surviving letters in the Clarendon state paper collection.[97]

The king certainly knew and approved of Bellings's correspondence with Montagu. Charles seems to have hoped that by giving Montagu assurances of his concern for English Catholics he would be able to obtain help from the French court. Hyde certainly knew of the correspondence too, for his endorsements are clearly visible on the decoded letters now in his collection of state papers. Montagu, however, was under the impression that he was dealing with Bellings and Charles alone; he clearly regarded Hyde as a stumbling-block to the

[95] Clarendon MS. 73, ff.175, 182, 192, 196, 200-1, 208.

[96] *Dict. Nat. Biog.*, and K. Feiling, *British Foreign Policy 1660-1672* (London, 1930), pp. 2, 30, 32.

[97] Ibid., pp. 24, 60-2, 271, 292; see also *Dict. Nat. Biog.*, *Notes which passed*, op. cit., pp. 41, 53, 57, 71, 88, and *Calendar of Clarendon State Papers*, op. cit., vol. v, *s.v.* Richard Bellings.

Catholic cause, and made some unfriendly remarks about him.

The first three letters are the most important and must be quoted at length. The first surviving letter, from Montagu to Bellings, was written on 15 August (25 August N.S.). The identity of 'Omen' is not clear; it was probably a code-name for a leading Catholic at court who was thought to have influence with the king.

We heare that Bishops are much now upon the stage and certainly Omens part ought to be very considerable in it. The king of England ought to keepe up the confusion as much as Omen can, for that order once settled will lesse yeeld to the king of Englands will. Wherefore it is without doubt best to hold that businesse in suspense as long as Omen can. The lord Hyde will certainly presse much the worke; but the king of England must be dextrous to delay that business.[98]

Bellings replied on 23 August:

I have receaved yours of the 25th . . . The King bidds me tell you that as far as he durst he still opposed the establishment of Bishops; and appearing too much in so important a business, his friends begun to be unsatisfied; of late he hath expressed more warmth, not upon that score though I imagine, but at an offer that Scotland absolutely refused to admit of an Episcopacy and England begins to speake the same language for London is drawing up of a Petition to resettle the honor of Presbitery wherefore He thought it absolutely necessary to countenance Bishops that they might better take heart to oppose that other faction, that would presently overrun all and proove a much greater obstacle to his designes then any settled ~~hated~~ [sic] Episcopacy can be. In the meane time Lord Hyde is reconciling all differences and hath written a Treaty which the King calls a strange potage.

If you can propose any expedient that embroyling Episcopacy, will not advance Presbitery, It will be most welcome.[99]

Two days later Bellings sent an additional note; the king would rather that Montagu enlarge upon the subject of Cardinal Mazarin's attitude towards the king's proposed marriage than upon that of the bishops: 'for money and a wife are the things he most wants. as for Episcopacy, you know it is his religion to promote it; but you need not feare he will proceed so rashly as to venture his Crownes'.[100] Three more

[98] Clarendon MS. 73, f.196. [99] Ibid., f.182. [100] Ibid., f.196.

letters were dispatched by Montagu in late August and early September describing other steps being taken to bolster the Catholic cause in Britain.

Charles's position is captured clearly in these letters. He realized that in public he must adhere to his father's religion ('as for Episcopacy, you know it is his religion to promote it'), but he was not going to appoint bishops until the time was ripe, partly because it might provoke opposition (he would not 'proceed so rashly as to venture his Crownes'), and partly because too well established an episcopate might prove a great 'obstacle to his designes' for helping the Catholics. (The notion that a 'settled Episcopacy' would obstruct any amelioration of their position was held by many Catholics at this time; in 1661 the earl of Bristol tried to prevent the bishops from regaining their places in the House of Lords for this very reason, and it is significant that he was then supported by Charles, for a while at least.)[101] By August 1660, however, Charles's inactivity had begun to cause discontent. There was growing dissatisfaction among his 'friends'—his father's strongest supporters—as we can see from a letter written by Bishop Duppa to Gilbert Sheldon on 11 August: there was 'never more need' for Sheldon to convince the king of the need to take positive action to revive episcopacy, 'for all the professed enemies of our Church look upon this as the critical time to use their dernier resort to shake his Majesty's constancy'.[102] These enemies were indeed gathering strength, and to Charles the activities of the Scottish covenanters and the petition to 'resettle the honor of Presbitery' circulating in London[103] represented a much more serious threat; for, as Bellings pointed out, if the Presbyterians were to 'overrun all' then they would 'proove a much greater obstacle to his designes' than the bishops ever would. Faced by this dilemma, Charles took two steps. He decided to appoint bishops without further delay, so that his 'friends' could 'take heart' and keep the extreme Presbyterians in check; the first episcopal nomination—ironically the translation of the despairing Duppa to Winchester—was made five days after Bellings wrote to Montagu.[104] But this was not to be the

[101] Clarendon, *Life*, ii, 263–5. [102] Tanner MS. 49, f.17.

[103] The petition is mentioned in *Hist. MSS. Comm. 5th Report*, Appendix, p. 168.

[104] See Appendix 6.

traditional type of bishop, for Charles was seeking some compromise solution ('embroyling Episcopacy' without advancing 'Presbitery') that would leave him in a strong enough position to advance the Catholics' cause at some future date. Charles's second step, therefore, was to order his chancellor to devise a 'Treaty' that would bring the two sides together. This treaty—caustically dubbed 'a strange potage' by Charles—must surely have been the first draft of the royal declaration on religious affairs, copies of which were circulating round London a few days after it was mentioned by Bellings.[105] The appearance of this draft marked an important stage in the settlement of the church, for in it Charles openly stated his support for a form of episcopacy that owed much to the moderate views of Ussher. By this one document, Charles paved the way for the restoration of episcopacy and ensured that many of the Puritans' grievances against the arbitrariness of that form of government were removed. At the same time he also ensured that he would not be at the mercy of any one religious element among his subjects, but would himself retain the initiative in ecclesiastical affairs, hopefully to the Catholics' advantage.

There were other straws in the wind. In October there was the altercation between Charles and Baxter at the penultimate meeting on the draft declaration. Charles, through Clarendon, suggested a clause which would have granted freedom of worship to those who were not members of the state church; Baxter asserted that such freedom might be permitted 'tolerable Parties' such as some of the sectaries, but not 'intolerable ones' such as Papists and socinians; Charles intervened to say that there were already '"Laws enough against the Papists"'.[106] In succeeding months, Charles listened sympathetically to pleas for toleration for his English and Irish Catholic subjects, and, through Clarendon again, started discussions on a new oath of allegiance which Catholics would be able to take.[107] Sometimes he was on the defensive, as in

[105] *Rel. Baxt.*, Lib. I, Pt. II, para. 105.

[106] Ibid., para. 110.

[107] Addit. MS. 41,846, ff.76-9; Clarendon MSS. 73, ff.175, 192, 200-1, 205, 208, 251, 284; 74, f.311; 78, ff.139, 155-64; Carte MSS. 68, ff.14-20, 23-33; 81, ff.183-4; 214, ff.202, 251, 292-3; Abernathy, 'English Presbyterians'. pp. 83-4. For the oath of allegiance and other activity, see chapter X below.

1663 when he opposed further victimization of Jesuits and Catholic priests by Parliament; M.P.s were then told that Charles had a 'just Memory of what many [Catholics] had done and suffered in the Service of His Royal Father of Blessed Memory, and of some eminent Services performed by others of them, towards His Majesty Himself in the Time of His greatest Affliction'.[108] On other occasions, he went onto the offensive, as in the proviso of 17 March and the declaration of 26 December 1662 both of which asserted that the king could dispense with the terms of the Act of Uniformity in the case of individuals who could not conform to the state church.[109] In later years, his support for bills against the sanguinary laws or in favour of toleration culminated in the declaration of indulgence of March 1672 which suspended altogether the penal laws against Catholics and nonconformists.[110]

From the very outset, then, Charles was determined to obtain fairer treatment for the Catholic community in his dominions, and in the opening months of the Restoration the most promising course seemed to be a compromise settlement. For some time it looked as though Charles might succeed. During the spring and summer of 1660 he received a stream of addresses from various religious groups, but beyond a promise that he would give them all his close consideration he did not commit himself.[111] The few moves he did make—the promotion of conferences, the issuing of the proclamation of 1 June, and support for the Ministers' Bill—were all designed to reassure the moderates and to keep a balance between opposing interests. Less publicly, Charles was also doing much to preserve the peace through the liberal use of his ecclesiastical patronage: clergymen of all standpoints were presented to the livings they sought or confirmed in the posts they already held, irrespective of their past actions.[112] In August, as we have just seen, this delicate balance of forces

[108] *J.L.*, xi, 503.

[109] Abernathy, 'English Presbyterians', pp. 82-3, 86-9.

[110] Clarendon, *Life*, ii, 270, 468-75; cf. R. Thomas, 'Comprehension and Indulgence', *From Uniformity to Unity*, ed. G. F. Nuttall and O. Chadwick (London, 1962), pp. 201-14.

[111] Bosher, p. 150; Tanner MS. 49, f.17; *Rel. Baxt.*, Lib. I, Pt. II, para. 91.

[112] These points are developed in the next two chapters.

was threatened by a resurgence of extreme Presbyterian activity, but Charles was equal to the crisis: he started to nominate bishops, offering sees to a wide variety of churchmen, and at the same time indicated his support for modified episcopacy in the draft declaration on ecclesiastical affairs. The initial draft was altered in a few respects, but there can be little doubt that in its final form the Worcester House declaration satisfied the king's political shrewdness as well as his personal inclinations.

Charles also demonstrated his determination and political skill in his handling of the Irish and Scottish churches during these first months. It must have soon become apparent to Charles that the compromise solution he favoured for England would not be received with much enthusiasm in his other kingdoms: those with power in Ireland favoured a much more traditional form of episcopacy, while many in Scotland were opposed to the return of even a modified form of episcopal government.[113] From Ireland Coote and Broghill urged the need for a rapid return to the old forms of church government in order that 'fanatics' should be speedily suppressed, and in this they were seconded by the Irish bishops and bishops-elect. The Irish bench differed from the English and Scottish benches of the Restoration in two ways: it was reinforced *before* the Worcester House declaration was conceived (due probably to Ormonde's influence), and it included a far higher proportion of men who had suffered considerably for their adherence to the episcopal church in the previous decades.[114] Clearly Charles was anxious to prevent the persecution of Irish Puritans, a move which would undoubtedly have had political repercussions in Scotland and England; on the other hand, he did not wish to alienate the Irish episcopalians altogether. His response was astute: he delayed the actual translations and consecrations of the Irish bishops until January 1661 (about six months after most of them had been nominated), and he sent over a copy of the Worcester House declaration which may have been published there in November.[115] By these means

[113] See above pp. 16–19.

[114] Eleven of the fifteen nominees had been sufferers; only Jones and Worth could be termed moderates. The nominations are in Carte MS. 41, ff.14–46.

[115] H. Cotton, *Fasti Ecclesiae Hibernicae* (Dublin, 6 vols., 1848–78); Carte MS. 31, f.59, and cf. ff.30, 58, and Carte MS. 45, f.44.

Charles ensured that the advent of persecution in Ireland was delayed long enough to give modified episcopacy a chance to take root in England.

Scotland required a different approach. The earl of Middleton and a sizable proportion of the Privy Council for Scotland pressed for the restoration of episcopacy, but as late as March 1661 Charles was still not convinced that 'the greater part of the Nobility and Gentry, and even of the Clergy themselves would be pleased with it'.[116] He seems to have agreed with Lauderdale that a politically emasculated kirk would be the best solution for Scotland; even a diluted form of episcopacy might cause a rebellion.[117] Twice, in August 1660 and after the passage of the Act Rescissory in March 1661, Charles sought to reassure the moderate Scots Presbyterians.[118] It was only in September 1661 that episcopacy was restored in Scotland, and then it was a very limited form: the new bishops were chosen from moderate Resolutioners such as Leighton, Guthrie, and Wishart rather than surviving episcopalians such as Sydserf, and public worship displayed remarkable continuity with the forms of the preceding era.[119]

The circumstances in which Charles made the decision to restore episcopacy in Scotland were very different from those in which he had taken the equivalent decision for England. For if it had been pressure from the 'left' which had pushed Charles into more positive action in August 1660, it was to be pressure from the 'right' which made him take further steps, and these much more unpleasant ones, in the second half of 1661. By then a decisive shift in political strength had occurred: those who had invited the king back had either changed their colours or been replaced by more reactionary elements, so that the new Parliaments of 1661 were without

[116] Clarendon MS. 74, ff.290-3.

[117] Burnet, i, 233-6.

[118] Wodrow, i, 13; *Acts of the Parliaments of Scotland* (12 vols., 1814-75), vii, 87-8. It is just conceivable that the Remonstrants would have accepted a Presbyterian settlement in Scotland and episcopal churches in England and Ireland (cf. Wodrow, i, Introduction, lvii); but it is difficult to see how Charles could have maintained this position permanently (cf. Burnet, i, 235).

[119] *Tudor and Stuart Proclamations*, ii, no. 2210;Donaldson, op. cit., pp. 360-6; W.R. Foster, *Bishop and Presbytery: the Church of Scotland 1661-1688* (London, 1958), chapters 1, 3, 6.

exception more conservative than the conventions which had recalled him. By the autumn of 1661, Charles was in no position to withstand the flood waters of reaction which in all three kingdoms were pressing for more traditional, authoritarian church settlements than he had fostered so far. Charles, therefore, changed his tack; henceforth he would accept the more conservative settlements demanded by his subjects, but where possible he would seek to moderate their severity and to preserve his own independence of action in church affairs.

The supporters of the Church of Ireland may actually have anticipated Charles's change of front. Certainly, they were the first to outlaw assemblies of Presbyterians and Independents, and the first to conduct visitations and to eject obdurate Puritans.[120] In England, the Cavaliers' sweeping victory in the spring of 1661 was soon followed by a series of measures which made clear their intention of blotting out the last traces of Puritanism.[121] Initially Charles managed to thwart some of the Cavaliers' schemes,[122] but in November he realized that he was in too weak a financial position to withstand them for long, and so made a tactical retreat. Henceforth he would not offer frontal resistance to the Cavaliers' bill for uniformity; instead he would submit provisos confirming his prerogative power of granting indulgences to individual dissenters, or seek other means of mitigating the severity of its effects.[123] The English bench of bishops was put in a dilemma by this turn of events. The more conservative took encouragement from the Cavaliers' lead, and succeeded in frustrating some of Charles's projects, for example the Savoy Conference summoned to produce a liturgy acceptable to Anglicans and Presbyterians, and the royal provisos to the bill of uniformity. The more moderate fought a rearguard battle for comprehension, or

[120] Clarendon MS. 74, f.98; *Tudor and Stuart Proclamations,* ii, no. 268; no. 3278 in vol. i does not mention Presbyterians or Independents. J. C. Beckett, op. cit., pp. 124–5; F.R. Bolton, *Caroline Tradition of the Church of Ireland* (London, 1958), Pt. 1, ch. 4; Carte MS. 45, ff.63, 131.

[121] *J.C.*, viii, 254, 256; 247; 261; 270; 279, 300 and *J.L.*, xi, 323; *J.C.* viii, 296, 321-2, 325, 330-2.

[122] For example he delayed the first uniformity bill and defeated the attempt to undermine the Ministers' Act of 1660: Bosher, pp. 224–5, 239–44.

[123] Abernathy, 'English Presbyterians', pp. 82–6.

failing that indulgence.[124] But in August 1662 all of the bishops were required by act of Parliament to eject those clergy who would not perform the tests laid down by the Cavaliers, and well over a thousand Puritan ministers were forced out of their churches.[125] In Scotland too, the first act of the new bishops—on the insistence of the Scottish laity—was the ejection of nearly 300 of the more extreme Presbyterian clergy.[126]

The second phase of royal policy, from the autumn of 1661, undoubtedly constituted a set-back for Charles. His hopes of a moderate, comprehensive settlement which would leave him room in which to work for greater toleration for Catholics, were frustrated. But he did not despair: for another ten years he pursued his policy of seeking an indulgence or a measure of toleration, until he was finally forced to abandon it by the fact that fear of Catholicism had begun to replace hostility to Puritanism as the driving force of the English Parliament.[127]

In retrospect it is tempting to compare the Restoration church settlement with that of Elizabeth I—the periods of bitter theological conflict preceding the settlement, the return of the exiled clergy at the start of the new reign, the royal attempts at a *via media* thwarted by vigorous Parliamentary intervention. But these parallels may conceal more than they reveal. Whereas Elizabeth was much more conservative than the Marian exiles and their supporters in Parliament, the exact opposite was true of Charles and the Cromwellian exiles. Furthermore, the relative mildness of the persecution of the 1640s and 1650s meant that Charles had a much wider selection of clergy from which to choose than Elizabeth. Despite her reservations about their progressive ideas, Elizabeth was forced to choose two-thirds of her first bench of bishops from Marian exiles; of Charles's first episcopal appointments, only three out of nineteen had been in exile.[128]

A more valuable comparison might be made between the

[124] Ibid., p. 83; Bosher, pp. 226-30, 250-3, and below chapter VI.

[125] See below chapter VII.

[126] Donaldson, op. cit., p. 365.

[127] R. Thomas, art. cit., pp. 192-222.

[128] P. Hughes, *The Reformation in England* (London, 3 vols. 1950-4), iii, 45, and cf. P. Collinson, *The Elizabethan Puritan Movement* (London, 1967), pp. 61-2; for Morley, Laney, and Cosin's period in exile, see below chapter IV.

events of 1660–1 and the restoration of the powers of the Scottish episcopate in the early seventeenth century. The first part of the reign of James VI was a period of Presbyterian domination during which the episcopate—though never extinguished— had a precarious existence. Later on, however, pressure from the king ensured the restoration of the bishops to their seats in Parliament, to their estates, and to some of their functions, though to secure the Presbyterians' co-operation James compromised on matters such as re-ordination and the diaconate on which their sensibilities were easily offended. The extreme of 'proud papal bishops' against which James warned his son was thus avoided, and according to Professor Donaldson 'the evidence all suggests that the combination of bishops with presbyters worked well'.[129] James had a manifestly better pupil in his grandson than his son. Charles's efforts to introduce a form of modified episcopacy into England in the first year of his Restoration suggest that he had inherited his grandfather's political opportunism and dislike of prelacy, rather than his father's rigid principles and devout churchmanship. Unfortunately for Charles, the sins of both father and grandfather were visited on his head, so that by the closing months of 1661 he was in no position to insist on a moderate settlement in open defiance of the wishes of Parliament.

[129] Donaldson, op. cit., pp. 205–7.

II

THE STABILIZATION OF THE PARISH CLERGY

Even before Charles reached England in May 1660, he was approached by many who sought some favour at his hands. After he landed, the press of suitors increased and soon became irksome.[1] Predictably, these petitioners generally fell into two groups: those who had shown commendable loyalty to the crown and who in return demanded restoration to an old post, or promotion to a new one instead; and those whose past services to the crown were negligible, but who as a reward for their acquiescence in the Restoration hoped to be confirmed in the office which they had held during the Interregnum. There were two groups of clergymen, for instance, who both tried to win the king's support. On the one hand, there were those ministers who, usually for their loyalty to the monarchy and the episcopal church, had been sequestered from their livings in the previous decades; in 1660 they were naturally eager to return to what they regarded as their rightful possessions. On the other, there were those who had accepted the changes in church government and worship during the 1640s and 1650s and been presented to livings by Parliamentary or Commonwealth authorities; notwithstanding this, they hoped that the new government would be sufficiently grateful for their co-operation in the Restoration to confirm them in their livings.

The interests of these two groups were clearly quite incompatible. The Puritans insisted that only scandalous clergy had been ejected, and that it would therefore be wrong to reinstate any of them. This was hotly denied by the sequestered clergy who in pamphlets and in petitions to the king defended their conduct and their right to their former livings. In several hundred parishes, this confrontation took the form of a sequestered minister and a Parliamentary

[1] *Cal. St. Pap. Dom. 1659-1660,* pp. 422-7, 447, and *1660-1661,* pp. 1-34; Clarendon, *Life,* ii, 8-9.

nominee vying for the same living. But it should be remembered in what follows that the conflict between the two groups was often much more complex than this and affected a sizable proportion of English parishes as a result. To take a case in point, there was disagreement over what should happen to those livings where the sequestered ministers had died before the Restoration (as in fact the majority of them had). Those who were in possession of these livings in 1660 saw no reason why their title should not be confirmed, but this assumption was challenged by some of the Cavalier gentry; they argued that certain tests of conformity should be imposed, and if these incumbents were unorthodox they should be ejected. Another complex situation arose where Royalist ministers had anticipated sequestration by resigning their livings in the 1640s. If the resignation had been performed with due forms of law, there were no legal grounds for recovery in 1660; but some of those who had resigned as a matter of principle felt that on moral grounds they were entitled to favourable treatment by the restored monarchy. There were other problems too, for instance a sizable minority of the sequestered clergy had bowed the knee during the Interregnum and been appointed to new livings before the king's return. These men really fell between the two camps, but this did not deter some of their number from trying to recover their original parishes in 1660. It is, of course, true that ejections had affected only a minority of English livings during the previous decades. Many others, however, had become vacant due to natural causes—promotion, resignation, death—and Parliament or the Commonwealth had helped to fill these livings too. Even here the two sides came into conflict: the incumbents naturally hoped that their titles would be confirmed, but some of the episcopalians again tried to insist that the government impose some test of orthodoxy as a precondition of confirmation. By this means, the controversy over titles was extended to include the great majority of parish livings.

This clash of interests placed the government in a very difficult position. Charles could not afford to ignore the claims of the sequestered clergy who had suffered for their loyalty to king and church; nor could he afford to alienate the influential body of ministers who were actually in possession of the parish churches at the time of his return. The exiled government had been aware of some of the problems created by these disputes over titles, though they carefully avoided all mention of this contentious subject in the soothing declaration from Breda. It was, however, in the spirit of that declaration (which left to Parliament the settlement of disputes over alienated property and the drafting of a form of indulgence for tender consciences)[2] that Charles allowed Parliament to take the lead in this matter. Accordingly it was the Convention Parliament which provided the solution in September 1660—the act 'for the Confirming and Restoreing of Ministers',[3] or the Act for Settling Ministers as it is usually known. This compromise measure restored sequestered ministers to most of their former livings, and with a few exceptions confirmed the titles of incumbents in all other livings. It is the purpose of this chapter to trace the development of this important piece of legislation and to examine the role of the king in settling the problem of disputed titles, one of the most pressing and difficult problems facing him on his return.

The first draft of the ministers' bill was prepared by the Convention Parliament before Charles reached England. It seems almost certain that the original bill was designed to support the claims of ministers in possession of livings against those of the sequestered clergy. The title of the bill at its first reporting on 9 May 1660 was a bill 'for establishing Ministers settled in Ecclesiastical Livings',[4] compared to the final measure 'for the Confirming *and Restoreing* of Ministers'. There are also references in contemporary letters to the Presbyterians' 'designe' to 'confirme all Ministers in . . . Sequestred livings' and to 'keep out the old ejected clergy'.[5] Furthermore, the pamphlet debate in the spring of 1660 suggests that the restoration of the sequestered clergy was by no means a foregone conclusion. The episcopalian Robert Mossom in his *Apology In the behalf of the Sequestered Clergy*

[2] *J.L.*, xi, 7-8.
[3] *Statutes*, v, 242-6.
[4] *J.C.*, viii, 19.
[5] Clarendon MS. 71, f.432; *Hist. MSS. Comm. 5th Report*, Appendix, p. 194.

was forced to countenance the idea that Parliament might confirm the 'intruders' in the 'unjust Possession of our Livings'.[6] The tone of the Puritan replies was militant and confident: rather than lose the prayers of 'so many powerfull godly Ministers', the king would confirm the titles of those in sequestered livings and thus render himself 'glorious in the eyes of all Parties'.[7] Recent work on the Convention Parliament suggests that the Presbyterians held the initative in ecclesiastical matters, at least during the early stages, and it looks as though intially they were prepared to use their numerical advantage to confirm the titles of all the Puritan clergy.[8]

Charles made his own attitude clear at an early conference with the Presbyterian clergy in June. In keeping with his avowed policy of abatements by both sides and a 'meeting in the Midway', Charles made two important points: 'all who had entred into Livings whose Incumbents are dead, should be continued' without being forced to adopt any particular religious practice ('until a Synod determined that Point'); secondly, those in livings to which a surviving minister laid claim would have to be 'outed', but those so ejected 'should be provided for'.[9] This statement of policy resembles the eventual settlement quite closely, and it seems clear that Charles's moderate standpoint must have influenced the moderate Presbyterians in the Commons. When the ministers' bill was next debated in late July, they had conceded the point that some of the sequestered clergy should be allowed back.[10] Again in early September the Presbyterians reminded Charles of his assurance to 'take care and provide' for such ministers as were ejected by the restoration of sequestered clergy.[11]

In addition to his remarks to the Presbyterian clergy,

[6] R. Mossom, op. cit. (London, 1660), p. 6.

[7] *An Humble Caution concerning the danger of removing godly . . . Ministers out of Sequestrations* (London, 1660), pp. 5, 8; cf. *A Plea for Ministers in Sequestrations* (London, 1660), e.g. p. 4.

[8] J. R. Jones, 'Political Groups and Tactics in the Convention of 1660', *Historical Journal*, vi (1963), 159-77; M. E. W. Helms, 'The Convention Parliament of 1660' (Bryn Mawr Ph.D. thesis, 1963), chapters 2, 3.

[9] *Rel. Baxt.*, Lib. I, Pt. II, para. 91; Wodrow, i, Introduction, xliv.

[10] 'Diary of Seymour Bowman', ff.103-8; as yet the Presbyterians baulked at the re-admission of all sequestered ministers—see below pp. 46, 48.

[11] *J.C.*, viii, 149.

Charles also issued a proclamation 'For Quieting Possessions'. This proclamation, prepared by Parliament and issued by Charles on 1 June 1660, expressed concern at the 'forcible Entries made upon the Possessions' of some of the king's subjects, lay and clerical, who had been 'setled in the said Possessions by any lawful or pretended Authority'. Charles commanded that 'no Person or Persons, Ecclesiastical or Temporal' should disturb an incumbent 'till our Parliament shall take order therein, or an Eviction be had by due course of Law'.[12] From the time of the king's return to the passage of the Act for Settling Ministers in mid September, this was the only official statement on the vexed issue of disputed livings, and as such deserves closer attention.

It seems clear, for example, that the clause in the proclamation allowing ejection 'by due course of Law' led to a certain amount of legal activity. On 21 July, 'sundry poor Ministers of the Gospel' in sequestered livings petitioned Parliament 'Concerninge the stoppinge of any further Proceedings in Lawe against them'.[13] We also know that a certain proportion of the sequestered clergy who petitioned the Lords for part of the revenue of their former livings in the summer of 1660, had begun proceedings against 'intruders' in their livings.[14] Some of these suits were heard at the assizes, and in early September it was reported from Winchester that 'not one Sequestred Minister, that brought his Action against the Intruder, but had a Verdict for him'.[15]

While it is apparent that many suits were begun, it is less clear how many 'intruders' were actually ejected as a result. The petition of 'sundry poor Ministers' has not survived, but its title suggests that it was the threat rather than the actual implementation of legal ejection which disturbed them. The assize records for this period are not full enough to permit an estimate of how many of these suits reached a verdict, but

[12] Ibid., 47; Bodl. Lib., *Vet. A.1.b.4/1*, no. 16; *Tudor and Stuart Proclamations*, i, no. 3217.

[13] *J.C.*, viii, 97; 'Diary of Seymour Bowman', f. 90.

[14] House of Lords Record Office, House of Lords Petitions—petitions presented in pursuance of Lords' orders of 22 and 23 June 1660 (see below pp. 44-6): vol. A-C, nos. 1, 5, 18, 22, 30, 55, 71, 72, 83, 84, 93, 103, 108, 125; vol. D-K, nos. 159, 178, 186, 187, 191, 2, 3, 19, 41, 50, 58, 103, 106; vol. L-P, nos. 133, 135, 139, 146, 5, 15, 16, 22, 60, 70; vol. R-Z nos. 7, 10, 13, 15, 34, 50, 67, 81, 82, 99, 106, 118, 120, 128.

[15] *Parliamentary Intelligencer* (1660), no. 38, 10-17 September, p. 608.

various factors incline one to believe that the numbers were small. It is noteworthy that the Winchester assizes which so favoured the sequestered clergy's pleas took place on 3 September, only a few days before the ministers' bill became law. In fact, half of the sessions of assizes in England took place *after* the ministers' bill had clarified the legal position of 'intruders' and sequestered clergy beyond all doubt.[16] Similarly, if we look at the petitions of sequestered ministers to the Lords, we find that only fifty out of over 600 specifically mentioned suits against 'intruders'. Indeed, the fact that the great majority of the surviving sequestered clergy had to petition the Lords during the summer of 1660 is in itself a strong indication that at the moment of petitioning they had failed to regain possession by legal means.

There were, it is true, other means than the 'due course of Law' of ejecting 'intruders'. Dr. Bosher has suggested that there was a restoration from below in many parishes, a wave of support for the old order which defied the proclamation of 1 June by driving out unpopular incumbents and restoring sequestered ministers long before Parliament got round to ordering this.[17] However, the authorities he cites are not all reliable. Thomas Rugge's chronicle may have been based on second-hand information and written some time after the event; his reference to the restoration of many sequestered clergy in June 1660 must therefore be viewed with some suspicion.[18] So must Sharp's report of the 'Ejection of many honest Ministers throughout the land'; as shown above, Sharp's reports were designed to drive a wedge between English and Scottish Presbyterians by persuading the Scots that they could expect little help from their English brethren.[19] Richard Baxter's account was written nearly five years after the event, and his memory was not infallible. Neither of his references to the ejections of 1660 is supported by a specific date.[20] The first could mean that the ejections

[16] *Parliamentary Intelligencer* (1660), no. 31, 23–30 July, pp. 482–3; *J.C.*, viii, 164–5. Sharp's prediction of over a thousand ejected (Wodrow, i, Introduction, xxx) was mere guesswork.

[17] Bosher, pp. 164–5.

[18] Rugge misplaces dates and varies the tense used in his chronicle: Addit. MS. 10, 116, f. 103, and cf. f. 43; see article on Rugge in *Dict. Nat. Biog.*

[19] Wodrow, i, Introduction, li; above p. 15.

[20] *Rel. Baxt.*, Lib. I, Pt. II, paras. 100, 151.

took place before the king's return (and we have other evidence that some incumbents were disturbed before the king's return, that is before the proclamation of 1 June was issued);[21] the second could mean that the ejections took place after the ministers' bill had become law. It is true that the Commons told the Lords that 'the Countries are much unquiet, by reason so many good Ministers have been ejected', but this statement was made on 8 September in an effort to goad the upper house into action on the ministers' bill which their lordships had been neglecting.[22] In the face of these contemporary or near-contemporary reports it would be foolish to deny that a certain number of incumbents were ousted between 1 June and 13 September, but their numbers may well have been exaggerated. Indeed, on one or two occasions when sequestered ministers tried to reinstate themselves unofficially, they ran into difficulties.[23]

There was one other means by which the security of a few incumbents was threatened during the summer of 1660. The king's proclamation stabilized the parish clergy as it stood on 1 June, but did not forbid presentations to vacant livings. Many patrons, including Charles himself, presented to livings during the summer, and a small proportion of these presentations—either through ignorance of the existence of an incumbent, or through wilful refusal to recognize an Interregnum nominee—had the effect of challenging the title of a minister who should have been protected by the proclamation. The system of episcopal institution, revived over much of England in July and August, carried this threat one stage further.[24] The threat may not have gone beyond this, however, for the system of episcopal induction was not restored as rapidly as that of institution. In the diocese of Canterbury, for example, the titles of five incumbents were

[21] H. Jessey, *The Lords Loud Call* (London, 1660), pp. 17, 20, *seqq.*; *A Plea for Ministers in Sequestrations*, op. cit., p. 7; *Cal Rev.*, p. 208.

[22] *J.L.*, xi, 162; the reference may have been to ejections likely to result from royal presentations to livings that were not in fact vacant, a subject under discussion a few days before; see below pp. 46–8.

[23] Robert Clarke did not regain complete possession of Andover until his title had been proved at law (*Walk. Rev.* p. 181); the 'intruder' Bowey hung on at Elwick Hall until September (*Correspondence of John Cosin*, ed. G. Ornsby, Surtees Society, lv (1870), pp. 5–6; *Cal. Rev.* p. 67).

[24] See below, chapter VI.

challenged by the institution of new ministers to their livings in July and August, but only one of these is known to have been inducted before the ministers' bill became law.[25] A similar situation prevailed in the diocese of Winchester.[26] It remains very difficult to find convincing evidence of ejections carried out between 1 June and 13 September, and unless a larger number of such ejections can be found it is surely wrong to talk of a national campaign to eject Puritan incumbents in defiance of the proclamation for quieting possessions.

Another major step affecting the parish clergy was taken in late June, this time by the predominantly episcopalian House of Lords.[27] During the period when Parliament was preparing the ministers' bill, it received many petitions from sequestered clergy anxious to obtain the fifth of the profits promised but not always paid to them during the previous decades.[28] On 22 and 23 June, the upper house made two orders which had the effect of securing the tithes and other profits of all sequestered livings brought to their attention; churchwardens or overseers of the poor were to take charge of such profits until the title of the living was determined.[29] Soon petitions were flooding in from sequestered clergy anxious to have the emoluments of their former livings placed in impartial hands. It is not possible to date the submission of most of these petitions, but from the minority which *can* be dated it seems likely that the peak of activity was reached in July and early August.[30] The degree of organization attained by this petitioning movement is well illustrated by the number of petitions bearing several names (often relating to livings widely separated in location) and by the existence of stereotyped

[25] *Lib. Inst.*—for institutions to Biddenden, Chartham, Ivychurch, Lydd (Kent), and Tangmere (Sussex); Cant. Cath. Chap. Arch., *F/B/1* 1564–1661, f.210 for induction to Biddenden.

[26] Only one institution, to St. Nicholas, Guildford (*Lib. Inst.*), threatened an incumbent's title; but the new minister does not appear in the parish register until October and did not compound until November (*Surrey Archaeological Collections*, xxvii, (1914), 91; *Cal. Rev.* p. 337).

[27] Abernathy, 'English Presbyterians', p. 56.

[28] *Walk. Rev.*, p. xxvi.

[29] *J.L.*, xi, 72, 73; the order of the 23rd was the more important of the two.

[30] Many petitions are marked with the date of the Lords' order (House of Lords Petitions, vol. A-C, nos. 14, 21, 35, 38, 47, *et passim*), but some are dated by the petitioners or bear an endorsement which is not '23 June' (ibid., nos. 3, 5, 9, 25–8, 40, 48, *et passim*).

forms on which the names of a petitioner and his living were later inserted.[31] It seems likely, in fact, that the great majority of the sequestered clergy who were still alive and in England sent post-haste to London to take advantage of the Lords' action. About 650 clergy (not all genuine cases as will be seen shortly) sought the benefit of the Lords' orders, and the number of surviving sequestered clergy was probably between 700 and 800.[32]

In one sense, the Lords had acted impartially in freezing the revenues of disputed livings and paying the sequestered ministers their fifth of the profits. But in other ways, their action may be deemed unfair: it seems to have been the whole revenue of disputed livings which was secured, not just a fifth; the seizures took effect just before the harvest on the glebe and the collection of tithes; and some of those who obtained the benefit of the Lords' orders had little or no right to a share of the profits. Not surprisingly, incumbents affected by the Lords' action were soon voicing dissatisfaction. Many presented counter-petitions (the first dating from early July); some read the proclamation of 1 June immediately after the Lords' order appeared in their churches; a few even offered violent resistance.[33]

Some incumbents had greater reason to be angry with the Lords than others, for the readiness with which the Parliamentary clerks put down the names of petitioners led to some abuse of the system. Some of those who claimed that they had been sequestered had in fact resigned their livings and so had no legal claim to them in 1660; others who had been presented but never instituted or inducted to livings during the troubles also had no right to a fifth of the profits.[34] Where the

[31] Ibid., vol. R-Z no. 123; vol. A-C, nos. 30, 31, 33, 45; the order of 23 June was printed in *Mercurius Publicus* (1660), no. 26, 21-28 June, p. 415.

[32] A. G. Matthews calculated that 'above 700' of the sequestered clergy were eventually restored (annotated copy of *Walk. Rev.* in the Bodleian Library, p. xvi), but it is clear from his text that other sequestered clergy did not seek restoration, owing to absence abroad, old age, or promotion.

[33] *Hist. MSS. Comm. 7th Report*, pp. 113, 114, 115,118, 119, 122, etc.; 119, 128; 125, 128.

[34] E.g. Maydwell, Greathed, Cordell, and Chase; Towers and Alexander; ibid., pp. 124, 130-2; 119, 128. All but Maydwell had their orders revoked—*J.L.*, xi, 154-5, 159, 163; 98, 140; and Maydwell does not seem to have ousted the incumbent (Cooper-*Cal. Rev.* p. 134).

Lords realized that the original petition had contained false or misleading information, they made amends.[35] But the general effect of the Lords' action must have been to lower the morale of incumbents in sequestered livings.

Meanwhile, the Commons were still trying to settle the terms of the bill to solve the problem of disputed titles. By late July, in accordance with the king's wishes, the Presbyterians in the Commons had conceded that the sequestered clergy should be allowed to regain their livings, though at this stage they still insisted that 'scandalous' clergy should not be restored, and that pluralists should be allowed to recover only one of their former livings. The Presbyterians also resisted a concerted campaign by what has been dubbed the 'church party' in late July and August. This consisted of a series of attempts to impose tests on all incumbents whose titles would be confirmed by the ministers' bill, tests which would effectively have prevented many Puritan incumbents from remaining in the church —taking the oaths of allegiance and supremacy, subscription to the Thirty-nine Articles, and reordination for those not episcopally ordained.[36] Spurred on perhaps by anxious ministers outside the Convention, the Presbyterians made a successful stand against these tests.[37]

The bill was nearly ready by late August, but then ran into fresh difficulties. As it then stood, the bill would have restored the more respectable members of the sequestered clergy (provided that they did not recover more than one of their former livings) and confirmed the titles of ministers in possession of all other livings on 25 December 1659. Then on 25 August the Commons read a new proviso which would have had the effect of confirming the titles of another group of ministers—those presented to livings by the king between his return and 26 August.[38] At first sight, this seemed innocent enough, but it was soon made clear to the Commons that some of these royal presentations, either by accident or design, were likely to eject incumbents appointed in the previous decades.

[35] As previous note, and *J.L.*, xi, 127, 152, etc.

[36] 'Diary of Seymour Bowman', ff.96, 103-8, 110-11, 113-14, 116-17, 120-1, 125, 135-6, for the debates.

[37] T. W. Evans, 'Hyde and the Convention Parliament of 1660' (London M.A. thesis, 1964), p. 186.

[38] *J.C.*, viii, 136-7.

What seems to have happened is that some enterprising clergymen had asked Charles to nominate them to a 'dead' living (that is, a living of which the last episcopally inducted minister had died before 1660) but neglected to inform Charles of the presence of a rival claimant, that is the incumbent put in by the Parliamentary or Commonwealth authorities to fill the gap left by the death of the original minister. The number of occasions on which the king or the lord chancellor had unwittingly slighted the claims of incumbents in 'dead' livings seems to have been small: if we compare a list of the livings to which Charles presented in the summer of 1660 with a list of the livings from which ministers were ejected in September we find that about forty incumbents were affected by royal grants to some other clergyman.[39] Nevertheless these grants were to prove a minor embarrassment to the government, at least until the situation was explained to the Presbyterians.

On 27 August the Commons received a petition from 'divers distressed Ministers, whose Livings, though in dead Places, are granted away under the Broad Seal of England'.[40] Feeling on this subject clearly ran high, for the Presbyterians gained an unusually large majority, 140 to 83, in favour of an enquiry into the offending appointments,[41] and a subcommittee was sent to see the chancellor. Hyde, however, managed to put their minds at rest by showing them two papers.[42] The first of these listed royal presentations to vacant or 'dead' livings, and it is likely that the Presbyterians were struck by two features of these nominations: the reasons for vacancy, and the identity of some of the nominees. If, as seems probable, Hyde's first paper quoted the reason for vacancy recorded on the Patent Rolls, then the Presbyterians would have been assured that the king had been under the genuine impression that all of the livings to which he presented had then been vacant 'by the death of the last Incumbent

[39] Royal presentations on the Patent Rolls (P.R.O., *C.* 66/2916–2919, 12 Chas. II, parts 1–4) have been conveniently if not always accurately summarized in *46th Report*. Ejections are provided by *Cal. Rev.* The names of the men involved are given in Appendix 3, Part 1.

[40] *J.C.*, viii, 138; the petition was said to include a list of those dispossessed, but unfortunately it has been lost.

[41] Ibid.

[42] *J.C.*, viii, 140.

there'—often the name of the last episcopalian minister was inserted here—'or any other Wayes howsoever now voyd'.[43] The Presbyterians may also have recognized the names of some of those who had received a royal grant as belonging to men of their own persuasion.[44] In addition there was Hyde's second, and unsolicited, paper which listed all those incumbents who had been confirmed in possession by the king during the summer of 1660. Together these papers must have convinced the Presbyterians that Charles was not deliberately or regularly ejecting incumbents in 'dead' livings; errors might have been made on a few occasions, but for the most part the king was protecting the titles of those in possession at his return.[45] Satisfied, the Presbyterians in the Commons dropped their opposition to the proviso of 25 August. Indeed, they later agreed to extend the deadline for royal presentations from 26 August to 9 September, having been told by Hyde that failure to do this might 'prevent the gratifying of their Friends, that had Presentations under the Great Seal'.[46]

The last obstacles in the path of the ministers' bill were placed there by the House of Lords. On 8 September, the upper house was exhorted to 'give Dispatch to the bill for the quieting and restoring of Ministers', and it responded by raising a host of objections, most of which seem to have been minor ones.[47] Clearly a certain amount of bargaining took place: the Lords persuaded the Commons to forgo their scheme to vet the sequestered clergy, and in return they conceded that pluralists should be restored to only one of their former livings.[48]

In its final form, the act granted unconditional confirmation to incumbents who had been serving cures on 25 December 1659, with the exception of those who fell into three categories. Those who were in livings to which sequestered ministers laid claim had to hand them back to the ousted

[43] P.R.O., *C.* 66/2916, no. 415, and below pp. 55–6, 57.

[44] See below, p. 59, and *J.C.*, viii, 164.

[45] The most puzzling feature of the whole episode is why Charles did not cancel the offending grants; perhaps he was unwilling to rescind grants at the behest of one group among his subjects. Cf. Hyde's strictures on the 'Indecency of . . . Repealing the King's Letters Patents' (ibid).

[46] Ibid.

[47] *J.L.*, xi, 162; *J.C.*, viii, 161–2, 164–5.

[48] *J.C.*, viii, 164.

ministers; those in livings where the lawful patron had made a presentation but his nominee had been refused admission by the Triers 'without lawful cause' had to give them up to the lawful nominee; and those who had petitioned for the death of Charles I, opposed the restoration of Charles II, or in doctrinal matters denied the validity of infant baptism were to be ejected as unfit to hold office.[49] The process of ejecting those who fell into these categories was to be supervised by commissions drawn from the local J.P.s and was to be completed by 25 December 1660.[50] Well over 700 parishes were probably affected by ejections or restorations, though as far as can be seen the enforcement of the act caused very little bother.[51]

Not surprisingly, it is the disruptive elements in the act which have caught the attention of historians. This is unfortunate, for its positive features are much more important that its negative ones. The final measure represents a triumph for moderation in an immoderate age: both sides made concessions, and both sides gained their principal objectives—the absence of incident in late 1660 tells us this. Focusing on the ejections obscures the fact that the most important effect of the act was to confirm the titles of several thousand parish clergy. This represented a major advance towards a settlement of the church, and for this reason alone there must be no doubt about the king's attitude to the act.

A recent interpretation has suggested that in fact Charles was opposed to the Act for Settling Ministers. Dr Bosher has suggested that the king regarded the unconditional con-

[49] In addition, the clause confirming royal presentations had the unintentional effect of ejecting a few ministers, as we have just seen. Peers, too, were allowed to make presentations for a period of six months after 1 September 1660 without limitation by the act.

[50] *Statutes*, v, 242–6.

[51] *Cal. Rev.*, p. xiii, gives 695 as the number of ministers ejected in 1660, probably mostly after the act had been passed. *Walk. Rev.*, p. xvi (annotated version), suggests that 'over 700' of the sequestered clergy regained their livings. The overlap was not exact: some of those 'ejected' were in newly created lecturing or cathedral posts or in 'gathered' churches; others were replaced not by a sequestered minister but by someone else—one of the nominees turned down by the Triers, or one of the king's erroneous nominations. Also a certain proportion of sequestered ministers returned to livings which seem to have been vacant in 1660. Isolated incidents did occur: *Cal. Rev.*, pp. 12, 42, 113, 264, but there is very little evidence of activity by the commissioners appointed by the act, ibid., p. xl, and the county record offices of Hampshire, Surrey, and Kent.

firmation of the majority of the parish clergy as a 'serious breach in the Laudian position'; he argues that Charles did all he could to emasculate the bill, both through his own powers and through a 'church party' of 'Laudians' in the Commons. In the end, however, Charles was forced to accept it.[52]

This interpretation is unsatisfactory in various ways. First of all, the exact aims and composition of the 'church party' are largely a matter of supposition. It cannot be denied that there was a sizable and well-organized group of episcopalians in the Commons, but it is doubtful whether they were as extreme or as close to the court as Dr. Bosher believes. The primary aim of these men was to secure the restoration of as many of the sequestered clergy as possible, and they pursued their aim with a good deal of vigour and not a little guile. It may be suggested that their campaign against unconditional confirmation of incumbents in non-sequestered livings was not a sign of extreme, 'Laudian' zeal, but a diversionary attack upon the Presbyterians' well-entrenched position. The Presbyterians were insisting that the ejected episcopalian clergy should be screened to prevent 'scandalous' ministers creeping back into the church; the episcopalians' reply was to challenge the fitness of those already in the church. As one of them put it, the effect of the ministers' bill (as it then stood) would be 'to Continue all scandalous ministers out and not to Remove all scandalous that were in'.[53] Their point was that either the same tests should be imposed on all clergymen, sequestered and incumbent, or there should be no tests at all. As a tactic it succeeded in forcing the Presbyterians to reduce the number of tests in the bill until there were none which would have prevented a sequestered minister from recovering at least one of his cures.

It may also be doubted whether the so-called 'church party' was acting as keeper of the royal conscience. It is true that a few M.P.s who acted as managers for the court on secular issues such as indemnity or finance occasionally made speeches hostile to the Puritan cause.[54] But other court spokesmen and

[52] Bosher, pp. 171–8.

[53] 'Diary of Seymour Bowman', ff.103–5 for speeches by Littlewood, Finch, and Charlton.

[54] For Finch and Charlton, see J. R. Jones, art. cit., 169 and 'Diary of Seymour Bowman', ff.63, 104, 106, 135.

royal supporters pursued a much more moderate line in religious matters. Thus Arthur Annesley (who was undoubtedly close to the king at this time) helped to defeat an episcopalian proposal to eject incumbents who had consistently failed to administer the sacrament.[55] Similarly, William Prynne who on many matters supported the court was always 'passionately in favour' of the ministers' bill.[56]

There are various indications that Charles was a strong supporter of the bill. There is the fact that the final measure corresponded quite closely to the solution he had outlined to the Presbyterians in June. There is also the likelihood that he helped the bill through its last stages in Parliament. A recess was due to start on 8 September, by which date the ministers' bill was still not ready for the royal assent; Charles, therefore, permitted an extension of five days during which the ministers' bill (and other bills including a grant of money) passed both houses.[57] One should also note the part played by Hyde in the last-minute negotiations between Lords and Commons which ensured that the bill was ready for the king's assent by the 13th.[58] Finally, there is the evidence of Hyde's speech at the closing of Parliament on that day.

> The King hath passed this Act very willingly . . . and hath done much to the End of this Act before . . . I may say confidently, His Majesty hath never denied His Confirmation to any Man in Possession who hath asked it . . . except such who upon Examination and Enquiry appeared not worthy of it.[59]

This passage, taken together with Hyde's answer to the subcommittee in late August, leaves no room for doubt about Charles's attitude to the confirmation of the majority of incumbents in their livings: even before the final terms of the ministers' bill had been known, Charles had been actively confirming the titles of all incumbents who had requested it.

Hyde's speech does, however, raise further questions. How many incumbents did obtain a royal confirmation during the

[55] Ibid., f.117, and cf. Abernathy, 'English Presbyterians', p. 70.

[56] J. R. Jones, art. cit., 169; 'Diary of Seymour Bowman', ff.116, 136; *Parliamentary History of England*, ed. W. Cobbett (London, 12 vols., 1806–12), iv, 80, 82, 94–5.

[57] *J.C.*, viii, 159; *J.L.*, xi, 164, 165.

[58] *J.C.*, viii, 164.

[59] Ibid.

summer of 1660? What did the process of 'Examination and Enquiry' entail? To answer these questions, we must take a closer look at royal patronage as a whole, not only confirmations to those in possession but also new grants to ministers not yet in possession, and not only parish but also capitular appointments.

It has not generally been realized that in the first four months of the Restoration the king made well over 800 ecclesiastical presentations under the Great Seal (and a few more possibly by the Signet). Of these over 600 were to parish cures, and the remainder were to cathedral dignities or other posts.[60] Analysis of the Patent Rolls shows that in June sixty-one presentations were made, in July 239, in August 357, and in September 180; thereafter the monthly totals dropped sharply to an average of about twenty in 1661. The reasons for this quite unprecedented number of presentations were partly the considerable number of church appointments in the royal gift, and partly the application of the canon law principle of lapse. If a lay patron did not appoint within six months, patronage devolved to the bishop of the diocese in which the living lay; if that bishop failed to present within six months, it devolved onto the archbishop of the province, and if he did not present within a similar period, the patronage lapsed to the crown.[61] Livings normally in the gift of churchmen lapsed in a similar way. Now since many laymen had failed to present (or been prevented from presenting) within the canonical period of time, and since both archbishops and two-thirds of the episcopate had been dead for some time, a vast amount of patronage had lapsed to the crown.[62] For a few months, Charles was by far the most important patron in the country, one of the few sources of a fresh appointment,[63] or a

[60] The exact figures are 837 presentations from June to September, of which all but 223 were to parish livings—P.R.O., *C.* 66/2916-2919, 12 Chas. II, parts 1-4. For endorsements suggesting Signet appointments, see *S.P.* 29/4, ff.94, 129; 29/5, f.28; 29/7, ff.84, 87, 89; 29/8, f.33.

[61] E. Gibson, *Codex Juris Ecclesiastici Anglicani* (Oxford, 2 vols., 1761), i, 763, 768-70.

[62] Both king and patrons realized this—cf. references to lapse in petitions (*S.P.* 29/10, ff.4,77; 29/12, ff.82, 86) and Patent Rolls (*C.* 66/2916, nos. 178a, 252, 282, 316, 325, 330, 442, 444).

[63] Charles allowed surviving bishops to exercise their normal patronage, though most of it had lapsed to the crown—*Lib. Inst.* and below pp. 63-4.

confirmation of an earlier title. Many of the incumbents appointed in the 1640s and 1650s were not sure of the legitimacy of their title in 1660, and petitioned Charles for confirmation; as we shall see, a considerable proportion of Charles's 614 'presentations' to parish livings were in effect confirmations of earlier titles rather than first-time appointments.[64]

Charles may himself have played some part in the distribution of the livings in his gift. Some petitions are said to have been examined 'in the king's presence' at Whitehall, and one of them bears a royal signature to a note ordering a grant by 'immediate Warrant'.[65] But for the most part it was almost certainly the chancellor and his officials who bore the brunt of selection and appointment. Charles had recognized Hyde's enormous capacity for work, and often exploited it;[66] it is obvious that Hyde was at the hub of ecclesiastical patronage from the speed with which he produced the two papers for the Parliamentary sub-committee in August, and from the confidence with which he spoke about royal presentations on 13 September. It has been suggested, however, that 'Control of these presentations under the Great Seal was . . . placed by Hyde in the hands of the Laudian leaders'; a 'standing committee' of three leading 'Laudians'—Sheldon, Earle, and Morley—was set up to 'ensure the appointment of clergy whose loyalty and orthodoxy could be guaranteed'.[67] While it cannot be denied that about a hundred petitions for clerical preferment were handled by these three royal chaplains, it would be unwise to exaggerate the powers and significance of this 'committee'.[68]

The genesis of this body need occasion little surprise. Faced by a barrage of claims and counter-claims for offices in his gift, Charles often referred petitions to officials or to peers who

[64] See below pp. 57-8.

[65] *S.P.* 29/4, f.94 (and others in Appendix 1); *S.P.* 29/7, f.85.

[66] Clarendon, *Life*, ii, 43-4, 49-50.

[67] Bosher, p. 159.

[68] Forty-two petitions were referred specifically to the three chaplains, and their verdicts are also visible (marked with an asterisk in Appendix 1); some of these petitions bear a third endorsement ordering a presentation to be made (appropriate column, ibid.). A further fifty-eight petitions bear signs of having gone through one or more of the three stages of referral, report, and appointment (ibid.).

might know more of the matter.[69] It should be noted that nearly half of the petitions handled by the 'committee' sought deaneries, archdeaconries, or capitular posts—offices indissolubly linked to the old order in the church, and it was natural for the king to turn to three episcopalians who had a wide acquaintance of their fellow churchmen through their own university and cathedral backgrounds. It should also be noted that most of the petitions referred to the 'committee' sought posts which would normally have been in the gift of bishops, deans or chapters, had they not lapsed to the crown by 1660.[70] In essence, the 'committee' was probably nothing more than an effort on the part of a hard-pressed government to delegate work to three royal chaplains who were regularly at court during the summer of 1660.[71]

The 'committee's' terms of reference were strictly limited. They were 'to certify their knowlige, att least their Information from Persons of very good creditt, whether the Petitioner for his Loyaltie, abilities, and merit, be capable, and fit'.[72] In none of the endorsements referring petitions to the chaplains was it suggested that doctrinal or liturgical tests should be imposed; on only one occasion did the endorsement demand proof of ordination.[73] Similarly, with one exception the chaplains' replies made no reference to the pre-war Church of England; they were confined to simple statements on the candidate's 'abilityes and good conversation' or the credibility of the referees who signed the petition or accompanying certificate.[74] Since the 'committee' does not appear to have interviewed petitioners, its members probably placed particular emphasis on the opinion of the laymen and

[69] *Cal. St. Pap. Dom. 1660-1661*, pp. 47, 49-51, 55-6; *Cal. St. Pap. Ireland 1660-1662*, pp. 3-6.

[70] See Appendix 1. By no means all lapsed ecclesiastical patronage was referred to the 'committee'; nor did the 'committee' deal exclusively with such patronage.

[71] A fourth, Humfrey Henchman, appears in five of the 'committee's' reports (ibid.). The idea of delegating may have been mooted by the overworked Hyde or by the experienced Secretary Nicholas who signed most of the initial endorsements referring petitions to the 'committee'.

[72] *S.P.* 29/5, f.26, and cf. 29/7, ff.56, 87.

[73] This was the very first case handled, *S.P.* 29/4, ff.94, 94.1; the demand was dropped from all subsequent endorsements.

[74] *S.P.* 29/7, f.86. The exception was again the first case where the 'committee' said they were satisfied of the candidate's 'Conformity to the Church of England as heretofore established by Bishopps'; thereafter such phrases cannot be found.

divines who supported the claimants. In view of the nature of many of the posts on which the chaplains were being consulted—capitular posts and livings normally in the gift of ecclesiastical patrons—it seems likely that the 'committee' was acquainted with many of the petitioners' referees.[75]

It should also be remembered that the 'committee' never had executive power, but could only recommend a presentation. This explains why the 'committee' recommended two men for the same living on more than one occasion.[76] It also explains why a fifth of the chaplains' favourable reports met with no response from the king; in many cases a rival claimant had got there first. The more one looks at the 'committee's' work, the more difficult it is to assign it more than a marginal role in the events of 1660. In the first four months of the Restoration, it handled petitions relating to about one tenth of the king's presentations to parish livings and to fewer than one fifth of his capitular appointments. Indeed, the amount of work done by the three chaplains dwindled as the number of royal appointments soared. Thus while the total number of royal appointments, parish and capitular, rose from 239 in July to 357 in August, the number of petitions handled by the 'committee' dropped from about fifty-five to about nineteen.[77] It is difficult to suggest a reason for this sharp decline, but it was clearly not overwork.

In only one sense can the 'committee' be said to have furthered 'Laudian' ends, in that a few of the royal presentations made on its recommendation had the effect of challenging the titles of incumbents who should have been protected by the proclamation of 1 June and the Act for Settling Ministers. About seventeen of the petitions approved by the 'committee' came from clergymen who had no prior claim to the living sought and who were consciously or unconsciously ignoring the claims of incumbents appointed during the civil wars or Interregnum.[78] But before this is

[75] This may explain the preponderance of episcopalian referees noted by Dr. Bosher (p. 160, and n. 3); however, by no stretch of the imagination can these men be termed uniformly 'Laudian'.

[76] E.g. Sudbourne and Worplesdon rectories.

[77] See Appendix 1 and above p. 52 n.60. The date at which a petition was handled has been gauged from the intial endorsement or from the subsequent presentation.

[78] The petitions of Burnett, Anthill, Davenant, White, Mallory, Blanchard,

claimed as evidence of 'Laudian' intent, two points should be borne in mind. First of all, it is doubtful whether the 'committee' was aware of the existence of an incumbent in the living sought. Only three of the seventeen petitions in question mentioned incumbents; most of them simply described the living as being vacant due to the death of the last episcopally instituted incumbent.[79] Secondly, it is clear that by no means all of the 'committee's' recommendations were adopted by the king. In some cases it would seem that the incumbents whose titles were being challenged fought back successfully. On 30 July, Sheldon and Earle endorsed the petition of Anthony Clifford for a rectory in Devon, but when the incumbent John Hill realized that he was 'threaten'd to be turn'd out of his Living, to secure himself he took out the Broad Seal for it, Sept. 6, 1660'.[80] Another incumbent, John Overed, succeeded in securing both the revocation of the royal grant recommended by the 'committee' and the confirmation of his own title.[81] Altogether seven incumbents who might have been ejected as a result of 'committee' reports managed to retain possession.[82] These seven should be borne in mind when considering the less fortunate incumbents who probably were ejected in September 1660 because of the 'committee's' endorsements and the king's erroneous grants.[83]

If the 'committee' played only a peripheral part in royal

Boldero, Robinson, Thurston, Sutton, Clifford, Butt, Bird, Brunsel, Bonner, Scott, and Huish. For incumbents affected, see following notes.

[79] The petitions of Burnett, White, and Thurston; the 'intruder' named by White does not appear in *Cal. Rev.* (though cf. John James, a lecturer ejected from this parish, ibid., p. 294); Thurston failed to gain possession from the incumbent John Overed (see n.82).

[80] Calamy, *Continuation*, i, 294.

[81] *Cal. Rev.*, pp. 375-6.

[82] Hill and Overed; Sam. Tomlyns, rector of Crawley, Hants., 1655-62; Is. Harrison, rector of Hadleigh, Suffolk, 1643-62; J. Fox, vicar of Pucklechurch, Glos., 1655-62; Ben. Burnand, rector of Warnford, Hants., 1648-66; and Phil. Nesbit, rector of Kirklington, Yorks., 1646-62. *Cal. Rev.*, pp. 264; 375-6; 488-9; 249; 211; *Lib. Inst.*, and F. T. Madge, *Hampshire Inductions* (Winchester, 1918), p. 51; *Cal. Rev.*, p. 366.

[83] T. Osmonton, M. Burkit, G. Faroll, W. Tray, H. Pierce, J. Cromwell, R. Ward, and E. Rolt (*Cal. Rev.*, pp. 375, 89, 191, 490-1, 384, 147, 509-10, and 416-17) were ejected as a result of presentations to Burnett, Anthill, Blanchard, Robinson, Bird, Brunsel, Bonner and Huish. Two more may have been ejected, but one was only a lecturer not an incumbent (see n. 79), and the other was replaced not by the 'committee's' candidate, Blanchard, but by another candidate not screened by them.

patronage, how were the great majority of the king's nominees selected? A categorical answer is not possible: many of the petitions which correspond to later royal presentations bear no endorsements to indicate the way in which they were treated;[84] in many other cases no petition at all has survived (though it is quite likely that there were oral requests for preferment, perhaps supported by those with influence at court on some occasions). The most likely answer, however, is also the most simple: hundreds of clergymen petitioned the king for a grant, their petitions were subjected to a cursory 'Examination and Enquiry' by the chancellor or his staff, and their requests were then granted. In view of the limited information at their disposal and the pressure of work in the summer of 1660, Hyde and his officials probably did no more than look for obvious errors or inconsistencies and try to prevent duplicate grants of the same living. They may have kept an eye open for regicides or notorious fire-brands ('such who upon Examination and Enquiry appeared not worthy of the king's blessing),[85] but few of these were likely to present themselves. For the most part, the chancellor and his staff rubber-stamped the petitions which came their way.

One final question may be asked: what proportion of royal grants to parish clergy had the effect of confirming the titles of incumbents appointed during the revolutionary decades, and what proportion gave completely new titles to ministers to enable them to take possession of vacant (or supposedly vacant) livings? The Patent Rolls do not make it easy to answer this query, for their entries tend to ignore appointments made by non-episcopal agencies, and thus to confound confirmations and fresh presentations. Even where we know from other evidence that a grant is in effect a confirmation, the Patent Rolls tend to describe the living as vacant 'by the death of the last Incumbent there or any other Wayes howsoever now voyd'. Only in a minority of cases do the entries contain the phrase *ad corroborandum titulum* or 'to Corroborate the tytle' when they should do so.[86] Nevertheless,

[84] E.g. *S.P.* 29/4, ff.39, 131; 29/6, ff.1, 2, 3, 13, 18, 20, 21, 23; and *C.* 66/2918, no. 166; 66/2917, no. 126; 66/2918, nos. 2, 122, 97; 66/2917, nos. 144, 130, 69; 66/2918, nos. 145, 136.

[85] *J.C.*, viii, 164.

[86] *C.* 66/2916, nos. 415, 444 (and cf. 200, 234, 239, 265); 252, 444.

this difficulty can be overcome by using other classes of records and the biographical aids at our disposal to trace the exact status of royal nominees in the summer of 1660. The very large number of Great Seal appointments precludes a complete analysis, but a sample survey of two large dioceses (Canterbury and Winchester) enables us to take a close look at over a tenth of royal presentations to parish livings between 1 June and 9 September—sixty-four presentations out of a total of 614.

Analysis of these sixty-four grants shows that a significant proportion of them did have the effect of confirming the titles of those in possession in May 1660. Eight of the twenty-nine grants to Canterbury livings and nineteen of the thirty-five grants to Winchester livings corroborated the titles of incumbents appointed in the previous decades.[87] This total of twenty-seven confirmations out of sixty-four grants is an impressive vindication of Hyde's statement to Parliament that 'His Majesty hath never denied His Confirmation to any Man in Possession who hath asked it'. If royal patronage was put to a similar use in other dioceses, Charles must have confirmed the titles of hundreds of parish clergy during the first few months of his reign. It seems likely that knowledge of the king's policy spread at parish level, for some of the incumbents confirmed by the king in Winchester diocese lived so close to each other, and the dates on their patents are so nearly simultaneous, that collusion seems certain.[88]

Presentations for ministers not in possession account for twenty-one of the twenty-nine Canterbury presentations and sixteen of the thirty-five Winchester ones. Of those presented, however, three in Canterbury and four in Winchester do not seem to have succeeded in obtaining possession, either because there was an incumbent who fought back or a rival aspirant to the living.[89] Thus the number who actually obtained livings in these dioceses was only marginally higher than the total of incumbents confirmed in possession.

[87] Details are given in Appendix 2, Part 1.

[88] The incumbents of four contiguous parishes received their patents in two pairs, 25th and 29th July, 30th and 31st August (Hinton Ampner, Warnford, Exton, Meonstoke); in between the rector of nearby East Meon obtained a patent. Similarly, the incumbents of Crawley, Houghton, and Wonston received confirmation on 16th, 19th, and 31st July (the first and third are contiguous, the second four miles away).

[89] Appendix 2, Part 2; Beeston, Dale, Stain; Clutterbuck, Gregson, Doughtie, and Goulston.

Nor do these figures convey the full extent of the king's generosity. By definition, those confirmed in possession by the king had conformed to the religious practice of the revolutionary decades; indeed, a minority of them were so determinedly Puritan in outlook that, having received a royal blessing on the continuation of their ministry in 1660, they were ejected two years later for refusing to conform to Parliament's notion of a church settlement.[90] But many of those given a completely new title in 1660 were also drawn from the ranks of the Commonwealth conformists. William Bicknell had been the assistant of the Puritan vicar of Newport, Isle of Wight, for at least five years before he was promoted by the king to the vicarage of nearby Portsea; he held the living for only two years, being ejected in 1662 for nonconformity.[91] Altogether eighteen of the thirty-seven ministers given new livings in these dioceses had served in the Interregnum church, or had taught at or graduated but recently from Puritan Oxford or Cambridge.[92] If we add together the patents confirming incumbents in their livings and those original presentations which were bestowed on Commonwealth conformists, we find that over two-thirds of the king's nominees in these dioceses had to some extent conformed to the practice of the Commonwealth church.

By contrast, the number of staunch episcopalians given livings by the king in these dioceses was very low—perhaps as low as seven.[93] One might have anticipated that a large number of sequestered clergy would have taken the opportunity to acquire another living (which could probably have been held with their old living if or when it was recovered). But if we compare the Great Seal appointments with the list of sufferers in *Walker Revised*, we find that over

[90] Seven in our two dioceses (marked with an asterisk in Appendix 2, Part 1). The national figure, produced by collating *46th Report* and *Cal. Rev.*, was at least thirty-three: Appendix 3, Part 2.

[91] *Cal. Rev.*, p. 53.

[92] Appendix 2, Part 2: Burnett, Cole, Dale, Harrison, Pindar, Pulford, Reading, Baker, Bicknell, Blanchard, Clutterbuck, Doughtie?, Gregson, Beeston, Drayton, Nightingale, Say, Stain, Thornborough.

[93] Six had probably been sequestered, Benskin, Harrison, Pindar, Smith, Doughtie, and Bp. of Galloway, but of these three later conformed; five had been ejected from the universities, Willys, Wilsford, Appleford, Clutterbuck, and Coles, but Clutterbuck later conformed. Ibid.

the whole of England only about fifty (or eight per cent) of the king's presentations were given to sequestered clergy seeking a new living; moreover, several of these were not experienced parish priests but fellows or scholars ejected from the two universities.[94] Thus, very few Anglican clergy of proven loyalty and experience received a royal grant in the summer of 1660.

It is the liberality of the king in the exercise of his patronage that stands out most clearly. Incumbents appointed by Parliamentary or Commonwealth authorities were readily granted confirmation. Other clergymen seeking a new appointment were given one, whether they were conformists or sufferers. As far as can be gauged, no doctrinal tests were imposed as a precondition of receiving a royal grant. Against this background, the considerable concessions to moderate Puritanism in the Worcester House declaration need occasion less surprise. They were an integral part of the king's efforts to secure a broadly-based parish clergy by the use of his prerogative powers. Against this background, it may also be possible to understand why the king chose to appoint cathedral clergy and even bishops not from one narrow group but from men of differing religious standpoints within the church.

[94] Appendix 3, Part 3. University men without experience as parish priests included Appleford, Coles, Comyn, Deane, Newlin, Reade, Ryves, and Samwayes.

III

THE RE-ESTABLISHMENT OF THE CATHEDRAL CHAPTERS

The cathedral chapters and the larger collegiate churches had suffered badly during the revolutionary decades.[1] After 1642 their work had gradually been rendered impossible by the attacks of parliamentary forces, the proscription of their traditional forms of worship, and the seizure of their possessions and revenues. During the civil wars and Interregnum a large number of the deprived cathedral clergy had died; though the sources are admittedly fallible, it appears that approximately 410 dignities, canonries, and prebends out of a total of just over 600 had fallen vacant by the Restoration.[2] In some cases, this left only one or two dignitaries or prebendaries to confront the 'intruders' preaching in the cathedrals or the purchasers in possession of capitular property in 1660.

Nevertheless, the chapters seem to have recovered their former strength and influence surprisingly quickly after the Restoration. There was considerable variation in the speed and ease with which different chapters were restored, but gaps in their ranks were being filled within weeks of the king's return, and by August or September general chapters were being held and the varied tasks of cathedral and collegiate churches resumed. Certain questions, however, need to be answered. Why, for example, did the king appoint so many men to cathedral posts in the early months of the Restoration, at a time when there were still Puritan lecturers in several cathedrals, and Presbyterian and episcopalian divines, under

[1] The four largest collegiate churches, Westminster, Windsor, Ripon and Southwell, will be included in the following discussion of cathedral chapters.

[2] Browne Willis, *A Survey of the Cathedrals of* [*England and Wales*] (London, 3 vols., 1742); Le Neve, *Fasti;* supplemented on individual churches by G. Oliver, *Lives of the Bishops of Exeter and A History of the Cathedral* (Exeter, 1861); W. H. Jones, *Fasti Ecclesiae Sarisberiensis* (London, 2 vols., 1879, 1881); *J. Le Neve, Fasti Ecclesiae Anglicanae 1541-1857: I St. Paul's London* compiled by J. M. Horn (London, 1969), *II Chichester Diocese* compiled by J. M. Horn (London, 1971).

his own chairmanship, were still discussing the eventual form of the church settlement?[3] What were the particular problems faced by the reconstituted chapters, and how did they overcome them?

In answering the first question, an examination of royal patronage again throws much light on the early stages of the church settlement. During the Interregnum, the exiled court had become acutely aware of the serious threat to the English episcopal succession posed by the dwindling number of bishops and the disruption of the chapters whose task was to elect new bishops: 'many of the deans being dead, some chapters extinguished, and all of them so disturbed, as they cannot meet in the chapter house, where such acts regularly are to be performed'.[4] We know from a series of lists preserved among the papers of Secretary Nicholas that the exiles made efforts to keep abreast of vacancies in the higher ranks of the Anglican church. These lists, which from internal evidence can be shown to have been drawn up in 1658 or 1659, stated which bishoprics, deaneries, dignities, and prebends had fallen vacant, and named eighty-six men worthy of promotion to them. A minority of these men were allocated a specific bishopric or benefice, but most were simply deemed worthy of promotion without having a specific post appended to their names. The lists clearly underwent revision when news of the death of more dignitaries and of some of their potential replacements reached the court,[5] so that the lists are probably an accurate guide to royal thinking at the moment of the king's return to England.

What emerges quite clearly from a comparison of these lists with the royal appointments actually made after the Restoration, however, is that the king decided to modify his plans. On the revised lists about a dozen translations and elevations were anticipated, but only two of these appointments were actually made in 1660.[6] A higher proportion of the capitular allocations of 1658–9 was followed by a royal grant in 1660; ten of the suggested appointments

[3] See below, pp. 72–3; Abernathy, 'English Presbyterians', pp. 68–73.

[4] Barwick, pp. 199–201, 414.

[5] Egerton MS. 2542, ff.265–70; cf. ff.265–6, 268–70 for deaths of Bishops Morton and Brownrigg, and of A. Clarke, J. Hewitt, E. Hyde, and H. Stringer.

[6] For a discussionof this point, see below pp. 81–2, 88–9.

were adopted, as opposed to six which were not.[7] However, of the many men on the lists in the more general category—worthy of promotion but not linked to a specific dignity—only eighteen received a royal grant in the first four months of the Restoration, as opposed to twenty-eight who received nothing at all.[8] Why did Charles pass by over half of those on the lists who were still alive in 1660 and not being considered for elevation to the episcopate?[9]

It is hard to find a feature common to the thirty-four men on the lists who were ignored. One or two may have incurred royal displeasure, for example Herbert Thorndike for his rather premature obituary of the episcopal Church of England; but others were notable loyalists, such as Joseph Crowther who had gone to serve the royal family in exile.[10] Some on the lists were perhaps little known or inexperienced, but the ranks of those passed over included an experienced dean (Bayley of Sarum), a learned archdeacon (Edward Layfield) and men of some standing in their own dioceses (for instance Edward Stanley and George Gillingham of Winchester).[11] A few of those ignored by the king were given a benefice by a surviving bishop—Crowther was made precentor

[7] Based on a comparison of Egerton MS. 2542, ff.266-70 and the presentations recorded on *C.* 66/2916-2919 (printed in *46th Report*). The ten were Edw. Aldey, Wm. Belke, Wm. Brough, Guy Carleton, Robt. Creighton, J. Earle, Pet. Hardres, Alex. Hyde, Jasp. Mayne and Geo. Morley; the six were J. Barwick, Jos. Crowther, Dr. (J?) Haywood, Wm. Paul, Robt. Sanderson and Edw. Wolley. A seventh—Mich. Honywood—received a deanery instead of the prebend originally allocated him; an eighth—Hen. Stringer—died in 1657.

[8] The eighteen were Rd. Allestree, J. Aucher, Wm. Barker, Geo. Beaumont, J. Castilion, Pet. Gunning, Ant. Hawles, Ben. Laney, Wm. Fuller, J. Lloyd, Rd. Meredith, J. Middleton, Dav. Mitchell, Robt. Mossom, J. Oliver, Barn. Oley, J. Reading and Thos. Warmestry. The twenty-eight were Rd. Baillie, Thos. Barlow, Is. Barrow, Thos. Browne, Rd. Drake, J. Gauden, Geo Gillingham, Nath. Hardy, Henry(?) Harrington, Jos. Henshaw, Pet. Heylyn, 'Mr. Hollis', Edw. Lamplugh, Edw. Layfield, Nich. Monck, Thos. Smith, Edw. Stanley, Rd. Sterne, Thos. Swadlin, Herb. Thorndike, Tim. Thurscross, Thos. Triplet, Tim. Tulley, Thos. Turner, Bri. Walton, Thos. Walker, Geo. Wishart, and Mich. Woodward.

[9] Eleven had probably died by May 1660: J. Alsop, G. Benson, A. Clare, E. Duncon, H. Hammond, J. Hewett, E. Hyde, J. Pottinger, R. Stuart, H. Stringer, and C. Wren. Ten were candidates for translation or elevation: Juxon, Warner; J. Cosin, H. Ferne, H. Henchman, W. Lucy, F. Mansell, M. Nicholas, B. Ryves, and G. Sheldon. Two—G. Wilde and J. Taylor—were nominated to Irish bishoprics in August.

[10] Barwick, pp. 401-2; Bosher, p. 287.

[11] *Walk. Rev.*, pp. 67, 53, 190, 183.

of St. Paul's by Juxon; some received posts in the second wave of appointments late in 1660, but those so favoured were in a minority.[12]

The reason for their neglect may have lain not in their own faults but in the pressure that new candidates, men not on the lists, brought to bear on the king. Over a hundred petitions for promotion to dignities, prebends, and archdeaconries in the king's gift were received in the first four months of the Restoration,[13] and their effect was probably to modify Charles's original plans in various ways. In the first place, the petitions must have provided the government with its first accurate information on the number and location of vacancies in the royal gift. The authors of the Nicholas lists were obviously unaware of the deaths of many churchmen of middling rank, such as the deans of Lichfield, Lincoln, Chester, St. Asaph, and St. David's; similarly, they knew of only seven canonries that were definitely vacant, and those all in south-east England.[14] The petitions of 1660 stated where the vacancies were—the eleventh prebend of Durham, the prebend of Ketton in Lincoln chapter—and the reasons why they were vacant (usually death, sometimes resignation or conversion to Catholicism).[15] They also informed the government how many livings had lapsed to the crown. The king's patronage in this field was traditionally large, and about a hundred dignities and prebends normally in his gift had fallen vacant by 1660. But this figure was more than doubled by the application of the principle of lapse, so that eventually Charles made 223 presentations to dignities, prebends, and archdeaconries between June and September 1660.[16] (Archdeacons were members of about half of the English chapters, and so may usefully be included in a discussion of royal patronage in the capitular field.)

[12] Le Neve, *Fasti*, ii, 351; Henshaw was made dean of Chichester by the king in October 1660, *46th Report*, p. 64.

[13] *S.P.* 29/1-17 *passim*, and Appendix 4 below; there may well have been petitions other than those preserved in the state paper collection.

[14] Four at Canterbury, one each at Oxford, Windsor, and Westminster: Egerton MS. 2542, ff.265, 268, 267, 270.

[15] *S.P.* 29/4, f.40; 29/12, f.38; 29/4, f.41; 29/6, f.23.

[16] Above p. 52 n.60; owing to duplicate grants the number of installations was slightly lower than the number of grants. It is not always clear from the sources used (p. 61 n.2) whether the king was the normal patron of certain benefices.

Another effect of the petitions was almost certainly to make Charles forget some of the allocations and 'worthy' men listed on Nicholas's papers. Thus, to judge from the lists, Dr. William Paul should have been given the Westminster canonry of an exile who had died in Paris; but before he was, John Sudbury, whose name does not appear on the lists, petitioned for the very same post and received a royal grant on 7 July.[17] It is surely significant that of the twenty-eight men on the lists who did receive a capitular post from the king, a third of them, probably unaware that they were on any list, petitioned the king for the benefice they received.[18] Moreover, the majority of the twenty-eight received their presentations in June or the first three weeks of July, that is, before the flood of clerical petitions for capitular livings reached its peak.[19] Thereafter only a handful of 'worthy' men were promoted, whereas two-thirds of the petitioners obtained the benefice they sought.[20]

The spate of petitions also serves to explain the speed and throughness with which royal patronage was exploited in the summer of 1660. Such was the pressure that nearly all capitular posts in the king's gift had been filled by August or September, and there was barely anything left for the new bishops appointed in the autumn. Archdeacons were normally appointed by the bishop of the diocese, but by 1660 twenty-two vacant archdeaconries had lapsed to the crown, and at least fifteen of these were filled—in part at least—because of the enterprise of clerical suitors. Furthermore these petitioners had moved so fast that all but two of them had received their grants by early September, before a single translation or consecration had taken place.[21] Indeed, such was the sustained

[17] Egerton MS. 2542, f.270; *S.P.* 29/6, f.28; *46th Report*, p. 111.

[18] Allestree, Aucher, Barker, Beaumont, Castilion, Hardres, Meredith, Middleton, Mossom; Warmestry petitioned for something else; Appendix 4.

[19] *46th Report* for the date of the grants of those listed above; *S.P.* 29/6-8 and 29/12 for the petitions.

[20] Meredith, Hardres, Laney, Oley, Aldey and Beaumont received grants between 25 July and 30 August. The 108 petitions resulted in sixty-two grants by September, and a further eight after September (Appendix 4); the failure rate for petitioners rose due to increasing rivalry.

[21] G. Hall, R. Meredith, W. Jones, E. Cotton, F. Fulwood, J. Smith, J. Middleton, G. Benson, G. Thorne, F. Davis, L. Womock, A. Sparrow, G. Roberts, J. Carter, and C. Breton (the last two received their grants in October)—Appendix 4.

enthusiasm of petitioners and the king's open-handed way with other people's patronage that at York Charles made over a dozen presentations to prebends customarily in the archbishop's gift *after* Frewen had been nominated and elected to that see.[22]

It has been suggested that one of the reasons for royal haste was the need for the chapters to perform their canonical role of electing new bishops as soon as possible,[23] but if this was one of Charles's motives it can have been only a minor one. Two of the bodies most rapidly reconstituted by royal appointments, Westminster and Windsor, were collegiate churches, and did not possess the right to elect a bishop.[24] Equally, the nomination of canons to Oxford and Rochester chapters in June and July bore little relation to the need for episcopal elections, for the bishops of both dioceses were still alive, and Skinner at least was in such disfavour with the court that he was unlikely to be translated.[25] Logically, the first appointment should have been to the chapters whose numbers had fallen lowest, but Carlisle with only one prebendary left and Gloucester with just the dean and a single prebendary were not reinforced until late July and not completely filled until September.[26]

It would also seem to have been possible for some chapters to have conducted episcopal elections within weeks of the Restoration (though it is perhaps unwise to generalize about the very diverse statutes of English chapters). At Winchester, seven of the twelve prebendaries who had attended the general chapter of June 1645 lived through to the Restoration, as did five of the six prebendaries at Chester and seven of the twelve at Durham.[27] The dean and four of the prebendaries of Peterborough were still alive and as early as June had come together to recover their muniments.[28] In such chapters, the

[22] *46th Report*, pp. 18, 40, 43, 44, 48, 52, 61, 65, 70, 74, 77, 110; *S.P.* 29/12, ff.54, 55, 58, 60.

[23] Bosher, p. 161.

[24] Le Neve, *Fasti*, iii, 349–60 and 375, 402–3; *46th Report*.

[25] Ibid., pp. 18, 45, 50, 83, 86, 95; 39, 40, 45, 75(2); Barwick, pp. 210, 218–19, 239–42, and below pp. 82, 91 on Warner.

[26] B. Willis, op. cit., i, 304–11, 730–45, and *46th Report*, pp. 33, 34, 107, 103; 119, 28, 61, 87.

[27] Le Neve, *Fasti*, iii, 33–44; B. Willis, op. cit., i, 345–52, 264–75.

[28] Kennett, *Register*, pp. 117, 218; only three prebendaries were active in June, but

appointment of a new dean or at most one or two prebendaries would probably have enabled canonical elections to have taken place in June or July had the king so desired, but the opportunity was not taken. Indeed, even after chapters had been raised to near their full strength, there was often a long interval before the *congé d'élire* was received. The chapter of Canterbury was raised to a strength of nine canons and the dean by 9 July, and was working as a unit within a matter of days; but two months elapsed before the *congé* to elect Juxon arrived.[29] Similar or even longer delays occurred at Norwich, Peterborough, Gloucester, and Hereford.[30] Thus, preparation for elections was probably much less important than the pressure from petitioners in accounting for the speed of royal grants.

It is hard to avoid the conclusion that most of the king's 223 nominees were presented in response to their own requests. No more than an eighth of royal presentations can be explained by reference to the Nicholas lists, and only twenty-seven petitioners for capitular preferment may be said to have owed their success to the favourable reports of the Sheldon-Earle-Morley 'committee'.[31] There are other factors which support this conclusion, for example the geographical pattern of royal appointments. The first chapters to be reconstituted by royal grants were those nearest to London; the majority of appointments to Westminster, Windsor, Oxford, Canterbury, Rochester, Norwich, and Winchester were made by July. Although traditionally in his gift, prebends in the chapters of Gloucester and Worcester were not filled until later; similarly, lapsed patronage in the important chapters of York and Lincoln, as well as Hereford, was not exercised until August or September.[32] It seems likely that this pattern reflected the greater length of time that it took provincial clergymen or their emissaries to reach the court. The proportion of men promoted by the king who had some connection with the locality in which their promotion lay is also striking. Five of

a fourth, Towers, was still alive.

[29] Le Neve, *Fasti,* i, 33, 47-61, and below p. 72 and Appendix 6.

[30] Capitular appointments from sources on p. 61 n.2 above, and *46th Report*; *congés*—Appendix 6.

[31] See above pp. 62-3 and Appendix 1.

[32] Sources on p. 61 n.2, and *46th Report*.

the new canons of Canterbury were incumbents of Kentish livings; two of the new prebendaries of Winchester had served parish livings in Hampshire, and the new archdeacon of Surrey had been ministering in London for several years.[33] Many other examples of this phenomenon could be given from all over England.[34] In normal times the appointment of local men would occasion little surprise, but their promotion in 1660—when two years earlier the court knew so little of the English clergy—does imply that many royal appointments were the product of a timely request by a provincial clergyman aware of a local vacancy.

Another feature of those promoted by the king was their relative inexperience. Nearly 200 members of the pre-war capitular clergy had outlived the troubles, but very few of them were promoted in the summer of 1660.[35] Only three of the eight surviving deans and four of the twenty-five experienced archdeacons were promoted to provide leadership in new posts or more important chapters.[36] Only one of the seven surviving prebendaries of Winchester was promoted (John Oliver, to be dean of Worcester); at Canterbury none of the five survivors was promoted in 1660. It might be argued that this was an act of policy, that the government felt that the

[33] Aldey, Belke, du Moulin, Hardres, Reading; Goulston, Waferer, and Pearson; their livings are given in *Alum. Oxon.*, *Alum. Cant.*, and *Walk. Rev.*

[34] Carlisle: Savage, West, new dean from next diocese (Carleton); York: Ainsworth, Bradley, Elcock, Hitch, Lister, Neale; Chester: Bridgeman, Mallory; Hereford: Benson, Good, E. Jones, Sedon, Wicherley; Worcester: Dowdeswell; Lincoln: Ashton, Coope, S. Cotton, Harwood, Naylor; Oxford: Allestree, Dolben, Fell, Morley; Rochester: Codd, Cooke, Dixon. The same is true of new deans (Bridgeman, Croft, Glenham, Honywood, Marsh, etc.) and archdeacons (Coke, West, Womock). Sources as in previous note.

[35] Above p. 61. Busby (Wells); Nicholas (Bristol); Henshaw and Paul (Chichester); Machon (Lichfield); G. Hall (Exeter); Coke (Hereford); Creighton and Pight (Lincoln); Morley (Oxford); Earle, Ryves, Hyde, and Pearson (Sarum); Laney (Westminster); Oliver (Winchester); Marsh (York); West (Carlisle). Sources as in previous notes. Some survivors were given an additional prebend e.g. Neale (York), Morgan (Chester); a few received grants confirming earlier presentations e.g. Brough (Gloucester).

[36] Deans of Bristol, Chichester, and Peterborough (to more important deaneries or a bishopric); deans of Bangor, Exeter, Hereford, Rochester and Sarum were not promoted. Three archdeacons were elevated (Brecknock, St. David's, and E. Riding), one was moved to a better archdeaconry (Cornwall); those not moved were the archdeacons of Bangor, Anglesey, Bath, Taunton, Lewes, Exeter, Derby, Leicester, Bedford, Stow, London, Essex, Colchester, Oxford, Berks, Worcester, W. Riding, Cleveland, Carlisle, Durham, Sodor and Man.

local expertise of the survivors would be wasted if too many were moved to new chapters. But the corollary of the fact that only twenty of the king's nominees had previous capitular experience was that nearly two hundred had none at all. Thus important deaneries such as Lincoln, Durham, and Norwich were filled by men with little or no experience of normal capitular procedures, let alone the abnormal problems created by the situation in 1660.[37] None of the new canons of Canterbury—the province's most important chapter—seems to have had any experience; at Winchester, only one had been a prebendary before.[38] Had the government known how many experienced men were still alive, it would surely have distributed them more evenly among the different chapters. But Charles was almost certainly unaware of the existence of many survivors: only a fraction of their names appear in the Nicholas lists or on the petitions preserved in the state papers.[39] Survivors may have trusted that their record and experience would speak for themselves, only to find that the brash importunity of younger and less experienced men was a more assured means of promotion.

Lack of experience was not the only remarkable feature of those promoted by the king; many of them also lacked a record of consistent loyalty to king and church. About a third of those nominated by the king do not appear in the lists of sufferers given in *Walker Revised*, which means that either they had conformed to Puritan practice in the 1640s and 1650s or they had been too young to be in positions of authority before the civil wars.[40] Perhaps a further quarter of royal nominees had been sequestered but had later conformed to hold a parish living, a university post, or a teaching post during the Interregnum.[41] Possibly half of the king's

[37] *Walk. Rev.*, pp. 237-8, 139, 332.

[38] J. Ryves had been a prebendary of Sarum and archdeacon of Berks. (*Alum. Oxon.*)

[39] Several deans and a certain number of prebendaries (e.g. Sheldon, Earle, and Morley) were on the lists; few petitions from survivors are extant—cf. *S.P.* 29/6, f.1, R. Marsh asking for confirmation of an earlier promise of promotion.

[40] See Appendix 5, Part 1. Many of these can be shown to have conformed during the 1650s.

[41] Ibid., Part 2; this list is almost certainly incomplete, as further research in two dioceses, Canterbury and Winchester, shows more conformity among surviving sequestered clergy than appears in *Walk. Rev.*

nominees, therefore, may have served under the Puritan regime for a time. Five of the eight men nominated to Canterbury chapter (and the new archdeacon) had conformed during the 1650s; four of the seven nominated to Winchester (and the archdeacon of Surrey) had done the same, for a while at least.[42]

It would be unwise to read too much into this state of affairs. Charles's choice was not boundless: there were probably very few devout episcopalians who had kept themselves strictly aloof from the Cromwellian church and were fit to hold high office in 1660. Furthermore, we cannot be sure that the king was aware of the recent behaviour of many of his nominees: petitioners for capitular preferment were naturally reticent on this point, and it is doubtful whether Charles had the machinery to check on the earlier careers of every one of his nominees. Nevertheless, the large proportion of conformists is of interest in the wider context of royal policy towards the church settlement. It confirms that Charles did not proceed inflexibly along the preconceived lines of the Nicholas lists; nor did he insist on proof of high standards of loyalty or a narrow definition of orthodoxy as a precondition of promotion. From the very fact that they had petitioned him for a cathedral post, Charles could safely assume that the petitioners believed in monarchy and a hierarchical church, but if it transpired that some of those promoted by this open policy had been moderate enough to conform during the Interregnum, this might well have been a source of satisfaction rather than dismay for the king.

For it seems quite possible that Charles was not anxious for the chapters to become the stronghold of the more extreme episcopalian clergy. In his declaration on religious affairs, Charles assured the Presbyterians that cathedral preferment would 'be given to the most learned and pious presbyters of the diocese', and that these dignitaries (together with an equal

[42] Aldey (appointed to St. Andrew's, Canterbury, in 1624), Belke (Wickhambreux, 1658), du Moulin (Adisham, 1658), Hardres (Upper Hardres, 1632), Reading (Cheriton, 1644); Archdeacon Hall, *Walk. Rev.*, p. 97. Clarke (N. Crawley, Bucks, 1644), Clutterbuck (Gt. Brickhill, Bucks, 1653), Goulston (Bishops Waltham, Hants, 1643), Manwaring (Norton, Derbyshire, 1643); Archdeacon Pearson, *Walk. Rev.*, p. 340. For the scale of Commonwealth conformity among the parish clergy of Canterbury and Winchester dioceses, see below chapter VIII.

number of parish clergy of the diocese) would 'advise' and 'assist' the bishop in the exercising of certain of his functions.[43] The king needed the confidence of the Presbyterian clergy in the impartiality of the chapters in order to ensure their co-operation with the bishop in each diocese. Accordingly, cathedral dignities were offered to leading Presbyterians at about the same time as a few others were offered bishoprics: Bates was offered the deanery of Lichfield, Manton that of Rochester, and Bowles that of York.[44] These offers were probably quite genuine, since the deanery of Lichfield was still vacant, that of Rochester soon would be on Laney's elevation to the episcopate, and that of York could have been freed by the elevation of Dean Marsh to one of the smaller sees still vacant, in order to make room for the very influential Bowles, 'our Presbyterian Primatt' as Frewen called him.[45] Although 'after some time' the deaneries were refused, Charles may have persisted in appointing men of diverging backgrounds to chapters, as the appointment of Thomas Gumble, the Presbyterian chaplain of the duke of Albemarle, to the chapter of Winchester illustrates.[46]

Arguably the offers came too late. With hindsight, it can be seen that the king's capitular appointments had not contravened the assurances given in the royal declaration; Charles had promoted 'presbyters of the diocese' and not given preference to any particular group such as the sequestered clergy. But to contemporary Presbyterians, royal policy must have appeared in quite a different light: Charles had filled vacancies in the chapters so quickly and so thoroughly that the prospective Presbyterian deans would have been isolated, or at most had only one or two allies appointed to give them moral support. When the offers came, the inherent Puritan suspicion of the capitular system had been confirmed, and an important element of Charles's scheme of modified episcopacy proved still-born.

Nominations were, of course, no more than a first step in the process of reconstruction. Two other important stages

[43] *English Historical Documents 1660-1714*, p. 368.

[44] *Rel. Baxt.*, Lib. I, Pt. II, para. 127; chapter IV for a discussion of the date at which the bishoprics were offered.

[45] Clarendon MS. 77, f.222.

[46] *Dict. Nat. Biog.*

were the holding of the first meetings of the chapters, and the repossession of their cathedrals. Two chapters had convened by mid-July, though in both cases there were exceptional circumstances. The chapter of Peterborough was (as we have seen) unusually well preserved, and inspired by the zeal of Dean Cosin and under pressure from anxious former tenants of their lands, the chapter had met by 7 June to send a petition to the Lords about their muniments. In succeeding weeks, the chapter ordered a new seal, leased properties, appointed to vacant livings in its gift, and handled other urgent business.[47] The dean and chapter of Canterbury first met in mid-July; conscious of their special role during the vacancy of the archiepiscopal see and reassured by a royal missive recommending the appointment of Sir Richard Chaworth as vicar-general of the province, they also were active quite soon after the king's return.[48] Other chapters did not reconvene so soon: Exeter held its first meeting on 31 August, Winchester held a meeting on 5 September and the first general chapter five days later. On the 10th, the dean and chapter of Winchester conducted the first episcopal election of the Restoration as well as appointing a new chapter clerk and other officials.[49] The collegiate church of Westminster was not far behind; in mid-September they inserted an advertisement in the journals:

> Whereas of late Business and Proceedings in Law have been obstructed in the City and Liberties of Westminster for want of establishment of Ministeriall Officers . . . the Dean and Chapter of Westminster have constituted a Bayliff and other Officers . . . So that all people may have . . . access to the Courts.[50]

It seems likely that some of these meetings took place before the cathedrals had been recovered from the Puritan lecturers put in during the previous decades. It is not clear whether cathedral preachers were protected by the proclamation of 1 June. Clearly some preachers retained possession for as long as they could, for example Cornelius Burgess at Wells, and four

[47] Kennett, *Register*, pp. 177, 218, 225, 229, 388–9.

[48] *Z.26*, ff.1–2, and *Z.27*, f.37; also see pp. 78, 103, 124 below.

[49] Whiteman, 'Re-establishment', p. 113; Winch. Cath. Lib., Dean and Chapter Act Book 1660–95, pp. 1–3, 5–6.

[50] *Parliamentary Intelligencer* (1660), no. 39, 17–24 Sept., p. 617.

preachers at York Minister who did not leave until September, the month in which the Act for Settling Ministers came into force.[51] Others may have sensed the direction in which events were moving, and surrendered possession before then: Simon Moor left Worcester Cathedral voluntarily on 1 July; the dean and chapter of Winchester had regained possession from two preachers by 19 August.[52] The date of recovery thus varied from place to place, but the process seems in general to have been comparatively peaceful.[53]

The next significant step was the re-introduction of the traditional forms of worship. There had been some services in the cathedrals to herald the king's return in May, but these were probably in the hands of conformist clergy rather than surviving dignitaries, and it is doubtful whether the Book of Common Prayer was used. The specific mention of the use of the Prayer Book at Westminster (by the House of Lords) and at Canterbury (by the king) indicates how unusual it then was.[54] The report of the thanksgiving service in Winchester cathedral on 10 May does not mention the Prayer Book, and the presence of the mayor and aldermen who had been in power since the re-modelling of the corporation in 1649 and their choice of a conformist minister to conduct the service would argue against its appearance on that occasion.[55] Three months later, however, when the chapter held a thanksgiving service to commemorate their repossession of the cathedral, the Prayer Book was almost certainly employed.[56] Within three weeks, vergers, lay-vicars, and bell-ringers had been admitted, and by December all prebendaries were being expected to preach on the appointed days during their

[51] *Cal. Rev.*, pp. 87-8; 67, 99, 387, 532. At Canterbury an existing institution, the Six Preachers, was taken over by the Puritans; it is not clear when the Cromwellian preachers left, but replacements were not appointed until October—*Z.26*, ff.206-7.

[52] *Cal. Rev.*, pp. 354; 182, 216, and next paragraph.

[53] Burgess made trouble at Wells, but he had long before acquired a reputation for ill-temper and litigiousness—*Cal. Rev.*, pp. 87-8.

[54] *Mercurius Publicus* (1660), no. 20, 10-17 May, p. 310; J. Stoughton, *History of Religion in England from the . . . Long Parliament to the end of the eighteenth century* (London, 6 vols., 1881), iii, 76.

[55] Above p. 6 n.14.

[56] E. Stanley, *Three Sermons Preached In the cathedral Church of Winchester* (London, 1662), sermon on 19 August 1660 (copy in the Morley Library, Winchester Cathedral).

course.[57] Winchester may have been among the first cathedrals to restore the statutory number and form of services: an above average number of old prebendaries had survived, the 'intruders' do not seem to have caused any trouble, and its proximity to London allowed new nominees to take up appointments quickly.[58]

The full restoration of choral music may have taken a little longer. The new dean of St. Paul's was said to have been reluctant to restore organs and choirs for fear of upsetting the Puritan tastes of Londoners.[59] Other cathedrals had to wait several months for repairs or for a new organ (though there are signs that organ-builders had been preparing stops in the spring of 1660 in anticipation of demand).[60] Winchester was fortunate still to have the services of Christopher Gibbons (son of the great Orlando) as organist, and of some of its former choirmen (including the octogenarian William Burt).[61] One problem for both organists and choristers must have been a shortage of service books and musical scores, a particular target for ransacking Parliamentarian troops. The choir at Wells does not seem to have received some of its new books until October 1661.[62]

Service books were not the only necessary items: the most essential covers, fittings, vestments, furniture, and vessels also had to be obtained if the services were to be conducted in a seemly fashion. At Winchester, the main damage seems to have been to the furnishings and fittings rather than the fabric, and this may have contributed to the delay in holding the first Anglican service after the Restoration. The chapter's later accounts show sums laid out for a new table, repairs to a chair, repainting and gilding, and the purchase of bibles, as well as for new glass and regular maintenance work.[63] At

[57] Dean and Chapter Act Book 1660–95, pp. 1–3, 25 (fine of £4 on those who failed to preach on appointed days).

[58] Similar conditions applied at Rochester: Kent Recd. Off., *DRc/Arb*. 2, ff.1, 2.

[59] Barwick, p. 311.

[60] Cant. Cath. Chap. Arch., *Y.14.2*, no. 102; *Hist. MSS. Comm. Dean and Chapter of Wells* (London, 2 vols., 1907, 1914), ii, 432; Kennett, *Register*, p. 270.

[61] Dean and Chapter Act Book 1660–95, p. 17 (Gibbons was soon tempted away to Westminster Abbey, *Winchester Cathedral Record*, no. 18, 1949, 16); Burt sang at 10 May proclamation ceremony, cf. p. 3 n.1.

[62] *Hist. MSS. Comm. Dean and Chapter of Wells*, ii, 432.

[63] Winch. Cath. Lib., 'Winchester Cathedral Accounts 1614 to 1663'.

Canterbury, too, the accounts of the treasurer show many sums laid out for the communion stools, mats for the Sermon House, and other items such as plate for the communion table and rich hangings.[64]

The cathedrals of Canterbury and Winchester must have witnessed some remarkable scenes in the opening months of the Restoration as treasures taken from the cathedrals in the previous decades, and preserved by the faithful in the intervening years, were returned to their proper place. At Winchester, the cathedral plate was returned by one John Dalsh, and the two statues of James I and Charles I cast by Le Sueur and sold to a Royalist in the 1640s were returned. These bronze statues had been buried for safety in the garden of a Mr. Newton, and in 1660 they were dug up, and at the expense of the bishop fetched and put back in their niches in the west end of the choir.[65] At Canterbury, the indefatigable antiquary and clerk of the chapter William Somner paid 10*s* 'for bringing the font bowle and other materialls of stone and yron' from the town into the cathedral, materials which he had preserved since the destruction of Bishop Warner's font some years before.[66] Similar scenes may have occurred elsewhere as concealed treasures were handed back to their guardians.[67]

The provision of the most basic utensils and vestments was accompanied by early efforts to restore the fabrics of the cathedral churches. That of Canterbury was in a 'sad, forlorne, and languishing condition' at the Restoration, according to Somner.[68] Through malicious damage, sale of lead and timber, and general neglect, only the bare walls and roof were left and the building was 'unserviceable in the way of a cathedral'. The dean and chapter later claimed that in the first years of the Restoration thousands of pounds had been spent on the 'Repairs of our almost ruined Cathedral,

[64] Cant. Cath. Chap. Arch., Treasurers' Books 1660-1, p. 87; 1663, p. 52.

[65] B. C. Turner, ' "The Return of the Church"; Cathedral and Close 1660-1662', *Winchester Cathedral Record* no. 29 (1960), 22.

[66] Cant. Cath. Chap. Arch., Treasurer's Book 1663, p. 61; J. M. Cowper, *The Lives of the Deans of Canterbury, 1541-1900* (Canterbury, 1900), p. 104.

[67] E.g. Kennett, *Register*, p. 202.

[68] Quoted in J. C. Roberston, 'The Condition of Canterbury Cathedral at the Restoration in A.D. 1660', *Archaeologia Cantiana*, x (1876), 95.

furnishing and recruiting of the rifled quire', and other necessary repairs and charges.[69] Other cathedrals, such as Lichfield and Exeter, may also have been unserviceable as cathedrals in the summer of 1660, but not all were in such a bad condition. Winchester, for instance, had survived the plunderings of the wars with its fabric quite sound; the main damage had been to the windows—glass valued by a contemporary at £1,000 had been lost.[70] Furthermore, during the Interregnum, friends of the cathedral had defeated a proposal to demolish it, and had raised money to carry out some maintenance work.[71] In May 1660 the nave was obviously safe enough to hold a congregation, and the accounts of the chapter show money spent on glazing and clearing drain-pipes, but no major structural repairs (apart from an addition—a dry walk from the cloisters to the dean's lodgings).[72]

The condition of the buildings in the cathedral closes was also an urgent problem, for until these were habitable some members of the chapter could not live close to the church whose services they had to maintain. At Winchester, the houses in the close were in such a bad condition that it was decided at once that five new houses should be built 'at the Common coste'.[73] At Canterbury, most of the houses were 'not recovered out of the invaders hands without the charge and trouble of a suit in law', and even when the houses were recovered the damage wrought by neglect or division into tenements had to be made good before they were fit to receive the canons.[74] As late as January 1661, one Captain Owen was resisting ejection; it was reported that he had 'pull'd down the Dean of Canterburies Chappel and part of his house', but that he 'yet forcibly lives in [the] rest of it'.[75] Some dignitaries at Lincoln who were kept out of their houses had to bear both the

[69] Tanner MS. 123, f.57.

[70] G. N. Godwin, *The Civil War in Hampshire 1642–45* (Southampton, 1904), pp. 47–50.

[71] *Documents relating to the History of the Cathedral Church of Winchester in the Seventeenth Century*, ed. W. R. W. Stephens and F. T. Madge (London, 2 vols., 1897), ii, 97–100.

[72] 'Winchester Cathedral Accounts 1614 to 1663'.

[73] Dean and Chapter Act Book 1660–95, p. 27.

[74] J. C. Robertson, loc. cit.

[75] *Mercurius Publicus* (1661), no. 2, 10–17 Jan., p. 31.

cost of law-suits to eject the intruders and the expense of renting alternative accommodation near the cathedral until they could return.[76]

Not only individual members, but also whole chapters became involved in law-suits to assert their rights. The collegiate church of Windsor, for instance, paid out £510. 3*s.* 4*d.* for this purpose in the opening years of the Restoration.[77] Gloucester chapter spent £345. 11*s* 1*d.* on law-suits, and a further £207. 14*s.* on 'securing diverse rights denied the church'.[78] Similarly, Hereford paid £76 in law-suits to defend the rights of the chapter.[79]

The chapters were also soon making attempts to trace their valuable collections of documents, especially terriers, rentals, and lease-books. On 7 June, the chapter of Peterborough asked the House of Lords to ensure the safe return of those 'Leidger Books, Registers, Court Rolls, Deeds, Counter-part of Leases, and other Writings and Evidences concerning the Lands and Revenues belonging to the said Church' that had been taken away by 'the Power of the late pretended Parliament'.[80] Some of the most important records had apparently been preserved by a friend of the church and were soon returned to Dean Cosin.[81] A similar foresight had been shown by the former dean of Ely who preserved the charters and terriers of the church. These were safely returned, by the dean's widow, to the church, who admitted that without these documents 'they had been in the Darke as concerneing the revenews of the Church'.[82]

Other chapters were less fortunate and were put to some trouble and expense to recover their records. The chapter of Canterbury had lost its common seal, registers and other records, and found in 1660 that many of them were 'irrecoverably lost, and the rest not retrived without much trouble and cost'.[83] The chapter clerk of Winchester had care-

[76] Tanner MS. 130, ff.68–9.
[77] Tanner MS. 140, f.168.
[78] Tanner MS. 147, ff.227, 229.
[79] Tanner MS. 147, f.83.
[80] Kennett, *Register*, p. 177.
[81] Ibid., p. 188.
[82] Tanner MS. 49, f.51.
[83] J. C. Robertson, art. cit., 96.

fully reorganized the chapter's documents after the cathedral was sacked. His work proved to be in vain, for the muniment house was ransacked a second time; some records were burnt, some used to make kites, some were thrown into the river, and many others together with the common seal were taken away.[84] A degree of continuity at Winchester may have been provided by Thomas Coward, who held the office of collector under Parliament and then under the restored chapter;[85] some of the documents concerning the estates of the chapter must have been preserved for his work to have been possible. At the 1663 visitation, however, the chapter had to admit that many of the muniments of the cathedral had been lost, though they had kept whatever they could lay their hands on.[86] Another church inserted an advertisement in the newspapers offering a reward of £5 for information on 'A Register belonging to the Church of Windsor, entituled *Liber Collegii,* beginning at the year 1614 . . . lost in the late troubles'.[87]

Another task facing the chapters was the resumption of their philanthropic activities. The return of the dean and chapter at Canterbury witnessed an extraordinary act of generosity: 'charity and almes at our first comeing' came to £148.[88] But the statutory acts of charity also required attention. At Winchester, eleven new paupers were admitted on 20 November, and soon the chapter was also handing out regular sums to the poor, as well as relieving the distressed widows of ministers, and other worthy cases.[89]

The responsibilities of the chapters did not end there, for they were also the patrons of many parish livings. As early as 20 July, the chapter of Canterbury made one appointment, and three days later a body describing itself as the custodians and vicars of the cathedral church of Hereford made a presentation to a living in their gift.[90] However, only half a

[84] G. N. Godwin, op. cit., p. 79 and Winch. Cath. Lib., 'Book of John Chase, 1623-50', p. 84.

[85] 'Winchester Cathedral Accounts 1614 to 1663'.

[86] 'Winchester Cathedral MSS. vol. ii'.

[87] *Mercurius Publicus* (1663), no. 19, 7-14 May, p. 297.

[88] Tanner MS. 128, f.57.

[89] Dean and Chapter Act Book 1660-95, pp. 19-21, and Tanner MS. 140, ff.117, 124.

[90] *Z.26,* f.13; *Lib. Inst.*

dozen more capitular presentations are recorded in the *Liber Institutionum* from July to late September, so it may be that the chapters generally did not resume this function until later in the year, perhaps after the Act for Settling Ministers had eased controversy in the field of parish appointments.

Even on the basis of this limited survey, certain features of the re-establishment of the cathedral chapters may be delineated. Although the gaps in the ranks of the capitular clergy were filled rapidly, it was several months before the chapters could be said to have recovered something like their former position. Hampered by damaged cathedrals and lost records, the chapters took some time to resurrect the full glory of their services and the full power of their administration. It is to their credit, however, that in overcoming a difficult set of problems, they acted with a blend of speed and discretion. Despite the fact that their activity was bound to offend certain sections of the population, there is little sign of any concerted opposition to their work; those who did obstruct them were treated with strict regard to the law. In view of the strength of Presbyterianism in England in the early months of 1660, the restoration of the cathedral chapters was remarkably smooth and rapid. It was certainly more rapid than the reconstruction of the episcopate and of episcopal administration.

IV

THE REVIVAL OF THE EPISCOPATE

During the 1650s, there was a real possibility that the English episcopal succession might be broken. The exiled court was acutely aware of the dwindling number of bishops and the poor health of some of those still alive. The 'business of the Church', as the appointment of new bishops was usually known during the Interregnum, became a matter of increasing concern.[1] Various attempts to secure the consecration of new bishops were made. In May 1659, for instance, Richard Allestree was sent from Brussels with a paper 'wherein were these names, Dr. Sheldon, Dr. Hammond, Dr. Lucy, Dr. Ferne, Dr. Walton with one other, which I have forgot, in cypher . . . The Dioceses they were to be consecrated to were also named'. When he reached England, Allestree was to give Bishop Duppa a stern injunction from the king that 'all pretenses whatsoever layed aside' he would without delay 'cause the bishops then alive to meet together' to consecrate these six men.[2] From the Nicholas lists it may be deduced that Sheldon was to be consecrated to Gloucester, Hammond to Worcester, Lucy to St. David's, and Ferne to Bristol; Walton's see is unclear, possibly it was Chester.[3] The sixth person, to judge from a letter sent by Barwick in September 1659, was possibly Dr. Mansell, designated bishop of Llandaff, or Dean Nicholas, destined for Hereford.[4]

The six nominations given in Allestree's paper did not represent the full complement of appointments envisaged in 1659. The Nicholas lists provide the names of several others considered by the court; indeed, at different stages of revision the lists suggest possible candidates for a large majority of the

[1] Barwick, p. 457; Clarendon MS. 68, f.168; Bosher, pp. 89–100.

[2] Worcester College, Oxford, MS. 54, pp. 252–3.

[3] Egerton MS. 2542, f.268; Walton was promoted to Chester in 1660, and it was vacant in May 1659.

[4] Barwick, pp. 438–9.

sees then vacant.[5] Other candidates can be found in the correspondence between Hyde and Barwick.[6] By May 1660, further revisions of the lists and the deaths of three prospective bishops had reduced the numbers of proposed appointments to about eight: two surviving bishops would be translated, Juxon to Canterbury and Warner to Norwich; Sheldon would then be elevated to London and Lucy to Rochester to replace the translated bishops; Cosin was to have Peterborough and Bruno Ryves St. Asaph, while the elevation of Ferne to Bristol and of Walton (to Chester?) possibly remained unchanged from the time of Allestree's mission.[7] Others who at one time or another had been allocated or offered a bishopric and were still alive in 1660 included Dr. Mansell, Dean Nicholas, Humfrey Henchman, and John Barwick.[8]

In some quarters, episcopal appointments were expected soon after the king's return. On 26 July, Sharp told his brethren in Scotland that English bishops would be 'speedily nominated', and on 11 August Duppa wrote to Sheldon bemoaning the slow progress of the 'business of the Church'.[9] But it was not until four months after Charles's return that the first translation was completed, and not until five months that the first consecration of a new bishop took place.[10] Furthermore, the translations and elevations announced from late August to late November differed markedly from the pattern suggested by the Nicholas lists.

The timing and the allocation of bishoprics in 1660 must be seen against the background of the events of that summer. As a practising Anglican, Charles was expected to reintroduce episcopacy; the chief problems were when, and what kind of bishops would they be? To have appointed bishops too soon would have been to court trouble, either a Puritan rising or possibly an episcopal reaction which would have suited

[5] Candidates were suggested for twelve of the seventeen vacant by May 1660; the exceptions were York, Chester (but see above), and Lincoln, and two that fell vacant late in 1659—Durham and Exeter.

[6] Barwick, pp. 247-8, 417-18, 427-8, 431, 438-40, 463-5.

[7] Egerton MS. 2542, ff.268, 270, omitting those who had died or are known to have refused before the Restoration.

[8] Ibid., and Barwick, pp. 247-8.

[9] Wodrow, i, Introduction, xlviii; Tanner MS. 49, f.17.

[10] Appendix 6.

Charles little better if he was going to do anything for the Catholics. In the event, Charles was nearly caught moving too late; by mid August, his episcopalian allies were becoming dissatisfied with his lack of action, and the more extreme Presbyterians were beginning to think that Charles might after all be persuaded to accept a settlement on Covenant lines. At once, Charles took steps to avert this crisis, and within days offers of bishoprics were being made, including some to leading Presbyterians; at the same time the terms of reference for a modified form of episcopacy were published in the draft declaration on ecclesiastical affairs that was circulating by early September.[11]

The offers of the see of Norwich to Edward Reynolds, of that of Hereford to Richard Baxter, and of Coventry and Lichfield to Edward Calamy were of considerable significance.[12] First of all, they marked a complete departure from the appointments planned in exile; none of the three men were on the Nicholas lists, and Norwich had been earmarked for Bishop Warner. Secondly, the offers represented an earnest of Charles's intention to implement the declaration, just as the offer of deaneries to other Presbyterians marked an attempt to make the system of limited episcopacy functional and impartial at all levels. Thirdly, it seems probable that the three moderate Presbyterians were among the first to be offered sees. It has generally been thought, on the basis of Baxter's narrative, that the offers to the Presbyterians were made in late October, by which date the great majority of vacant sees had been filled and the offers could have been dismissed as an afterthought which would have had little influence on the character of the restored episcopate.[13] However, a closer look at Baxter's account and some other items of information suggests quite a different conclusion: not only were the Presbyterians among the first offered sees, but also they took the suggestion very seriously, and gave it much thought and time before (with the exception of Reynolds) refusing the bishoprics.

As early as April, the Presbyterians may have been assured

[11] See above pp. 28-30.

[12] *Rel. Baxt.*, Lib. I, Pt. II, paras. 118, 127.

[13] Ibid., paras. 118-25, 127, and Appendix 6 below.

of 'present good preferments in the Church' by Morley, acting on Hyde's instructions. Morley then told Hyde 'I doe not perceive that any of them desires to be a Bp, at least not at first'.[14] In June, Charles appointed several Presbyterians as royal chaplains, four of them preached before him during the summer, and were allowed much latitude as to forms and ceremonies.[15] The chaplaincies given to the Puritans are important: they show the king using his patronage openly to balance the episcopalian forces at court by Presbyterians; also it was very common in the seventeenth century for a royal chaplain to be elevated at a later date. Certainly, of the ten chaplains appointed, three were offered bishoprics and two were offered deaneries.[16] Bates and two other Puritans also had doctorates of divinity conferred on them at Cambridge by royal letters.[17]

At least one offer of a bishopric was made in early September. News of Reynolds's prospective promotion was abroad by 9 September, and he was nominated officially later that month.[18] Reynolds had been one of the moderate clergymen who had worked for a compromise solution to the religious problem in the early 1640s, and in the spring of 1660 Morley had found him 'fully satisfied' with an episcopacy that was governed by the canons and laws of the church and answerable to a free synod. In the autumn Reynolds was one of the supporters of the declaration who tried to persuade Baxter to modify his criticisms of it. An offer to Reynolds when the draft declaration first appeared was predictable.[19]

Unofficially, bishoprics were also offered to Baxter and Calamy by late September. A letter written from Cumberland on 8 October refers to the fact that these two had been offered

[14] Barwick, p. 525; Clarendon MS. 72, f.199.

[15] *Rel. Baxt.*, Lib. I, Pt. II, para. 88; Abernathy, 'English Presbyterians', p. 68.

[16] Baxter, Calamy, Reynolds; Bates, Manton; *Rel. Baxt.*, Lib. I, Pt. II, paras. 118, 127.

[17] Kennett, *Register*, p. 308.

[18] *S.P.* 29/14, f.62, and P.R.O., *S.O.* 1/4, p. 128.

[19] Clarendon MS. 71, f.233. Baxter's account is confusing here (*Rel. Baxt.*, Lib. I, Pt. II, para. 106): he implies that Reynolds received his offer at the same time as Calamy and himself, was pressed to accept by Baxter, and then 'suddenly' accepted saying a friend had taken out the *congé d'élire* without his knowledge. There is no evidence of an offer to the other two in *early* September, but if the rest of Baxter's account is correct then all three knew of the offers by 30 September when Reynolds's *congé* was issued.

bishoprics but 'make a little nice of accepting them'.[20] Allowing at least a week for the news to have reached the far north-west, the offers must have been known in London in late September or early October. There is also the meeting between episcopalians and Presbyterians described by Baxter:

> Dr. Morley, Dr. Hinchman, and Dr. Cosins, met Dr. Reignolds, Mr. Calamy, and myself . . . and they being at that time newly elect . . . we called them 'My Lords' which Dr. Morley once returned with such a passage as this 'we may call you also I suppose by the same Title'.[21]

If by 'newly elect' Baxter was referring to the *congés d'élire* issued for their election, then this meeting could have taken place in late September; if on the other hand, Baxter meant the capitular election, the meeting may have taken place in about the second week of October.[22] It would seem more likely that it was the royal nominations that were being referred to: Morley knew very well that the Presbyterians had not been actually elected, but implied that they had been offered sees, and in one case, that of Reynolds, had already accepted and been nominated. Morley's reply is very significant: it suggests that the offers to the Presbyterians were known to have been made at about the same time as offers were made to four episcopalians; it also implies that he expected them to accept.

There is further evidence of an early offer to the Presbyterians in Baxter's narrative. 'A little before' the Worcester House conference on 22 October, he says,

> Collonel Birch came to me as from the Lord Chancellor, to persuade me to take the Bishoprick of Hereford . . . After this (having not a flat denyal) he came again and again to Dr. Reignolds, Mr. Calamy, and myself together, to importune us all to accept sees.

The three Presbyterians, he adds, had 'some speeches oft together' about the offers.[23] These repeated meetings with the Presbyterian Birch and among themselves must have been spread over a space of days if not weeks before the day when the final declaration was issued and Baxter received an official

[20] *S.P.* 29/18, f.42.
[21] *Rel. Baxt.*, loc. cit.
[22] See Appendix 6.
[23] *Rel. Baxt.*, Lib. I, Pt. II, paras. 118-19.

offer from Hyde on 29 October.[24] Finally, one may note that Baxter had sufficient warning of his possible elevation to compose a carefully selected list of seventeen alternative candidates for the see of Hereford, and put it in his letter of refusal on 1 November.[25]

That the offers were put forward in good faith and accepted as such by the Presbyterians is beyond doubt. Perhaps in 1665, after years of unhappiness, Baxter could write that one of the reasons he had turned down a bishopric was that he 'feared that this Declaration was but for a present use'.[26] But in November 1660 he was clearly far less suspicious and much more optimistic about the potential benefits of moderate episcopacy. Indeed, both he and Calamy came very close to accepting and joining Reynolds on the bench. Baxter told Hyde that the day before the royal declaration came out, he was prepared to refuse, but having read it he was 'exceedingly beholden to his Lordship for these Moderations' (the extra concessions made in the final declaration) and was determined to do all he could to promote the church's happiness. After a little more time to consider his decision, however, the objections that had made him refuse Birch's offer (objections that were partly personal, partly doctrinal) re-asserted themselves and he again refused.[27] In May 1660 Calamy had been prevailed upon by Morley to 'comply as to Episcopacy and the Liturgy with little alteration', and in the autumn he—like Reynolds—had found Baxter's objections to the draft declaration too strong.[28] Calamy almost accepted Lichfield, but was dissuaded, perhaps by his wife and brother-in-law Matthew Newcomen, or perhaps by the turn of events in Parliament when the declaration came under attack from the episcopalians.[29]

The refusals were not the end of the matter, however, for

[24] *Rel. Baxt.*, Lib. I, Pt. II, paras. 118, 123; the declaration was sealed on the 25th, but was not published until the 29th (according to Baxter's account) or 30th (*The Diary of Samuel Pepys*, i, 278).

[25] *Rel. Baxt.*, Lib. I, Pt. II, para. 123.

[26] Ibid., para. 121; cf. the remark (para. 106) about the proffered sees: 'I perceived that they had some Purposes to try that way with us'.

[27] Ibid., para. 121.

[28] Clarendon MS. 72, ff. 284–5; *Rel. Baxt.*, Lib. I, Pt. II. para. 106.

[29] Ibid., paras. 120, 127; Abernathy, 'English Presbyterians', p. 77.

there are indications that both sides were genuinely concerned to press the possibility of bishoprics being accepted by Presbyterians. In his letter of refusal Baxter told Hyde that he hoped 'by Letters this very Week to disperse the seeds of Satisfaction into many Counties of England'; he also thought it worthwhile to 'offer some choice to your consideration' in the form of a list of seventeen men worthy of the bishopric of Hereford.[30] His nominees do not seem to have been chosen at random. Although perhaps only two of the seventeen were to conform in 1662, twelve of the other fifteen had been episcopally ordained. Most of them had been parish priests since the 1620s or 1630s, and several had published works to their credit. Of those not episcopally ordained, all had degrees; Richard Gilpin and Edward Bowles were prominent figures in the north, while Benjamin Woodbridge was eminent enough to be a royal chaplain in 1660 and one of the Savoy commissioners in 1661.[31] It looks as though Baxter was choosing ministers of experience and reputation, who would not need re-ordination, and who would be acceptable to moderate episcopalians. That Baxter regarded the offer of a bishopric as being a genuine one is also suggested by his urging Hyde to 'put as many of our Persuasion as you can into Bishopricks, (if it may be, more than three)'.[32] Furthermore, in November 1660, Baxter defended the new style episcopacy at some length and at some risk of personal unpopularity at a meeting of London Presbyterians.[33]

On their side, the king and Hyde may not have abandoned the idea of attracting Presbyterians into the episcopate after the refusals of Baxter and Calamy. Their repeated kindnesses to Baxter after his refusal may be significant in view of the statement by Antony Wood that Coventry and Lichfield, originally designed for Calamy, was kept vacant until November 1661 in the hope that Baxter would eventually

[30] *Rel. Baxt.*, Lib. I, Pt. II, para. 123.

[31] Sources: *Cal. Rev.*, *Walk. Rev.*, *Alum. Cant.*, *Alum. Oxon.*, *Dict. Nat. Biog.*, and A. Wood, *Athenae Oxonienses* (London, 2 vols., 1721). The mention of Gilpin seems to have given rise to the impression that he was offered the see of Carlisle: see prefatory memoir to *Daemonologia Sacra; or a Treatise of Satan's Temptations, by Richard Gilpin, M.D.*, ed. A.B. Grosart (London, 1867), p. xxxii.

[32] *Rel. Baxt.*, Lib. I, Pt. II, para. 123.

[33] Ibid., para. 128.

accept a bishopric.[34] Most of Baxter's ministry had been spent at Kidderminster, only a few miles from the boundary of Lichfield diocese.

Between 28 August and 29 November, three surviving bishops were translated and sixteen new bishops were nominated.[35] The first observable feature of these appointments is how radically they differ from the allocations on the Nicholas lists. In only two instances were the appointments projected before the Restoration implemented: the translation of Juxon from London to Canterbury, and the elevation of Sheldon to Juxon's former see.[36] In a further three cases, it could be argued that there was a degree of forethought in the nominations: Cosin was given a bishopric, though not the one suggested on the list; Henchman was elevated, though not to the diocese originally allocated him; the promotion of Walton was not mentioned on the lists but had been anticipated in Allestree's paper.[37] Apart from these appointments, the nominations suggested in the lists were a dead letter. Bishop Warner was not translated to Norwich, which as we have seen went to Reynolds instead; this meant that Lucy could not receive Warner's see of Rochester (though in mid-October Lucy did receive the see of St. David's allocated him in 1659).[38] Ferne and Ryves were disappointed of elevation, and others who at one time had been considered for elevation, Mansell, Nicholas and Barwick, were passed over, or perhaps refused.[39] The corollary of this situation was that thirteen of those nominated by the king (fifteen if we include the offers to Baxter and Calamy) had not been allocated a see in 1659 or early 1660.[40] Admittedly some of these men had been deemed worthy of a dignity, and one, possibly two, had been destined for a deanery.[41] But seven of

[34] Ibid., paras. 130, 155, and A. Wood, op. cit., ii, 1147; Calamy's grandson thought that Lichfield was kept vacant for Calamy himself: Calamy, *Account*, i, 55.

[35] See Appendix 6.

[36] See above p. 82.

[37] See above pp. 81-2.

[38] Ibid.

[39] Ibid.

[40] The translations of Duppa and Frewen were not anticipated on the lists, and eleven others were not considered for sees in 1659.

[41] Gauden, Sterne, Laney, and Monck; potential deans—Sanderson and Morley (on one list designated Master of the Savoy); Egerton MS. 2542, ff.266-70.

those offered bishoprics in the sutumn of 1660 were not on the Nicholas lists at all—Reynolds, Calamy, Baxter, Griffith, Lloyd, Nicholson, and Ironside. How was the revised allocation made?

It has been suggested that 'the principal part in the selection of new bishops' was taken by Sheldon,[42] but the sources employed to prove this do little more than show that Sheldon was *thought* to have influence in 1660, or that he was used as a messenger to offer a see to an individual divine.[43] Episcopal appointments were undoubtedly supervised by the king and chancellor in person. Baxter states clearly that both unofficial and official offers came from the chancellor.[44] John Gauden's elevation to Exeter was the king's personal decision and (according to Burnet) was taken despite Sheldon's disapproval.[45] Nicholas Monck's promotion to the episcopate owed less to his own singularly unremarkable attributes than to the debt Charles owed his elder brother—General George Monck.[46] Henchman's rapid rise to the major see of Sarum owed much to the help he gave the king when he was escaping in 1651, though one also notes that just before his nomination he had been arranging a lease of church lands for Secretary Nicholas as part of a campaign to press his claims to the see.[47] Similarly mundane considerations may have affected other appointments: Anthony Wood suggests that William Nicholson offered money to secure the see of Gloucester, and that Gilbert Ironside was appointed to the poor see of Bristol because his private wealth would enable him to maintain the dignity of a spiritual peer.[48]

Charles's pragmatic approach to church affairs is demon-

[42] Bosher, p. 183, and n.2 and pp. 233-4, 39 (Lucy and Griffith) for total of eighteen allegedly 'Laudian' bishops.

[43] Tanner MSS. 49, f.23; 48, f.46. Two biographies stressing Sheldon's role date from a later period when his influence was greater—Sanderson's life was not published till 1678, Ward's not till 1697; Nicholson's preface to *A plain, but full Exposition of the Catechism* (London, 1661) when read *in extenso* stresses the king's part more.

[44] *Rel. Baxt.*, Lib. I, Pt. II, paras. 106, 109-11.

[45] Burnet, i, 87-8, 324; cf. Brit. Lib. Birch MS. 4104, ff.333-9 for Gauden's use of his part in producing the *Eikon Basilike* in an attempt to gain promotion in 1662.

[46] *Dict. Nat. Biog.*

[47] R. Ollard, op. cit., pp. 102, 118-20; *S.P.* 29/16, f.42.

[48] A. Wood, op. cit., ii, 494-5, 489 and Bliss edition (London, 4 vols., 1813-20), iv, 825.

strated in another way. An examination of the earlier careers of the nineteen divines nominated in 1660 shows that they were drawn from widely differing backgrounds; some were Arminians, exiles, staunch Anglicans, others were Calvinists, Low-Churchmen, Commonwealth conformists, and yet others had few discernible links with either side. It is not easy to accept that this pattern was haphazard; it seems much more likely that the 'politique' Charles was trying to balance different interests within the episcopate and to reconcile as many people as possible to the emerging settlement. This was an essentially erastian policy, to ensure that the king was the prisoner of no one party in the church, or as Bellings put it to 'embroyle' episcopacy without advancing Presbyterianism. The diverse nature of the restored bench emerges more clearly on a closer examination of their backgrounds, but it is important that these men should be seen as contemporaries saw them in the autumn of 1660 and not through the distorting image of the intervening years—the years of the 'Clarendon Code'.

To contemporaries, the new bishops must have seemed a very elderly body of men; their average age was 65.[49] Sanderson fell prey to a prolonged 'distemper' each winter; Ironside called himself 'an old man, much decayed in Strength, Lungs, Parts, plundered of Abilities as well as Books'; Nicholson signed an epistle to his former parishioners 'Your aged Pastour'.[50] The nine surviving bishops were, of course, even older, with an average age of 74. The point is of more than academic interest, for vacancies would soon occur, and the king would be able to keep the balance between the different viewpoints on the bench. Three of the youngest bishops appointed in 1660 were Low-Churchmen, Gauden (55 years old), Griffith (59), and Reynolds (61). Had Calamy (aged 60) and Baxter (a mere stripling of 45) accepted the king's offer, there would have been a nucleus of younger, moderate

[49] Ages in this paragraph taken from the relevant articles in *Dict. Nat. Biog.* The comparable age of bishops on the bench in January 1640 and January 1680, at the time of their consecrations, was fifty and fifty-six respectively.

[50] I. Walton, *The Life of Dr Sanderson* (London, 1678), pp. 178–9; G. Ironside, *A Sermon Preached at Dorchester* (London, 1660), Preface; W. Nicholson, op. cit., Epistle dedicatory.

bishops, who could have been reinforced, or balanced by High-Churchmen, as the older bishops passed away.

Contemporaries may also have been struck by the fact that despite their age very few of the new nominees had held positions of authority in the church when Archbishop Laud had been at the peak of his power. There was no shortage of such men in 1660, but only two of the bishops who had helped enforce Laud's policies in the 1630s (Juxon and Duppa) and one archdeacon (Cosin) were promoted at the Restoration.[51] The government was deliberately neglecting churchmen closely associated in the public mind with Archbishop Laud. After Laud, Matthew Wren had been Charles I's most hated and vilified bishop; his execution had also been demanded by the Long Parliament and he had spent many years in the Tower. Rumour linked him with the primacy in 1660, and he was not without ambition—at least in 1663 on the death of Juxon.[52] But in the autumn of 1660 he received neither York nor London, nor any of the other sees above Ely in rank if not in wealth. Bishops Warner of Rochester and Piers of Bath and Wells had also received their share of abuse and criticism in the early 1640s for enforcing Laud's policies, but both were passed by in 1660.[53] Warner was bitterly disappointed, and in a letter to Sheldon listed his services and sufferings for the church; Sheldon was unable to help him.[54] Others close to Laud were similarly ignored, for example two of his personal chaplains Edward Martin and William Heywood. The neglect of Peter Heylyn was particularly striking: few had been closer to Laud, or written so much in defence of the High-Church position. Although his sight was poor by 1660, he was still active enough in 1661 to agitate for the calling of a Convocation. As his fellow High-Churchman and disciple of Laud, John Cosin, said 'I wonder, Brother Heylyn, thou art

[51] Those active in the 1630s and still alive in 1660 included the bishops of Ely, Bath and Wells, Chichester, Oxford, and Bangor; the deans of Sarum, Exeter, Bristol, and Bangor; the archdeacons of Anglesey, Bedford, London, Essex, Oxford, Peterborough, Berks, East Riding, Cleveland, and Durham.

[52] P. King, 'The Episcopate during the Civil Wars', *Eng. Hist. Rev.*, lxiii (1968), 525; Barwick, p. 496; *Hist. MSS. Comm. 5th Report,* Appendix, p. 184; W. G. Simon, *The Restoration Episcopate* (New York, 1965), p. 43 and n. 23 (though the Clarendon MS. there quoted cannot be traced).

[53] P. King, art. cit., 527; *Dict. Nat. Biog.* on Wm. Piers.

[54] Tanner MS. 49, f.23.

not a Bishop, but we all know thou hast deserv'd it'.[55]

Neglect was also the fate suffered by many lesser clergy who had risked persecution during the 1650s by using the Book of Common Prayer or by writing in defence of the Church of England. Admittedly, some of them received Irish bishoprics, while others accepted deaneries or university preferment.[56] But many had to be satisfied with less, such as Herbert Thorndike's prebend or Matthew Griffith's living.[57] As in the field of secular preferment, many acknowledged loyalists saw what they regarded as their just reward being usurped by lesser sufferers, conformists, and even Presbyterians.

Those who were promoted in 1660 were on the whole not such controversial figures. There had been little criticism of a personal nature against Juxon in the previous reign, only against his office; he seems to have taken no part in the Anglican schemes of the 1650s and was left undisturbed by the Cromwellian government. His presence at the execution of Charles I made him a hallowed symbol of the martyred king, and he was the obvious choice for Canterbury, 'the old peaceable Archbishop' as Baxter called him.[58] Duppa was also unlikely to have aroused Puritan fears: elevated only at the end of the personal rule of Charles I, chaplain and mentor of Charles II when he was Prince of Wales, Duppa for the most part protected himself during the Interregnum 'as the tortoise doth, by not going out of my shell'.[59] Frewen had not been elevated until 1644, being one of the moderate bishops appointed by Charles I (on Juxon's advice) to calm the fear of prelacy then felt by many Puritans. His tenure of Coventry and Lichfield had been too short for the character of his episcopate to be revealed, but during the Interregnum he too had an undistinguished record. Despite (or perhaps because of) his moderation and inexperience, he was promoted to York, where he impressed Baxter as 'a peaceable man'.[60]

Many of the new nominees would probably have been best

[55] P. Heylyn, *Ecclesia Restaurata*, op. cit., clxxviii–clxxxii; *S.P.* 29/18, f.42.

[56] J. Taylor, G. Wild, and R. Mossom; B. Ryves, J. Barwick, and T. Pierce; R. Allestree was made regius professor of divinity at Oxford; cf. Bosher, pp. 29–30

[57] *46th Report*, p. 113; *Alum. Cant.*

[58] *Dict. Nat. Biog.*, and Bosher, p. 26; *Rel. Baxt.*, Lib. I, Pt. II, para. 425.

[59] *Dict. Nat. Biog.* and *Duppa-Isham Correspondence*, pp. xxv–xxvii, 52.

[60] *Dict. Nat. Biog.; Rel. Baxt.*, Lib. I, Pt. II, para. 171.

known for their roles in university life in the reign of Charles I. As in the Elizabethan appointments of 1559-61, the universities provided several members of the bench, though the Caroline bishops boasted more senior academic rank than their Elizabethan counterparts.[61] Sterne and Laney were probably most widely known as the former heads of Jesus and of Pembroke Hall, Cambridge, Sheldon as warden of All Souls, Oxford. Sanderson had been regius professor of divinity at Oxford, in name at least, from 1642 to 1648. Three, Cosin, Laney, and Reynolds, had acted as vice-chancellor of their university, while Sheldon had been pro-vice-chancellor twice. Admittedly some of these men had been associated with introducing High-Church innovations into their colleges; Laney, for instance, had been called 'one of the professed Arminians, Laud's creatures to prosecute his designs in the university of Cambridge'. But this was not true of all the academics later elevated, Sanderson and Reynolds for instance; in the 1630s Sheldon and Morley had been members of the Tew Circle, a group of whose views Laud positively disapproved.[62] It may also be suggested that in the flush of royalism which coloured most sections of the population in 1660, the strong royalism exhibited by some of these men—the sending of the college plate to Charles I by Sterne, the ministrations of Sheldon and Morley to Charles I in captivity—probably helped to erase the memory of other, more controversial deeds.[63] Moreover, if the suggestion that Charles was trying to balance interest in the episcopate is correct, then he needed one or two more obdurate figures such as Cosin and Sterne to act as a counterweight to the moderates and Low-Churchmen.

What is remarkable about Charles's nominees is that so few of them seem to have undergone particular persecution. With the exception of Sterne and possibly one or two others,[64]

[61] P. Hughes, *The Reformation in England* (London, 1967), iii, 45.

[62] Most of the information in this paragraph was derived from the relevant articles in *Dict. Nat. Biog.*; on Tew, cf. Clarendon, *Life*, i, 50.

[63] Royal chaplains to Charles I elevated in 1660 included Sanderson, Laney, Sheldon, Morley, and possibly Walton and Reynolds; other chaplains elevated to Irish sees or English after 1660 included Bramhall, Ferne, Croft, and possibly Hacket; P. King, art. cit., 535, ns. 6, 8, and *Dict. Nat. Biog.* articles.

[64] *Dict. Nat. Biog.* on Sterne, Walton, and Ironside.

Charles II's first nominees had suffered no more than thousands of other churchmen, academics, or royalists who had lost their livelihood or had to compound for their estates. The great majority of those nominated in the autumn of 1660 had not felt it necessary to go into exile or to stay there; only three of the new creations stayed abroad rather than live under a Puritan government, Cosin, Laney, and Morley.[65] Although most of the new bishops had lost parish livings, some had resigned rather than been dismissed from them.[66] Moreover, four seem to have continued ministering in their parishes throughout the troubles, while William Lucy did not lose his livings until the mid 1650s.[67] Sterne and Nicholson were allowed to keep schools, and Walton was helped by the government in his preparations for the polyglot bible.[68] Even those such as Sheldon and Henchman, who corresponded with the court in exile, who organized financial aid for Anglican sufferers, and encouraged others to defend their faith in print, went unmolested.[69] Those who had suffered most conspicuously, such as Wren in the Tower and those who had been in exile, were on the whole ignored.[70]

Far from being great sufferers, several of the new bishops had been allowed to publish during the Interregnum. Sanderson's multitudinous sermons, Griffith's attacks on the Welsh visionary Vavasour Powell, and Gauden and Reynolds's various works were probably well received by many moderates.[71] Walton was involved in the polyglot bible, an uncontroversial venture on the whole, though in a reply to a critic of the polyglot Walton did complain that the text of the bible was suffering from 'the wilfull corruptions and falsifications of Sectaries and Hereticks, which never more

[65] Bosher, pp. 286, 290, 291.

[66] E.g. Sheldon and Ironside, *Walk. Rev.*, pp. 76, 134.

[67] Gauden, Griffith, Reynolds (and Lucy), *Dict. Nat. Biog.*; Monck, *Walk. Rev.*, p. 119.

[68] Relevant articles in *Dict. Nat. Biog.*

[69] Bosher, chapters 1-3.

[70] Cf. Hyde's argument against promoting exiled Scots episcopalians—'by their long absence out of Scotland, [they] know nothing of the present generation: and by the ill usage they had met with . . . they would run matters quickly to great extremities' (Burnet, i, 236-7).

[71] For their publications in the 1650s, see D. Wing, *Short-Title Catalogue of Books Printed in England . . . 1641-1700* (New York, 1945-51).

boldly nor in greater numbers than now, endeavoured to deprave or corrupt it'.[72] Nicholson's *Apology for the Discipline of the Ancient Church* (1659) stated his preference for the traditional Church of England, but the work is notably mild in tone: 'Far more comfort it were for us (so small is the joy I take in those strife) to labour under the same yoke, as them that look for the same eternal reward of our labours, to be joyned with you in the bonds of indissoluble love and amity'. He reserved stronger words for the sectaries, whose factiousness made the work of the Pope easier, he thought.[73] Most of the works written by Cosin during the Interregnum were not published till later, but his *Scholastical History of the Canon of Holy Scripture* (an attack upon the Catholic not the Puritan position) appeared in 1657.

The majority of the Restoration nominees, however, seem to have published nothing at all. Indeed, the behaviour of some of the new bishops in the preceding decades was so innocuous that their views were probably as hard to discover then as they are now. Obscurity is perhaps the best word to describe the origins and background of men such as William Lucy, Hugh Lloyd, William Nicholson, Gilbert Ironside, and Nicholas Monck. In one or two cases there are glimmers of light: two of these men had risen to the heights of Welsh archdeaconries in 1644; Ironside's wealth may have been needed to uphold the dignity of the poor see of Bristol; Monck was fortunate to have a much abler elder brother.[74] But in many respects one is reminded of the phrase used, approvingly, by Archbishop Parker to describe the early Elizabethan bishops—'reverent mediocrity'.[75] These men may have had some claim or influence that is not apparent today, or they may have been compromise candidates, put in to act as makeweights between High- and Low-Church parties. But their elevation is the more striking in that at the Restoration there was no shortage of more senior, experienced men or of men who had done more for their ailing mother the Church of England in previous years.

[72] *The Considerator Considered* (London, 1659), pp. 292-3.
[73] W. Nicholson, op. cit., p. 238.
[74] See above pp. 68, 89.
[75] P. Collinson, *The Elizabethan Puritan Movement* (London, 1967), p. 64.

One further feature of the new nominees, and one which may help to explain the promotion of little known figures, is the close relationship which often existed between them and their new dioceses. George Griffith had been chaplain to a previous bishop of St. Asaph, a canon of that cathedral, a minister in Montgomeryshire, and a stout upholder of Welsh traditions and language, before he was elevated to St. Asaph. Gilbert Ironside had held livings in Dorset for many years before becoming bishop of Bristol, and Hugh Lloyd had held livings in Glamorgan and been archdeacon of St. David's before becoming bishop of Llandaff. Better known figures also had long-established links with the dioceses to which they were elevated—Cosin with Durham, Henchman with Sarum, and Sanderson with Lincoln.[76] This pattern was undoubtedly deliberate. We can see the efforts that the exiled court was making to match bishops and dioceses,[77] and in 1660 we may observe the care taken in choosing sees for the three Presbyterians. The diocese of Norwich, with the high incidence of Puritanism which had caused Wren so much trouble, was given to Reynolds; Coventry and Lichfield with its several Puritan centres was offered to Calamy; and Hereford, part of the West Midland area influenced by the Association Movement, was offered to that movement's leading light—Baxter. It is also interesting to note that many of the sees which received moderate bishops in the early 1640s, in an effort to allay Puritan dislike of prelacy, again received moderates in 1660. Reynolds's predecessor at Norwich was the conciliatory Joseph Hall, whom Laud thought too inclined to Calvinist notions. In 1642 the diocese of Exeter received a strict Calvinist, Ralph Brownrigg, who had been prominent in the opposition to Laud at Cambridge; at the Restoration, he was succeeded both in his chaplaincy at the Temple and in his bishopric by the Low-Church conformist Gauden. Lichfield was given to the moderate Frewen in 1644, and at the Restoration having been refused by Calamy and possibly

[76] Articles in *Dict. Nat. Biog.*

[77] Dr Clare was allocated Carlisle partly because of his 'great benefice' in the next county; Cosin was first allocated Peterborough of which he was then dean; Hammond had close links with the royalist gentry in Worcestershire and had he lived would have become their diocesan; Egerton MS. 2542, ff.270, 268; *Walk. Rev.*, p. 217.

Baxter was at last given to John Hacket, who had stayed in his living at Cheam throughout the troubles and written an admiring biography of his former mentor and Laud's greatest enemy—Archbishop Williams.[78]

It may be suggested that Charles's choice of bishops was shrewd. To re-assure the ecclesiastical right he had chosen one or two hard-liners, Cosin and Sterne, who reinforced surviving disciplinarians such as Wren and Pierce. But for the most part he had chosen moderates or conformists, men who had been closer to the martyred king than the martyred archbishop, men whose inactivity or conformity during the Interregnum would have calmed Puritan suspicions. It is surely significant that Baxter, speaking in November when nearly all the episcopal nominations were known, still felt capable of defending the experiment of modified episcopacy.[79] It is also significant that nearly all of the bishops-elect who attended the Worcester House conference acquiesced in the compromise settlement that was emerging.[80] Indeed, in the important case of Morley, it was welcomed in a very positive manner: he wrote off to Scotland to spread the glad tidings of the approaching settlement.[81] Only one bishop-elect—predictably it was Cosin—protested that Charles would 'Unbishop' his bishops if he insisted on their sharing their authority with the parish clergy.[82] In other words Charles had managed to find bishops whose reputations did not alienate Puritan sympathy from his scheme for limited episcopacy, and whose consciences allowed them to support the form of church government outlined in his declaration.

By late October, it must have seemed to Charles that his scheme had a more than reasonable chance of success. The parish clergy had been stabilized on a broad basis, the cathedral chapters had been reconstituted with little fuss, and

[78] Articles in *Dict. Nat. Biog.;* on Brownrigg, N.R.N. Tyacke, 'Arminianism in England, in Religion and Politics 1603 to 1640' (Oxford D. Phil. thesis, 1968), p. 82.

[79] *Rel. Baxt.*, Lib. I, Pt. II, para. 128.

[80] There is some doubt as to who was present at the first meeting (Whiteman, 'Restoration', p. 70, n. 2). Probably present and already nominated or elected were Sheldon, Morley, Henchman, Cosin, and Reynolds; possibly there and already nominated were Gauden and Sterne.

[81] Whiteman, 'Restoration', pp. 69-70.

[82] W. Bates, *Works* (London, 1723), p. 725.

an amenable bench of bishops had been selected. His prospects of success soon began to fade, however; by the spring of 1661 he would be forced onto the defensive and by the autumn he was forced to abandon the scheme. But before turning to this second phase of the settlement, we must examine the church's financial recovery, for without this it would have been very difficult for any church settlement to have advanced much further.

V

THE FINANCIAL RECOVERY OF THE EPISCOPATE AND CATHEDRAL CHAPTERS

The land question was potentially one of the most explosive issues of the Restoration. Naturally, the purchasers of confiscated crown, church, or royalists' lands did not want to hand them back, or at least not without some form of compensation such as their purchase money repaid with interest or a long lease of the same lands at low rents. The deprived owners of these lands tended to nurse an even greater sense of grievance, but although they hoped for immediate recovery they did not relish the prospect of recovering estates encumbered by heavy debts or long leases. In the event, as will be seen, church lands were recovered with surprisingly little bother. Indeed, so successful were some ecclesiastical landlords in recovering their estates, and so great were the amounts of money which some of them received, that they soon faced criticism from their supporters as well as their enemies. Efforts had to be made to correct the impression of 'vast summs received, and nothing issued out',[1] and Sheldon circulated two questionnaires, one in 1662, the other in 1670, gathering information on bishops' and chapters' leasing policy and on how they spent the unusually large sums then received.[2] Over forty replies have survived in the Tanner manuscript collection, and together they constitute a mine of information on Restoration church finance.[3] Probably after the second set of replies had been received, Sheldon's secretary, Miles Smyth, prepared an apologetic work, 'The State of the Clergy of England', to demonstrate how

[1] Tanner MS. 140, f.178.

[2] *Correspondence of John Cosin*, ed. G. Ornsby, Surtees Society, lv (1870), 101, prints the 1662 letter; for replies echoing it, see Tanner MSS. 144, ff.14, 153–4; 147, f.87; 150, f.24. For 1670 letter, see Tanner MS. 128, ff.58–9, and Winch. Cath. Lib., 'Winchester Cathedral MSS' vol. i.

[3] Concentrated in Tanner MSS. 140, 141, 144, 146, and 147, with isolated accounts in 92, 123, 128, 129, 130, 131, 134, 137, 143, 148, 150, and 217.

generously the restored bishops and chapters had treated their tenants, how great were the expenses facing them, and how small their personal share of the church's revenues had been.[4] The validity of Smyth's conclusions can be tested by reference to the individual accounts in the Tanner collection or by examining diocesan material. The chapters of both Canterbury and Winchester, for example, have preserved fine collections of estate records for this period.[5] Episcopal finances, or at least the records kept of them, were to some extent private matters, but the evidence produced in dilapidation suits against Juxon of Canterbury and Duppa of Winchester provides much useful information.[6]

The position of the purchasers of church lands remained obscure throughout the summer of 1660, despite much political manoeuvring.[7] When some ecclesiastical landlords began to grant leases, Parliament showed its displeasure in a bill to prevent further leasing by bishops or chapters.[8] By coincidence, three days later on 9 August Charles sent a letter to church leaders ordering them to augment the value of poor vicarages and curacies when these formed part of a lease, a move which seemed to give qualified approval to continued leasing of church properties.[9] The legal position was not completely clarified until 7 October, when Charles issued a commission to enquire into the 'pretended Sales and Purchases' of church and crown lands, the task of the

[4] Tanner MS. 141, ff.79-105, 111; for an assessment of Smyth's work, see my 'Process of Re-establishment' pp. 221, 271-2.

[5] Cant. Cath. Chap. Arch., Accounts New Foundation, Receivers' and Treasurers' Books and accounts for early 1640s and early 1660s, Registers *Z.26* and *Z.27*, miscellaneous items such as Domestic Economy 91, Rentals 22, 57, Rural Economy 117, 127, and Canterbury Letters *Y.14.2* and *Y.14.3* have all proved of value. In Winch. Cath. Lib., 'Winchester Cathedral MSS' vols. i, ii, 'Winchester Cathedral Accounts 1614 to 1663' and '1664 to 1670', the Receivers' books for 1661 and 1662, the isolated Receiver's account (1663) and Treasurer's account (1663), and 'An abstracte of the Accompts of the Cathedral church of Winton since . . . 1660' (by the chapter's auditor Edward Traffles, and cited hereafter as Traffles's 'Abstracte') have provided much evidence.

[6] J. Aubrey, *The Natural History and Antiquities of the County of Surrey* (London, 5 vols., 1719), v. 273-4, and cf. Smyth's assessment of Juxon's finances in Tanner MS. 141, ff. 101, 111; for Duppa, Tanner MS. 140, ff. 39-88.

[7] J. Thirsk, 'The Restoration Land Settlement', *Journal of Modern History*, xxvi (1954), 315-28.

[8] *J.C.*, viii, 112.

[9] Ibid., 113.

commission being to supervise the recovery of alienated lands and to settle any differences as amicably as possible.[10] At the same time, he issued a letter urging bishops and chapters to be generous in their treatment of purchasers and former tenants.[11]

Two factors eased the process of recovery considerably. First of all, many of those who had purchased parcels of church land in the revolutionary decades had in fact held the same lands as tenants of the church in the late 1630s or early 1640s. All that was needed was for the former tenant to surrender his deed of purchase and negotiate a new lease with the bishop or chapter concerned. Just how common this situation was can be gauged from the correspondence of the restored landlords; tenants pleaded that they had been 'forced to kisse the Rod' and purchase the estate they already rented in order to prevent 'a great Captaine of the Armie' from getting it.[12] It can also be seen in the indentures of new leases made at the Restoration; on over twenty occasions at Canterbury, the indentures refer to the simultaneous surrender of an old lease from the chapter and of a deed of purchase 'from the late pretended state or their Trustees'.[13] Replies to Sheldon's question about leasing policy tell the same story: the chapter of York described purchasers as being 'moste of them olde Tenants'.[14]

The second factor was the apparently favourable treatment meted out to many purchasers. Various landlords reported an 'exact observance' of the king's orders to treat purchasers considerately.[15] At Canterbury, in addition to the twenty-one indentures mentioning a double surrender, there are a further thirty-five leases stating that the surrender of a deed of purchase was taken into consideration when the lease was granted.[16] The chapter of York halved the fines of purchasers, that of Winchester reduced them to six years' purchase (six

[10] D. Wilkins, *Concilia Magnae Brittaniae et Hiberniae* (London, 4 vols., 1737), iv, 557-60; for echoes of their work, Kennett, *Register*, pp. 376, 388-9, 391.

[11] Ibid., p. 279.

[12] Canterbury Letters, *Y.14.2,* nos. 90, 95; cf. Kent Recd. Off. *DRc/Egz* 29, and Tanner MS. 49, f.18.

[13] *Z.26,* ff.37, 41, 44, 45, 46, 57, 60, 82, 90, 118, 123, 142, 143, 146, 166, 194, 199, 200, 217; *Z.27,* f.8.

[14] Tanner MS. 150, f.102.

[15] Tanner MS. 140, f.140; Harleian MS. 3789, f.76.

[16] *Z.26,* ff.63, 67, 74(2), 78, 81, 84, 89, 91, 93, 116, 117, 119, 120, 127, 131, 132,

times the yearly profit of the land).[17] The canons of Windsor said that they had sacrificed £9,000 'In abatements to tenants on account of being Purchasers'.[18] The chapter of Durham suggested that their allowances to purchasers were probably greater in value than the original purchase-money paid for the land, not to mention the profits taken since then.[19]

Not all purchasers could be given leases at the Restoration. Some of those who had obtained possession at the expense of former tenants were ousted to allow the old tenants to return; others were replaced by a new tenant who had the ear of the bishop or chapter. But in all these cases, Sheldon was assured, purchasers were dealt with fairly. The bishop of St. David's and the chapter of Gloucester described the generous terms offered to two men who had been evicted; the chapter of Lincoln spent £700 in 'buying out of Purchasers'.[20] Some of the sums described as 'allowances' to purchasers are so specific that they too may have been devoted to this end: the chapter of Ely 'allowed' purchasers £2,691, the bishop of Norwich 'allowed' them £702.[21]

The process of ejecting a proportion of the purchasers seems to have been relatively peaceful. At Canterbury, Rochester, Lincoln, Peterborough, Oxford, and Wells, difficulty was experienced in recovering properties in the cathedral close, and in some cases legal action was taken in order to regain possession.[22] There also survive a few letters from disgruntled individuals, and at least one petition to the king (which Charles merely passed on to the commissioners for 'pretended

139, 141, 154, 156, 169, 173, 183, 185, 203, 204, 222, 224, 234, 237, 248; *Z.27*, ff.8, 9, 50.

[17] Tanner MSS. 150, f.102; 140, f.51. In most leases the reserved rent paid annually was small, but to compensate landlords exacted a large lump sum, or 'fine', when a lease was first taken out or when it was renewed.

[18] Tanner MS. 140, f.168. Several replies put abatements to purchasers in with allowances to other people—royalist sufferers, ousted tenants, etc—e.g. Tanner MSS. 129, f.31; 130, f.66; 141, f.166; 146, f.159; 147, f.227. Thus Canterbury chapter claimed to have foregone 'some thousands of pounds' by 'kind and moderate usage' of their tenants, Tanner MS. 123, f.57.

[19] Tanner MS. 144, f.153.

[20] Tanner MSS. 146, f.133; 147, f.113; 130, f.68.

[21] Tanner MSS. 141, f.45; 137, f.34.

[22] J. C. Robertson, art. cit., 95-6; Kent Recd. Off., *DRc/Arb.* 2, ff. '22', '23'; Tanner MSS. 130, ff.68-9; 147, ff.87, 71; *Cal. Rev.*, p. 88.

sales').[23] In most dioceses, however, the work of these commissioners may have been minimal. Bishop Sterne of Carlisle claimed that not one purchaser had summoned him to appear before the king's commissioners, and Archbishop Frewen of York told Sheldon that 'not any Tenant (great or small) hath as yet complained of hard usage from me'.[24] Frewen's technique was a passive one: he 'oft left it to the old Tenants to compound with' those purchasers who were to be ejected, and then deducted the sum paid by the old tenant from the fine which he paid on his new lease. The chapter of Peterborough also reduced the fines of 'severall Loyall and well-affected Tenants' on account of their 'great charges in recovering their Leases from the intruders'.[25] This picture of peaceful recovery is drawn largely from clerical sources, but if we look at state papers, newspapers, and secular correspondence, there is a singular absence of criticism of the methods by which churchmen regained their estates.

A few reverend landlords were in the fortunate position of being able to give new leases and levy fines within weeks or months of the Restoration. The chapter of Canterbury granted eighteen leases within days of its re-assembling in mid-July, and a further ten in September and early October. Significantly, all of these leases referred to the surrender of former leases; as the chapter's Receiver noted, former tenants were anxious to renew their titles as soon as possible.[26] Similarly, Dean Cosin of Peterborough had barely returned from exile when he 'was earnestly invited and pressed by several Tenants heretofore belonging to the Cathedral Church . . . to repair unto that Church, and there to hold a Chapter for the renewing of their leases which were then expired'; accordingly, a chapter was held, and leases were issued in late July.[27] Before their respective translations to Winchester and York (both confirmed on 4 October), Bishops

[23] Canterbury Letters, *Y.14.3*, nos. 119, 131; Tanner MS. 144, ff.88–9.

[24] Tanner MSS. 144, f.8; 150, f.24. Cf. the valuable article by Dr W. J. Sheils, 'The Restoration and the Temporalities: Archbishop Frewen's Commissioners 1661–1662', *Borthwick Institute Bulletin*, i (1975), 17–30.

[25] Tanner MS. 127, f.53.

[26] *Z.26*, ff.1–31 (early folios damaged), 41, 156; *Z.27*, ff.28–30; Receiver's Book 1660–1.

[27] Kennett, *Register*, pp. 388, 218, 225.

Duppa and Frewen had been actively leasing out the episcopal estates of their old dioceses.[28] These instances of early leasing may, however, have been exceptional: only a third of the episcopate was still alive, and the prebendaries of Canterbury and Peterborough resumed their work much earlier than their fellows.[29] For most chapters and for most of the bishops, the work of financial reconstruction cannot have begun in earnest until the closing months of 1660.

To try and assess the speed with which ecclesiastical revenues returned to normal is to some extent a misleading exercise. The typical revenue of 1640–1 consisted for the most part of rents and other regular receipts (from tithes, pensions, court fees, etc.); only a small part of it was derived from fines which fell in very sporadically. That of 1660–1 was quite the reverse, consisting largely of fines with only a small amount from rents. The reasons for this are quite simple: it took time to reconstruct the administrative machinery to collect rents on a regular basis, but in 1660 many tenants and purchasers were very anxious to pay fines in order to secure a legal title to a particular piece of land. It is interesting to note that many of the old tenants of the chapter of Canterbury who received new leases at the Restoration held unexpired leases from the reign of Charles I. Well over a third of the leases surrendered in the opening years of the Restoration had been sealed in the years 1639 to 1643, and since twenty-one years was the normal length for a lease of a larger property and thirty years was quite common for a tenement, it may be deduced that many of these leases had not actually expired by the time of surrender.[30] However, years or lives still in being were almost certainly sacrificed in 1660 in order to obtain the reassurance and legal security of a fresh lease. When we bear in mind that not only old tenants but also purchasers were usually very anxious to obtain leases, the volume of fines received in 1660 and 1661 is not surprising.

The amounts received in fines at the Restoration were clearly unparalleled in the history of the English church,

[28] Whiteman, 'Re-establishment', pp. 128–9; A. Wood, *Athenae Oxonienses* (London, 2 vols., 1721), ii, 1147. Cf. *S.P.* 29/16, f.42 for September leasing at Sarum.

[29] Above pp. 66–7 and below p. 117.

[30] Based on an analysis of indentures 1660–3 (*Z.26, Z.27* ff.1–288 *passim*).

perhaps reaching a million pounds in value.[31] But this 'faire and more than ordinary crop of profit and treasure' was both short-lived and unevenly distributed throughout the country. It seems clear that the most lucrative period of leasing was the first two years of the Restoration. Juxon may have received £54,000 in fines in the two and a half years after his translation, but his successor derived only £19,000 from this source in the fourteen years that he held the see.[32] The dean and chapter of Winchester received over £31,000 in the two and a quarter years after their first meeting in September 1660; by 1670, the total was only £12,500 higher.[33] We do not possess accurate figures for the chapter of Canterbury, but we have a rough guide to their receipts from fines in the numbers of leases granted each year: seventy-three in 1660, 152 in 1661, thirty-nine in 1662, forty-six in 1663, and similarly low figures thereafter; it seems likely that the chapter had received over £20,000 by late 1662.[34] Similar evidence could be cited from other dioceses: having creamed the episcopal estates at Lichfield, Frewen received a further £20,000 during his three and a half years at York; over £20,000 was taken by the dean and chapter of Exeter between 1660 and 1663 and nearly £14,000 by that of Wells in the same period.[35]

It would be unwise, however, to assume that these figures were representative of the country as a whole. The chapter of Chester, Sheldon was told in 1663, was so meanly endowed that it had 'seal'd but one lease, and that for £300'. Their bishop was little better off: only four leases of episcopal estates had expired (though some tenants had added a life or two to

[31] Smyth's estimate, though he said £216,000 of this had been abated-Tanner MS. 141, f.103.

[32] Tanner MSS. 123, f.57; 140, f.111; 127, f.151 (for a slightly lower estimate, Lamb. Pal. Lib. 'Lambeth Payments', book 3).

[33] Tanner MS. 140, ff.118-19.

[34] For leases, see *Z.26* and *Z.27*. From Peter du Moulin's 'Letter to a Person of Quality, Concerning Fines Received by the Church at its Restoration', it may be deduced that well over £17,000 worth of fines had been received by November 1661 (printed in *Harleian Miscellany*, ed. W. Oldys (London, 8 vols., 1744-6), iv, 92-3), and from the Treasurer's Book 1662 we know that a further £3,592 was received in the following year. By 1663-4, however, fines had dropped to a mere £1,121-Treasurer's Book 1664.

[35] University of York, Borthwick Institute of Historical Research, *CC Ab 3/2;* Whiteman, 'Re-establishment', p. 129; Tanner MS. 140, f.12; and cf. allegations at Sarum mentioned below p. 113.

existing leases).[36] Cosin found few fines to be taken at Durham, since his predecessors had leased for lives, which were often still in being, or for long periods up to ninety-nine years, and even an incredible 450 years 'which will outweare 20 Bpps'.[37] His chapter made only one dividend of fines between Michaelmas 1661 and June 1663, and that 'not greater, then was ordinary in former yeares, before the late troubles'. Similar complaints were heard from Norwich, Ely, Bristol, Hereford, and St. David's.[38]

There seems to have been similar variation in the speed and ease with which ordinary revenues (rents, tithes, etc.) were recovered. The chapter of Canterbury made an early start, appointing officials in July 1660 and demanding the rents due at midsummer 1660. Within a matter of months it was in receipt of an income comparable to that collected in 1641 or 1642.[39] At Winchester, both bishop and chapter began collecting rents a little later, but within a couple of years they were back to the pre-war position.[40] Not all ecclesiastical landlords were so fortunate; some found that their incomes were temporarily depressed by the damage done to their properties during the Interregnum. Half a dozen of them had lost valuable timber, while at Hereford the value of the chapter's tithes had been reduced almost to nothing 'through the vast conversion of Arable to pasture, Sowing Clover grass, where good Wheat, Rye and Barlie and Pease and Oats grew' together with 'fruits and 1000s of acres of Hops'. The value of one property had dropped from £32 to £8. 10*s*., so that even at a reduced rent the chapter had been unable to find a tenant, and in the end had been forced to lease it for nothing for a

[36] Tanner MS. 144, f.15.

[37] Tanner MS. 92, f.11.

[38] Tanner MSS. 144, f.154; 137, f.34; 134, f.139; 141, f.45; 129, ff.27, 29; 147, ff.81, 84, 102; 146, f.127.

[39] Domestic Economy 91; Casaubon's notes in Receiver's Book 1660-1; Rental 22. Comparison of Receiver 54(1641), 55(1642) with Receivers' Books 1660–1, 1661, 1662, and 1663 suggests that over £1,000 had been received by September 1660 (a sum equivalent to half of the total receipts of 1641 or 1642), that over £3,000 was received in 1660–1 (a total swollen by arrears?) and about £2,400 in the two succeeding years (about the same as pre-war figures).

[40] Duppa's receipts from rents 1660–2 compare very favourably with Morley's annual rental—Tanner MS. 140, ff.83-5, 65–76; the chapter's recovery can be traced in Receiver's book 1661, Receiver's account 1663, and Thomas Coward's acounts in 'Winchester Cathedral Accounts 1614 to 1663'.

year.[41] It would take much longer for losses such as these to be made good.

Financial recovery, therefore, would seem to have been uneven. Some bishops and chapters were soon receiving far more in fines than they had ever received before the troubles, while others were struggling against the natural poverty of their endowments, the reckless leasing of a previous generation, or the damage done to their property during the revolutionary decades. All landlords, however, both rich and poor, had to face a variety of extraordinary expenditure, some of it very onerous: episcopal palaces, cathedrals, and closes had to be repaired or refurbished, augmentations to poorer vicarages and curacies in their care had to be made, and charitable gifts on an unusually heavy scale were expected of them.

The cost of restoring the houses in which they lived was often a major item of expense for the restored episcopate. Juxon spent over £14,000 on building repairs at Lambeth Palace and Croydon House; even then, his executors were sued by Sheldon for his failure to do more, and had to pay out £800 to the new archbishop.[42] Duppa probably spent about £4,500 on three episcopal houses destroyed or nearly demolished by 'the late rebels', but his successor claimed that none of the three was habitable, that he himself had spent over £12,000 on repairs to two houses and on building a new one, and that Duppa's executors should reimburse him for some of this expenditure. Their reply raised the interesting ethical and legal problem of how far the first Restoration bishops were responsible for making good damage for which they were not responsible. Duppa's executors said that those who were to blame for the poor condition of the palaces at Morley's accession were 'the late rebels', but since they had been pardoned by the Act of Oblivion, they could not be sued, and the offence itself was pardoned.[43] The same problem embittered relations between successive bishops in other dioceses too. Sparrow of Exeter alleged that Gauden had

[41] Rural Economy 127; Tanner MSS. 140, f.124; 134, f.20; 147, ff.83, 113; 150, f.24; 147, f.94.

[42] J. Aubrey, op. cit., v, 273-4.

[43] Tanner MS. 140, ff.39-41, 58-61, 83-5, 63-4; both sides agreed that full repairs to the three houses would have cost £30,000.

received much in fines, but had then 'carried his money away with him, and left his successors to repair the Palace'; Henshaw of Peterborough claimed that his predecessor had 'stayed here but a little while (yet long enough to reneiw the estates) and not living here, bestowed nothing upon repaires'.[44]

In fairness, it may be pointed out that some of the bishops gave generously to the refurbishing of their cathedrals. Juxon left £2,000 to St. Paul's, and £500 to Canterbury; Duppa helped to recover the statues of James I and Charles I which had adorned Winchester cathedral before the wars, and also left it money in his will; Morley converted a fine of £300 into equal gifts to Worcester cathedral, St. Paul's, and Christ Church, Oxford.[45] Hacket said he had given £3,500 to Lichfield cathedral, one of the most badly damaged in the country, and then he had collected a further £15,000 for an organ, stalls, altar ornaments, pavements, etc. Cosin gave the chapter of Durham some plate, a lectern, and a litany desk.[46]

The greatest share of the burden of restoring the cathedrals naturally fell on the chapters. That of Canterbury reported in 1670 that they had spent £7,921 on 'reparacons, utensills and ornaments' for their cathedral, though this figure may include payments for work done outside the cathedral.[47] The bulk of the work was done in the early years of the Restoration, for in 1662 the cathedral was described as 'very well repaired' with 'the windows all new glazed'. In the early Treasurers' books, we can also trace the purchase of 'damask linnen for two tablecloths for the Communion table', hangings for the choir, and a set of Communion plate.[48] Other chapters faced similar

[44] Tanner MSS. 141, f.132; 147, f.56. Also Rainbow brought a dilapidation suit against Sterne at Carlisle, Till, 'Ecclesiastical Courts of York', p. 86.

[45] Harleian MS. 3790, ff.14, 20; B. C. Turner, *Winchester Cathedral Record* (1960), p. 22; Tanner MS. 140, f.87; *Mercurius Publicus* (1661), no. 37, 12-19 September, p. 591.

[46] Tanner MSS. 131, ff.44, 45; 92, f.4.

[47] Tanner MS. 128, f.57. It is not easy to see how this figure was reached since the accounts do not make a clear distinction between repairs to the close and to the cathedral; even allowing for this, the payments for materials, wages, and fittings recorded in the Treasurers' books do not account for more than a fraction of the chapter's figure.

[48] *Mercurius Publicus* (1662), no. 13, 27 March-3 April, p. 207; Treasurers' Books 1660-1, p. 87; 1663, p. 52.

payments: Exeter spent over £6,000 on their cathedral, Worcester £3,500 on theirs, and Wells nearly £3,000 on theirs.[49]

At Winchester, the greatest expense was repairing the close. In the decade after their return, the chapter spent £17,275 on repairs to cathedral and close, of which all but a few hundred pounds was devoted to the close.[50] Nine of the thirteen houses in the close had been demolished or partly destroyed during the troubles, and the burden of building new stone or brick houses, though done 'at the Common coste', was considerable, consuming about a third of the chapter's total income in the first three years of the Restoration. By late 1662, however, most of the new houses were ready.[51]

Another task facing bishops and chapters was the augmentation of the stipends of the vicars and curates under their supervision. The royal letter of 9 August had suggested that this be done when these livings formed part of a lease: the landlord would make some concession (usually the reduction of the fine) in return for which the tenant would guarantee to pay the incumbent a higher salary than before. Juxon set a good example, making augmentations in thirty-two leases which had the effect of raising the stipends of over forty vicars and curates by a total annual value of £955. 16*s*. 8*d*.[52] According to Smyth, Juxon sacrificed £11,000 to this end.[53] Bishop Sterne of Carlisle reckoned that he had foregone £1,800 in fines in order to ensure augmentations, and it cost Sanderson of Lincoln nearly £1,000 to raise the value of some of his poor livings by a total of £124 a year.[54] Chapters also acted quite generously: Winchester raised the value of over a

[49] Tanner MSS. 141, f.169; 140, ff.140, 12; and see above pp. 75–6.

[50] Tanner MS. 140, f.123. The cathedral needed few repairs (see above p. 76); payments for cathedral and close in 1660 and 1661 are combined in Traffles's 'Abstracte', but from a loose folio entitled 'Expended by the Deane and Chapter', bound in 'Winchester Cathedral Accounts 1614 to 1663', we can see that in succeeding years work on the cathedral cost only a minute fraction of work on the close.

[51] B. C. Turner, *Winchester Cathedral Record* (1960), pp. 18, 20–3; Traffles's 'Abstracte'; Receiver's book 1661; Receiver's account 1663.

[52] Lamb. Pal. Lib., *VC1B/2* (Register of Augmentations); W. Kennett's figure is slightly higher, *The Case of Impropriations and of the Augmentation of Vicarages* (London, 1704), pp. 256–7.

[53] Tanner MS. 141, f.101.

[54] Tanner MSS. 144, f.8; 130, f.66.

dozen livings by a total of £500 per annum, Canterbury raised thirteen poor vicars' incomes by £315. 13*s*. 4*d*., while even the relatively poor chapter of Rochester raised vicars' stipends by £150 a year in all. Windsor estimated that they had foregone £6,100 and Ely £2,427 by augmenting vicarages and curacies.[55]

To judge from the Tanner accounts, bishops and chapters responded well to the king's letter. The point made later by Burnet—that the basis for 'a great and effectual reformation' would have been laid if the restored landlords had devoted half of their fines to raising the value of poorer livings—is probably true.[56] In their defence, the restored landlords might have argued that some of their poorer livings had already been augmented before the troubles;[57] furthermore, poor vicars were not the only recipients of their generosity at the Restoration. In at least three cathedrals, Canterbury, Winchester, and Wells, the stipends of the choirs were raised, while at Exeter £300 per annum was settled on sixteen prebends.[58] They would also have argued that to have devoted much more to augmentations might have left them with insufficient money for pressing needs such as building materials or new fittings, or for the charitable donations which they made so freely at the Restoration. The city gates of Canterbury, torn down in 1648 after the Kentish rising, were replaced at Juxon's personal expense; not far behind, the chapter gave the corporation a 'considerable sum of money by way of stock' so that corn could be 'brought in and provided at reasonable rates, for the supply of the necessity of the poor'.[59] Two chapters undertook to bear the cost of lectures for the benefit of their corporations, and Bishop Hacket made a

[55] Tanner MS. 140, ff.122-4; Treasurer's Book 1663; Tanner MSS. 147, f.10; 140, f.168; 141, f.45.

[56] Burnet, i, 329-30; cf. Dr. Whiteman's point ('Re-establishment', p. 129) that this proposal was 'less feasible at the time than in retrospect it was to appear'.

[57] E.g. by the chapters of Canterbury and Winchester, Treasurer's Book 1663, Tanner MS. 140, f.123.

[58] Tanner MSS. 140, f.123; 128, f.57; 140, f.12. The figure of £250 for augmentations to Canterbury choirmen and other inferior officers is higher than would appear from the treasurers' accounts, even if we include augmentations already paid before the wars. Exeter—Tanner MS. 141, f.169.

[59] *Mercurius Publicus* (1662), nos. 23, 5-12 June, pp. 358-60, and 13, 27 March-3 April, pp. 207-8.

donation to the fund for church bells in the city of Lichfield.[60] Ecclesiastical landlords were also called upon to make other gifts in the early years of the Restoration: first of all, there were the two gifts to the king in 1661, and then there were the contributions to the fund for ransoming English prisoners out of captivity in North Africa in 1662. All three sets of payments deserve fuller treatment than they can be given here,[61] but their value at least may be indicated.

Bishops and chapters gave two presents to the king in 1661, one completely unsolicited, and the other in response to a statute designed to help Charles pay off his debts.[62] The highest unsolicited gifts were made by the archbishops (£3,000 and £2,000) and by three chapters who gave £2,000 apiece, but even the poorest bishops and chapters made a generous contribution. Many churchmen also gave the highest amount permitted by the statute (£400 for a peer and £200 for a commoner).[63] The grand total for the two sets of presents was well over £42,000—a useful sum, especially since it was paid over in the first eighteen months of the Restoration at a time when the king was anxious not to sacrifice his prerogative powers in return for Parliamentary funds. Like his father in 1640, Charles was being given practical proof of the readiness of a hierarchical church to support monarchy.[64]

Shortly afterwards, reverend landlords again dipped into their pockets in order to pay the ransoms of English sailors captured during hostilities against the privateers of North Africa.[65] Again Juxon and the chapter of St. Paul's set an example with contributions of £1,000 and £500 respectively. Altogether £8,750 was given to 'this truly Christian and pious Designe',[66] and in the closing months of 1662 two churchmen travelled to Algiers and secured the release of most of the

[60] Tanner MSS. 140, ff.143, 123; 131, f.44.

[61] A fuller account may be found in 'Process of Re-establishment', pp. 259–65.

[62] 'An Act for a Free and Voluntary Present', *Statutes*, v. 307.

[63] Cf. Tanner MS. 141, ff. 106, 108, and Brit. Lib., Lansdowne MS. 805, ff.71–4; full details may be found in 'Process of Re-establishment', pp. 259–63.

[64] S. R. Gardiner, *History of England . . . 1603–42* (London, 10 vols., 1883–4), ix, 143, for free contribution of £120,000 offered in 1640.

[65] S. R. Gardiner, *History of the Commonwealth and Protectorate* (London, 4 vols., 1903), iv, chap. xlvi; K. Feiling, *British Foreign Policy 1660–1672*, op. cit., pp. 50–1.

[66] *Mercurius Publicus* (1662), no. 26, 26 June–3 July, pp. 404–5.

captive sailors.[67] As Sheldon had anticipated in his circular letter urging support for the venture, the whole episode provided 'a fair Opportunity . . . of taking off that injurious Obloquy, which is commonly cast upon the Clergy, that we receive much and do but little Good with it'. At the same time, it provided a further opportunity of assisting Charles, 'the exigence of whose Affairs at present renders him in want of Money'.[68]

The particular circumstances of the Restoration also necessitated other payments. Service books lost or destroyed during the civil wars had to be replaced; a sealed copy of the new Prayer Book had to be bought; sometimes libraries had to be replenished.[69] Royalist sufferers were given financial aid. In answer to Sheldon's question about expenditure on pious uses, Frewen said that his charity had been aimed principally at the 'relief of distressed cavaliers' and the poor. The chapter of Exeter settled a house and £6 per annum on each of six families who had suffered for their loyalty to king and church 'to their utter undoing'.[70]

It can readily be seen, therefore, that at the same time as resuming regular payments such as taxes and stipends, bishops and chapters faced a wide range of extraordinary expenses. Taken together, the costs of restoring and rebuilding, of augmenting salaries, and of making generous gifts to various worthy causes could amount to a sizable sum, and these expenses must have swallowed up a significant proportion of many bishops' and chapters' extraordinary income. In the light of this situation, it is easy to comprehend the indignation felt by churchmen at the accusations of selfish behaviour levelled against them by laymen. Sheldon's letter about captive redemption in June 1662 and the questionnaire he sent out later that year demonstrate his awareness of these accusations and his concern that they should be answered. In this he was not alone. In 1662, the dean of Lincoln bemoaned the 'excessive charges' and the 'small residue left us', adding that 'notwithstanding we shall by diverse be thought too rich,

[67] 'Process of Re-establishment', pp. 263–5.

[68] Kennett, *Register*, p. 720.

[69] *Hist. MSS. Comm. Dean and Chapter of Wells*, ii, 432; Cant. Cath. Chap. Arch. Treasurer's Book 1663, p. 52; Tanner MSS. 92, f.4; 147, f.227.

[70] Tanner MSS. 150, f.24; 141, f.169.

till we be seen to beg, or dye in debt'. In the same year, the chapter of Winchester felt that the public should be informed that capitular revenue did not 'wholy centre in the Prebendaries Purses, but hath its diffusions in the support of great companies of men, and the Fabrick of the Churches'.[71]

Expressions of indignation are not in themselves proof of innocence, and it must be admitted that there are a few disturbing features about the church's financial re-establishment. Charges of illegal or injudicious leasing were made against various bishops: Croft of Hereford, for example, alleged that his predecessor 'not long after falling desperately sick, and, as I conceive, being past any good sense when he did it', put all the remaining unleased properties into two great leases which were made over to his brother (the duke of Albemarle) and to Colonel Birch (a leading Presbyterian).[72] Disputes over leasing and the dividend from fines occurred in at least five chapters: at Hereford the dean and two prebendaries were accused of illegal leasing and profiteering by five of their fellows; at Wells, three of the chapter suspended five others over the division of the fines; and at Sarum, it was alleged that 'only 3 persons had the dispose' of the capitular estates in 1660, that these three had received £24,000, 'but what they laid out upon publique uses is not visible to us, nor does any thing appeare upon our Bookes'.[73] A disturbing feature about these and other cases was the haphazard way in which records, especially of fines, were kept. The dean of Canterbury later admitted that 'our Audit Bookes, at our first coming, were not soe exactly kept, as they ought'; his counterpart at Worcester apologized for the 'obscure and imperfect' condition of their accounts as far as fines were concerned.[74]

All of these features suggest that a few individuals *may* have benefited unfairly from the positions they held in the early 1660s, though it is hard to be sure. Detailed work in two dioceses suggests that their diocesans and chapters probably

[71] Tanner MSS. 48, ff.21, 71; 140, f.178.

[72] Tanner MS, 147, f.102; cf. allegations against Frewen, Gauden, and Laney—above pp. 103-4, 107-8.

[73] Harleian MS. 3789, f.76; Tanner MSS. 147, f.94; 140, ff.6-8, 19-27, 31-7; 143, f.263; Lichfield—Tanner MS. 131, f.45; York—Borthwick Institute *V. 1662-3*.

[74] Tanner MSS. 123, f.68; 140, f.138 (and cf. f.176).

received far more from fines, rents, stipends and other sources than they had to pay out in dues or charity. Extraordinary payments (repairs, gifts, etc) account for less than half of the fines received by Juxon or Duppa; both left large sums of money in their wills, and both of their successors brought dilapidation suits against their executors.[75] Dean Turner of Canterbury probably received nearly £2,500 from fines between 1660 and 1662, and Dean Hyde of Winchester over £2,100 over the same period; other members of their chapters received about half as much during the same period. Individual expenses and acts of charity that can be traced do not account for much of these sums, especially when it is remembered that certain expenses such as house repairs were met from common funds.[76] The Tanner accounts suggest a similar situation in one or two other chapters. The extraordinary cash payments made by the chapter of Wells by 1663 accounted for less than a third of their income from fines, which suggests sizable dividends.[77] At Exeter, £16,190 of the £20,972 received between 1660 and 1663 was shared out among the residentiary canons.[78]

To balance this picture, it should be remembered that many churchmen probably made very little personal gain or were even out of pocket. To take a few examples, Cosin received £19,800 in fines during his first seven years at Durham, but laid out £54,385 in 'Public and Charitable Works'.[79] Ward complained that he was 'more than £2,000 the worse' for being bishop of Exeter, and had to spend £300 per annum of his own 'small pittance'; Henshaw of Peterborough claimed to be '£400 poorer then when I came'.[80] At least three factors had to operate if an individual bishop was to make a large profit: he had to be nominated to a relatively wealthy see, he had to be its first occupant after the Restoration, and

[75] 'Process of Re-establishment', p. 272-5.

[76] Ibid., pp. 278-83.

[77] Tanner MS. 140, f.12, but cf. Tanner MS. 150, f.45; cf. the allegations at Sarum also.

[78] Whiteman, 'Re-establishment', p. 129.

[79] Tanner MS. 92, ff.4-5; the latter figure does include some items of regular expense, e.g. clerical dues, and some payments for new building rather than restoration.

[80] Bodl. Lib., MS. Addit. c. 305, f. 194; Tanner MS. 147, f.56; cf. Hacket also. W. G. Simon, *Restoration Episcopate* (1965), p. 37.

his patrimony had to be sufficiently well preserved to permit a rapid influx of fines and rents and to obviate the necessity of spending large sums on repairs. Similar factors determined the scale of reward that a prebendary might receive. In both cases it seems possible that only a minority were lucky. It was one of the ironies of the church settlement that those churchmen who inherited a badly damaged patrimony often had to do far more work for much less return.

Nevertheless, contemporary churchmen were quick to defend such profits as were made. One argument was that such returns represented compensation for financial losses suffered in the previous decades. Du Moulin said that though he was not the greatest sufferer in his chapter he had lost over £3,000 by sequestration and other penalties. The dean of Bristol told Sheldon that all members of his chapter had suffered, 'some of us to the loss of two or three thousand pounds, and he that suffered least, to the loss of a thousand pounds'.[81] Sometimes there were individual legal costs to be borne, as at Lincoln.[82] Others would have agreed with Bishop Henshaw that 'reason and Christian religion doe require us to provide for our family . . . the estates being but during life'.[83] Then there was the standard defence of ecclesiastical property—the church would not attract able or well-educated ministers 'if it were not for the hope of obtayning some one of the Few dignities and better provisions for learning and merit in the church'.[84] The profits made by capitular clergy could also act as a reward or as a support for other, less remunerative duties, acting as archdeacons, as surrogates in church courts, or as parish priests in poorly paid urban livings.[85]

It could also be argued that in so far as bishops and canons fulfilled the functions for which they were chosen, they deserved some return for their labours. The evidence suggests that the diocesans of Canterbury and Winchester administered dutifully and relatively efficiently; perhaps they

[81] *Harleian Miscellany*, loc. cit.; Tanner MS. 129, f.25.

[82] See above pp.76–7.

[83] Tanner MS. 147, f.56; for other examples of concern for family, see Clarendon MS. 77, f.222 and Tanner MSS. 129, f.29 and 131, f.47.

[84] Tanner MS. 141, f.80.

[85] E.g. in Bristol, Tanner MS. 129, f.29.

were negligent in the matter of repairs, but their charities went well beyond the call of duty.[86] The chapters of Canterbury and Winchester put their cathedrals into working order soon after their return, and shared their financial good fortune with others, especially those under their supervision. The mild outburst of anticlericalism provoked by the personal gains of a few churchmen should be kept in perspective. For most laymen, such profits probably constituted no more than a minor blemish on the character of the restored hierarchy; they were a small price to pay for the return of the traditional forms of church government.

[86] Juxon left over £10,000 to two cathedrals, St. John's College, Oxford, and the poor of several parishes (Harleian MS. 3790, ff.5-22); Duppa left over £4,000 to various good causes (Tanner MS. 140. ff.87-8).

VI

THE RECONSTRUCTION OF EPISCOPAL ADMINISTRATION

By May 1660 the church in England had split into several thousand units. Although certain religious practices had been proscribed, there had been no machinery capable of ensuring that uniform standards of worship and behaviour were maintained in every one of these units during the Interregnum. The restored episcopate must have been ignorant of the most basic facts about their dioceses, such as the identity of their parish clergy.[1] Administrative reconstruction was hampered by other difficulties. In only nine out of twenty-six dioceses did the former bishops live to be restored, and since three of these were soon translated, a total of twenty dioceses received a new bishop in 1660 or 1661.[2] Some of these bishops were well acquainted with their new dioceses,[3] but others had no such links, and where a bishop was both a stranger to his see and unused to the ways of governing a diocese, recovery may have been difficult indeed. Another problem was that some of the ordinaries were unable to proceed straight away to their dioceses. Delayed by business at court, by a summons to the Savoy Conference, or by the duty to attend Convocation from May to July 1661, some bishops, such as Morley and Walton, do not seem to have reached their sees until September 1661.[4] Others consecrated in December or January may have been

[1] Some of the surviving bishops had continued to make appointments during the late 1640s and 1650s, though their nominees had little prospect of taking office: Le Neve, *Fasti,* i, 354, 357, 361, 362; ii, 626; *J. Le Neve Fasti Ecclesiae Anglicanae 1541-1857 II Chichester Diocese,* compiled by J. M. Horn (London, 1971), 11, 22, 27, 45; Lamb Pal. Lib., *VX 1A/2E;* and see Bosher, p. 38.

[2] The survivors were the bishops of London, Sarum, Coventry and Lichfield (translated), Bangor, Bath and Wells, Chichester, Ely, Oxford, and Rochester.

[3] See above p. 96.

[4] *Mercurius Publicus* (1661), nos. 37, 12-19 Sept., pp. 588-91; and 38, 19-26 Sept., pp. 598-600.

delayed well into the new year by wintry conditions on the roads.[5]

In the early stages of reconstruction, the role of the bishop's officials was obviously crucial. It was upon their shoulders that there fell the tasks of finding out the state of the diocese, of advising a new bishop of the traditions of that see or even initiating him into the procedures of episcopal administration, and of acting as surrogates when the bishop was delayed or called away.

The most senior officials in any diocese, the bishop's right-hand men, were the vicar-general and the official-principal, or, where these two offices were combined in one man's hands, the chancellor. Where a chancellor outlived the Interregnum, his experience would be most useful. Whether his patent had granted him the office for life, or whether he was simply in the position of offering the bishop-elect renewed service in his see, a surviving chancellor offered the prospect of continuity and a smooth return to normality. Not surprisingly, the services of experienced chancellors were often called upon. Robert Mason, who had served as chancellor under two bishops of Winchester before the civil wars, was soon back in harness under Bishop Duppa.[6] Francis Baker seems to have been chancellor of Gloucester from 1630 until his death in 1669.[7] Some held positions in two dioceses: Sir Richard Chaworth appointed vicar-general of Canterbury in 1660 continued to hold the office of vicar-general of the bishop of London which he had held before the wars; similarly, Thomas Burwell retained the chancellorship of Durham when appointed to that of York.[8]

Not all surviving chancellors may have proved of equal worth; the chancellor of St. David's appointed by one bishop in 1641 was accused by the next of being ignorant of the law and incapable of holding the office.[9] Moreover, many chancellors seem to have been new to the position in 1660.

[5] Though Gauden managed to reach Exeter within seventeen days of his consecration: ibid. (1660), no. 54, 27 Dec.–3 Jan., pp. 833–4.

[6] Lambeth MS. 958, p. 109; see below, p. 120 n.17.

[7] Ibid.

[8] Below p. 124 and *Alum. Oxon.*; Till, 'Ecclesiastical Courts of York', p. 3.

[9] Lamb. Pal. Lib., Court of Arches, Act Book *A.2*, ff. 195, 240.

Doubtless some of these men were highly qualified in the law. The new official principal of Canterbury was Dr. Giles Sweit, an experienced member of Doctors' Commons and professor of law at Oxford after the Restoration.[10] Other eminent members of Doctors' Commons who became chancellors at the Restoration included Robert King, the restored master of Trinity Hall and Wren's new chancellor at Ely; Timothy Baldwin, principal of Hart Hall and apparently chancellor of both Hereford and Worcester after the Restoration; and William Turner who may have served as vicar-general under Duppa at Winchester.[11] The fact that some of these men held another major office demanding residence elsewhere or held posts in two dioceses at the same time suggests that in many cases their appointments were nominal ones, and the heaviest burden fell on lesser officials such as registrars or surrogates. It should also be borne in mind that chancellors in sees of medium or lower rank were less likely to be well qualified in the law, and for different reasons to have been especially reliant on their officials. The new chancellor of Chichester, Lambrock Thomas, possessed a doctorate of dignity and had served the cure of Pevensey from 1642–60,[12] but otherwise seems to have had no administrative experience or legal qualification for the post.

There may, however, have been considerations other than legal experience which influenced bishops in their choice of chancellors. In those testing times, it was important to have a good personal understanding between bishop and senior official, and in some cases such an understanding was perhaps best guaranteed by family ties or personal friendship. There is a remarkable chain of family connections which links Bishop Duppa with senior officials in four dioceses of the south-east. Sir Richard Chaworth, vicar-general of London and Canterbury in 1660, had married one of Duppa's nieces before the troubles; though the niece had died, Chaworth had remained sufficiently close to Duppa to be named as one of his executors in 1662.[13] When Lambrock Thomas was chosen as

[10] Lambeth MS. 958, pp. 110–11.

[11] Ibid., pp. 112, 116, 112–13; below p. 120 n.17.

[12] *Duppa-Isham Correspondence*, p. 195.

[13] Ibid., p. 196.

chancellor by Bishop King of Chichester, it may well have been a factor in his favour that Thomas had married another niece of Duppa, for Duppa and King were old friends and King had been sheltered by yet another of Duppa's numerous nieces during the Commonwealth period.[14] Finally, the man who may have served Duppa himself as vicar-general was William Turner whose wife was the step-child of Duppa's sister-in-law. The couple had been married in 1655, first at the civil ceremony ordained by the government of the day, and later at a clandestine Anglican service held by the bishop in his own house.[15] Yet another of Duppa's nieces married Miles Smyth, later secretary of Archbishop Sheldon.[16]

Within each diocese, family ties often influenced the allocation of offices considerably. Duppa's vicar-general, as we have just seen, was a distant relative of his; the registrar of the consistory court, John Lowen, was a relative of Duppa's cousin; the new clerk of the episcopal estates was the first cousin of Duppa's wife, and the new auditor-general was probably a nephew of his.[17] In the diocese of Canterbury, two of Juxon's relatives were made registrars and a third apparitor-general.[18] The appearance of Sandersons among officials at Lincoln, of a Sheldon at London, and later a Sterne at York and Morleys at Winchester probably indicates the same trend elsewhere.[19] At least two archdeacons appointed in 1660–1 were also related to their diocesans.[20] Arguably nepotism would be too strong a word for this phenomenon. There was probably a shortage of experienced senior officials at the Restoration, and since most bishops were new to their dioceses

[14] Ibid., pp. 195, 196; on the death of Thomas his wife dutifully married the next vicar-general of Chichester—ibid., p. 195.

[15] Ibid., pp. 108, 200 (and next paragraph).

[16] Ibid., p. 199.

[17] There is some confusion in Lambeth MS. 958, pp. 109, 112–13, as to whether Mason or Turner was chancellor of Winchester under Duppa; in 1661 Mason first appears in the court records as official principal, so it is possible that Turner was vicar-general. Lowen was also registrar of the archdeacon of Winchester. Hants Recd Off., *Liber Decimus Quartus Briani Winton*, ff. 14, 9, 3; *Duppa-Isham Correspondence*, pp. 199–201.

[18] Richard Swain (nephew), George and William Juxon: Harleian MS. 3790, f.10; *Z. 26*, ff. 102–4, 34.

[19] Kennett, *Register*, p. 309; Tanner MS. 142, f.144; Till, 'Ecclesiastical Courts of York', p. 20; *Liber Decimus Quartus*, ff. 35, 43, 44, 45, 47, 48.

[20] Rochester and Norfolk—Le Neve, *Fasti*, ii, 581, 485.

they did not know which of the lesser officials to promote. Under these circumstances, bishops may have considered that their relatives were as well qualified as most people to undertake such work, and probably more reliable or responsive in overseeing the work of lesser officials. However, one could not have expected a high standard of skill from most of these relatives.

Archdeacons were potentially of great value at the Restoration. Nearly half of the Caroline archdeacons were still alive in 1660, though resignation and promotion reduced the proportion of those actively involved in diocesan administration to a third.[21] Three of the six archdeacons of the diocese of Lincoln (the largest in the southern province and scattered over several counties) outlived the Interregnum, and the fact that they had obtained some knowledge of their archdeaconries before the civil wars must have been of assistance to the new bishop, Robert Sanderson, elevated straight to this major see.[22] Similarly Sheldon and Laney must have benefited from the experience of Thomas Paske, archdeacon of London from 1626, Edward Layfield, archdeacon of Essex from 1634, and John Quarles, of Peterborough from 1629.[23] On the other hand, some of the surviving archdeacons had been appointed so near to the civil wars that they probably had not had the opportunity to conduct a visitation before their authority had disappeared.[24] It may also be remembered that many of the new archdeacons appointed in 1660 had no administrative experience; nor do they appear to have been selected because they showed signs of administrative ability.[25]

The officials who were probably the most important in the reconstruction of episcopal administration are also the men who are most difficult to trace through the revolutionary

[21] See p. 68 above. At least two archdeacons resigned: Lewes and Carlisle, Le Neve, *Fasti*, i, 264, iii, 250; at least seven were promoted by 1661: Brecknock, St. David's, East Riding, and Cornwall (above p. 68 n.36), Leicester, Bedford, and Richmond, Le Neve, *Fasti*, ii, 62, 75, iii, 267. Two died in 1661: Oxford and Bath, ibid., ii, 516, and *Walk. Rev.*, p. 311.

[22] Bedford, Leicester, and Stow: Le Neve, *Fasti*, ii, 75, 62, 81.

[23] *J. Le Neve Fasti Ecclesiae Anglicanae 1541–1857 I St. Paul's London*, compiled by J. M. Horn (London, 1969), 8, 9; Le Neve, *Fasti*, ii, 542.

[24] E.g. Taunton, Exeter, Northumberland: ibid., i, 168, 396; iii, 308.

[25] See above pp. 64–5.

decades—the registrars, surrogates, clerks, and other lesser officials. There are occasional glimpses of chapter officials at work during the civil wars and Interregnum,[26] but for those officials who had worked in episcopal administration before the wars there were hardly any opportunities to use their specialized knowledge during the troubles. Only a few of the officials at Canterbury and Winchester can be shown to have worked in both the pre-war and post-war administration, but the unevenness of the materials makes it difficult to know if these were all that survived from the earlier period. Of the survivors at Canterbury, undoubtedly the most useful were William Somner, deputy registrar of the consistory and archidiaconal courts in the 1640s, and William Stede, official of the archdeacon from 1628 to 1672.[27] Others of lesser rank, surrogates, apparitors, and proctors, returned to their former work, as the opening meetings of the revived church courts demonstrate, both at Canterbury and Winchester.[28] In other dioceses, too, recovery was helped by the continuing labours of lesser officials. A registry official at Exeter was busy at work in October 1660, weeks before the new bishop was elected; in the diocese of Sarum, not only the archdeacon of Berkshire, but also his registrar resumed the work they had done before the revolution.[29] In many cases, surviving officials probably took on different or additional work in the same diocese. In 1660 William Somner was appointed clerk and auditor of the chapter of Canterbury, and registrar of the consistory court and a collector of tenths in the diocese of Canterbury by the archbishop.[30] Similarly, the chapter clerk of Wells before the wars became the bishop's registrar after the Restoration.[31] But some of the survivors who were promoted in 1660 were

[26] See above pp. 77–8 and below p. 126.

[27] Kent Recd. Off. *P.R.C.* 22/18, f.206; 22/19, ff.84–94; Cant. Cath. Chap. Arch. *Y.6.5.-Y.6.16.*

[28] Canterbury: James Lamb (a surrogate), *P.R.C.* 22/18, f.206; 22/19, f.94; Thomas Shindler and Leonard Browne (notaries public), *P.R.C.* 22/18, f.206; 22/19, f.95; and *P.R.C.* 2/1 (no foliation, see entries for 24.12.47 and 24.11.60); apparitors, Cant. Cath. Chap. Arch. *Z.2.4*, f.133. Winchester: see below; also cf. Mr. Foell and Henry Foyle, seneschals in 1640 and 1663, possibly the same man, Winch. Cath. Lib., Treasurers' Books 1640, 1663.

[29] Whiteman, 'Re-establishment', pp. 114, 115. For York examples, Till, 'Ecclesiastical Courts of York', chaps. 1, 2.

[30] *Z.27*, ff.42–3; Domestic Economy 91; *Z.26*, ff. 34, 104.

[31] *Hist. MSS. Comm. Dean and Chapter of Wells*, ii, 418, 431.

relatively inexperienced. John Harfell, appointed chapter clerk and then registrar of the consistory court at Winchester after the Restoration, had been only a proctor in the consistory court before the wars; Edward Traffles, appointed registrar of the archdeacon and auditor of the chapter in the same diocese had been an actuary in the same court as Harfell.[32]

The appointment of new officials sometimes brought with it its own problems. Some of the new men were obviously ill-acquainted with the forms and terminology of episcopal administration. The scribe making the first entry in the instance act book of the consistory court of Winchester in 1661 had forgotten, or did not know, the correct form of the title given the bishop in those records, and had to make two or three attempts to get it right.[33] The communar of the chapter of Wells had similar problems: 'Perditions to be payd *in fine anni*. What are they? *Super*; what is it? and A.B.C. *Quid significat*?'[34]

Worse than ignorance was inefficiency, and the occurrence of various cases of this would seem to suggest that the choice open to the restored bishops was sometimes limited. Richard Butler, appointed registrar of the consistory court of London in January 1661, and then deputy registrar of the commissary court as well, was later accused of neglect of his duties on a serious scale.[35] In 1664 one well-informed critic deemed that the following were 'Matters fit to be reformed' in the church courts: that ignorant clergymen should not be employed as surrogates to keep courts, that accurate and up-to-date records should be kept, and that registrars should not take excessive fees.[36] Such abuses were not new, but their mention in 1664, taken together with the serious dereliction of duty proved against Richard Butler, suggest that restored bishops may sometimes have been unable to appoint men of the experience or the integrity they would have hoped for to the lesser offices in their administration. Even where a bishop

[32] Winch. Cath. Lib., Dean and Chapter Act Books 1622–45, pp. 69, 83–4, and 1660–95, p. 1; Hants Recd. Off., Consistory Court Books 125, f.1 and *passim*, and 126, f.3; *Liber Decimus Quartus*, f.17.

[33] Court Book 126. f.3.

[34] *Hist. MSS. Comm. Dean and Chapter of Wells*, ii, 431.

[35] Tanner MS. 142, ff.152–91.

[36] Tanner MS. 315, ff.66–7.

tried to replace an insufficient official inherited from a predecessor, there could be trouble. When Bishop Lucy tried in September 1661 to supplant the chancellor appointed in 1641 by his predecessor, he was forced to take part in a protracted legal battle in the Court of Arches with the disgruntled Awbrey.[37]

The timing of officials' appointments is a matter of some interest. Only two weeks after he had set foot in England, Charles wrote to the surviving members of the chapter of Canterbury recommending the appointment of Sir Richard Chaworth as vicar-general, and in mid July the appointment was duly made.[38] A second letter from the king, dated 11 July, secured the appointment of Sir John Birkenhead as registrar of the court of faculties (a post he soon exchanged for that of commissary).[39] Further appointments were made in July, for example William Mericke to be judge of the Prerogative Court, though most offices were left vacant until Juxon was translated.[40] In acting this quickly, the court may have been trying to pave the way for a rapid return of episcopacy, but there were probably other considerations. Sir John Birkenhead seems to have been promised promotion by Archbishop Laud shortly before his death; Mericke had been judge of the Prerogative Court under Charles I until he was ejected by the Parliamentarian authorities; Chaworth was well qualified and the obvious candidate for the post of vicar-general.[41] These appointments were also necessary to end the anarchy into which the organization of the English church had fallen. The appointment of Chaworth as vicar-general ended the confusion into which the institution of clergy in the southern province had fallen; the re-appointment of Mericke took the control of probate out of the hands of a lay body served by officials appointed during the Commonwealth; the nomination of Birkenhead permitted the court of faculties to

[37] Court of Arches, Act Book *A.2*, ff.129–316 *passim*.

[38] *Z.27*, f.37; the exact date of appointment is not clear, since the register is damaged at this point, but other evidence points to this time: *Z.26*,ff. 1-2, 206; *Parliamentary Intelligencer* (1660), no. 32, 30 July–6 Aug., p. 520.

[39] *Z.27*, f.37; Harleian MS. 3797, f.153; and *Z.26*, f.100.

[40] P.R.O., Probate 12/37 f.104; *Z. 26*, ff. 2, 3.

[41] Lamb. Pal. Lib., *Comm. I*, f.145; *Prerogative Court of Canterbury Wills 1653–56*, Index Library, liv (1925), xiv-xv; and above p. 118.

restart work, such as registering those important figures in church administration, notaries public, thirty-three of whom were licensed in the six weeks before Juxon's translation.[42] The king's intervention ensured that the unacceptable methods used by the Commonwealth authorities were soon replaced by the traditional ones, but only at provincial level. The majority of appointments at diocesan level were not made in most dioceses until the autumn or later, in other words after the declaration on religious affairs had been drafted and the new bishops chosen.

At Canterbury, for example, permanent appointments by the archbishop (as opposed to temporary ones by the chapter) could not start until the formalities of his translation had been completed on 20 September. Even then there was no great flurry of activity. A few of the chapter's appointments were confirmed in late September or early October, but important offices in the Court of Arches were not filled until late October or November.[43] The majority of Juxon's officials were appointed in November, both for public and for private functions, but this still left many lesser offices to be filled. Further appointments continued into the summer of 1661, or even later in the case of minor posts in the restored church courts.[44] The pattern of events at Winchester was similar: Duppa's translation was confirmed on 4 October, and most of his appointments were made from October to December, though lesser posts were left vacant till June or August 1661, or later.[45]

How soon other bishops appointed their officials varied according to circumstance. A surviving bishop restored to his old see, Piers of Bath and Wells, appointed his vicar-general as early as 2 July, but a new bishop, Sanderson of Lincoln, could not appoint before late October, though he was active from the day of his consecration.[46] Since the number of bishops who were new to their dioceses was more than twice

[42] See below p. 129 and *Parliamentary Intelligencer* (1660), no. 32, 20 July-6 August, p. 520; previous notes; Lamb. Pal. Lib., *F I/C*, ff.1-6.

[43] *Z.26*, ff.34-6, 97-8, 102-4; *Z.27*, f.40.

[44] *Z. 26*, ff.100-101; *Z. 27*, ff.25-6, 35, 39-40, 49; *Z. 2.4*, f.134; *Y. 6.13*, f.246: Harleian MS. 3798, ff.27-8, 31.

[45] *Liber Decimus Quartus*, ff.1-26, and Court Book 126, ff.3, 9.

[46] *Hist. MSS. Comm. Dean and Chapter of Wells*, ii, 430; Whiteman, 'Re-establishment', p. 115.

that of the bishops who were not, and since many of the new were not consecrated until December 1660 or January 1661, it may fairly be assumed that most dioceses were without permanent officials until late 1660 or the new year. Coventry and Lichfield, possibly kept vacant for political reasons, cannot have received permanent officials until December 1661.[47]

The survival of old records obviously helped to expedite the reconstruction of episcopal administration. Such records were useful as sources of both information and precedents, especially for the forgetful or inexperienced clerk. The diocese of Canterbury was particularly well served in this respect. It is noticeable that in several classes of records the first post-Restoration entry follows straight after the last one made in the 1640s or early 1650s.[48] The preservation of many of these records was probably the work of that dedicated antiquarian and inveterate collector, William Somner.[49] A register of wills has survived which was clearly prepared by him in the 1650s. In it he arranged in alphabetical order and made a fair copy of wills proved in the 1640s; the last of these was copied out and attested as accurate in May 1654.[50] Other records may also have been in his possession: in the instance act book of the consistory court he appears as the deputy registrar at the first meeting on 14 July 1660; and in a volume of caveats he appears as registrar both at the last business transacted during the troubles (in February 1651) and at the first after the Restoration (on 1 September 1660).[51] Few dioceses can have been as fortunate as this. Most of them probably had the same experience as Winchester, where few records survived from the immediately pre-war period. At Winchester this may have been due to the relatively junior position of the surviving officials or to the damage done to the episcopal palaces and to the cathedral's archives during the wars.[52] After the Restoration, not one important class of episcopal records was

[47] Above pp. 87–8.

[48] Kent Recd. Off., *P.R.C.* 22/19, 5/3, 7/8, 8/3, 15/12, 43/7, 43/8; Cant. Cath. Chap. Arch., *Z.2.4, Y.6.13, F/B/1, X.7.2, X.7.3, X.7.1, X.6.11*, pt. 2.

[49] W. Kennett, 'Life of Mr. Somner', prefixed to W. Somner, *A Treatise of the Roman Ports and Forts in Kent* (Oxford, 1693), and *Dict. Nat. Biog.*

[50] *P.R.C.* 17/70/2, f.721.

[51] *P.R.C.* 22/19, ff.90, 94; *P.R.C.* 5/3, f.18.

[52] See above pp. 77–8, 123.

resumed in the volume that had been in use before the wars.

There was another problem facing bishops and their officials: should they revive the forms and procedures of the 1630s or adopt new ones? The Restoration should have seen the emergence of a new form of church government. The king's declaration of October 1660 stipulated that in future bishops and archdeacons would be assisted by the senior clergy of their dioceses in matters such as ordination and correction.[53] In practice, however, the procedures which were revived in the early 1660s differed little from those employed three decades earlier. The king's instructions appear to have been taken seriously by one or two bishops, but in most dioceses they were to prove a dead letter. Why was this so?

Ironically, Charles himself was partly to blame for the failure of his scheme. Each bishop was to be advised by an equal number of ministers drawn from the parish clergy and the cathedral chapters. But as we have seen Charles had been so precipitate in filling the chapters that by the autumn there were not enough places left to give the Puritans reasonable representation in them.[54] Without this, the Puritans probably felt little confidence in the impartiality of the king's scheme. Further doubt arose as a result of an incident in November 1660. In that month the Presbyterians in the Convention proposed that the Worcester House declaration be turned into an act of Parliament, but Charles blocked the bill. He had perfectly valid reasons for doing so. The bill was a challenge to his prerogative in ecclesiastical affairs, implying that the declaration by itself had insufficient authority to establish modified episcopacy. Furthermore, if the bill had been passed, a precedent would have been created which would have made it very difficult for Charles to secure greater freedom of worship for Catholics simply by issuing a similar declaration at some later stage.[55] The Presbyterians, however, could not be expected to see the matter in this light, and they were obviously disappointed and not a little suspicious of Charles's reaction.

Charles is also to blame insofar as he allowed matters to

[53] *English Historical Documents 1660–1714*, pp. 367–8.

[54] Above pp. 61–71.

[55] Abernathy, 'English Presbyterians', p. 78; Whiteman, 'Restoration', pp. 71–2.

drift. As far as can be seen, neither he nor the archbishops issued any further instructions on the implementation of the proposals in the declaration, with the result that many questions were left unanswered. How were the representatives of the parish clergy to be elected? What were the specific areas in which co-operation should take place, and how should it be arranged? It may be supposed that many bishops were too busy with practical problems such as recovering their estates to give much thought to these questions, while the more conservative bishops who did not wish to see a dilution of the episcopate's traditional authority took advantage of the king's inactivity simply to ignore his proposals.

What seems to have happened is that the old forms were brought back in two stages. In the first year of the Restoration, some of the less contentious procedures were resurrected quietly and with little apparent opposition. Most of the work carried out at this stage fell outside the areas of 'assistance' specified in the declaration; indeed, some of these forms had been revived even before the declaration was issued, for example institution, induction, and the probate of wills. The king's declaration must have created a period of confusion which was eventually ended not by the king or the bishops, but by the Cavalier Parliament. From the very outset, the Cavaliers demonstrated their determination to restore the old order in the church, and their behaviour probably gave heart to those who opposed the king's proposals and gave a sense of direction to those who were not sure which way to go. In July 1661, Parliament passed an act which not only restored the church courts' corrective powers (with one or two changes),[56] but also by implication endorsed the legality of the traditional procedures of episcopal administration. Thereafter, the bishops began to reintroduce the more contentious elements of their authority, prosecutions in the church courts, excommunication, and visitation. More liberal bishops such as Gauden and Reynolds seem to have made genuine attempts to enter into the spirit of the October declaration, but they were almost alone in trying to swim against the tide of reaction.

It seems likely that the first episcopal forms to re-appear

[56] The Ecclesiastical Causes Act outlawed the Court of High Commission and the *ex officio* oath: *Statutes*, v, 315–16.

after the Restoration were revived in response to demand from one quarter or another. Institution and induction may be taken as illustrations of this point. Institutions were being performed by eight of the surviving bishops from June and July 1660, and from 20 July institutions were being made in all the vacant sees in the southern province by the officials appointed by the dean and chapter of Canterbury.[57] The rapid revival of episcopal institution may have reflected the inadequacy of the Commonwealth system of institution,[58] or it may have been stimulated by the desire of many clergymen to obtain episcopal institution as a means of safeguarding their titles. Concern with the legitimacy of their title was of paramount importance to thousands of incumbents in 1660, and it seems clear that many of those who were 'presented'—and instituted—in the summer of 1660 had an existing claim or were actually in possession of the living to which they were appointed.[59] There were other incumbents appointed by Parliamentary or Commonwealth authorities who do not seem to have bothered with a fresh presentation, but did secure episcopal institution in the early months of the Restoration as a means of protecting their titles.[60]

Archdeacons were often among the first to be instituted, as at Ely and Chichester.[61] This was a natural step in view of the fact that archdeacons would soon be needed to induct the parish clergy instituted by Chaworth or one of the surviving bishops. Since many archdeacons outlived the troubles and new ones were appointed rapidly by the king, it would seem

[57] *Lib. Inst. Press* 9/71 f.556; 9/69 f.66; 9/71 f.477; 9/74 f.57; 9/69 f.113; 9/70 f.290; 9/74 f.167 (though cf. Warner's grant to a relative on 4 May 1660, f.182); 9/70 ff.264, 277; Frewen did not institute until October—9/69 f.37. *Sede vacante* institutions: 9/69 ff.22-34.

[58] It is not clear what happened after the death of the conformist Vicar-General Brent in 1652 (W. A. Shaw, *A History of the English Church During the Civil Wars and Under the Commonwealth,* (London, 2 vols., 1900), ii, 282-6). From early June to early August, Dr. Mericke, the former judge of the Prerogative Court of Canterbury, was performing institutions, *Lib. Inst.*, Press 9/69 ff.21, 22, 33, but what his status was is far from clear.

[59] See above pp. 48-9, 57-8.

[60] For the institution of the incumbents of Chevening, Hernhill, Meopham, Sundridge, and Warehorne, Kent, see *Lib. Inst.* and 'Process of Re-establishment', pp. 387-9; other examples in Kent include Deptford, Farningham, Nutsted and Sundridge (sources: ibid., pp. 358-9, and *Lib. Inst.*).

[61] *Lib. Inst.*

possible that archidiaconal inductions were taking place regularly by the late summer or autumn of 1660. The archdeacon of Winchester was inducting in mid August, shortly after his own installation. The induction records of the archdeacon of Canterbury recommence on 4 September, about three weeks after the archdeacon was himself collated.[62] Again the supply was probably stimulated by the demand, both from Commonwealth incumbents anxious to protect their titles, and from ministers recently presented to livings by the king or some other patron.[63]

The same may be said of ordination. The early re-appearance of episcopal ordination is of particular interest because it was one of the few forms specifically mentioned in the king's declaration: bishops were to ordain candidates with the assistance of an equal number of parish clergy and prebendaries. At least one bishop took this formula seriously: in January 1661, Bishop Gauden told his candidates that they had been ordained 'by the hands, prayers, and benediction of a Bishop, assisted with the Company and Counsel of his venerable Presbyters'.[64] Bishop Reynolds took a similar position: from subscriptions in his register we can see that some of the clergy who were ordained by him in the early 1660s accepted that rite on the basis of the terms in the October declaration.[65] There were also some Scottish and Irish bishops temporarily resident in England who were notoriously liberal in their attitude to ordination. They may not have observed the communal ceremony envisaged by the king, but they almost certainly obeyed that clause in the declaration which said that ordinands should not be forced to take the oath of canonical obedience previously demanded by the episcopal authorities.[66] As we shall see later, quite a few of the Puritan clergy ejected in 1662 had accepted ordination from one of

[62] Hants Recd. Off., Induction Mandates 35M 48/6/133; Cant. Cath. Chap. Arch., *F/B/1*, f.210; Le Neve, *Fasti*, iii, 27; i. 44.

[63] For the induction of the incumbents of Alton, Bedhampton, Monkston, and Weyhill, in Winchester diocese, see Hants. Recd. Off., Induction Mandates 35 M 48/6/125; 35 M 48/5/1, f.1 (twice), and 35 M 48/6/139 and 'Process of Re-establishment', pp. 390, 392, 394.

[64] Quoted in Whiteman, 'Restoration', p. 75.

[65] *Cal. Rev.*, p. lxi.

[66] *English Historical Documents 1660-1714*, p. 370.

these bishops in the early months of the Restoration.[67] There was probably a certain amount of regional variation in the availability of episcopal ordination. Neither Juxon nor Duppa seem to have ordained while at Canterbury and Winchester, and Frewen did not ordain at York until the summer of 1662; Juxon does not seem even to have issued letters dimissory until December 1661.[68] It should be remembered, however, that there was no need for those in possession of livings at the Restoration to receive episcopal ordination until the Act of Uniformity was passed in May 1662. Some incumbents may have done so before then, encouraged by the liberal attitude of a few bishops to strengthen their title in this way.[69] Otherwise those who received ordination in the first two years of the Restoration were ministers who had been recently appointed to livings, and in certain parts of the country they were probably asked to perform less than previous generations of ordinands.

The other area of projected participation was the church courts. The declaration was really not very precise about the means by which this was to be effected. The parish clergy were to assist the bishop in 'every part of jurisdiction which appertains to the censures of the Church', but did this mean that they were to advise him throughout the legal proceedings or merely be present when an excommunication or other censure was being considered or pronounced?[70] In the event, the point was to prove academic, for by the time that the powers of the church courts to inflict punishment had been restored, in July 1661, the prospects of effective participation by the lesser clergy were wilting fast.[71]

There were three procedures commonly followed in the church courts—summary (the prosecution and correction of

[67] *Cal. Rev.* p. lxi.

[68] See below p. 150; Lamb Pal. Lib. *VC 1A/1/1*, f.115. For ordinations elsewhere, cf. Whiteman, 'Re-establishment', p. 114; Bodl. Lib., MS. Oxf. Dioc. Papers d. 106, f. 1 (and Brit. Lib. Landsdowne MS. 986, f.89); A. J. Willis, *Winchester Ordinations 1660–1829* (Folkestone, 2 vols., 1964–5), ii, 68.

[69] Ibid., ii, 73, 106, 118, and below p. 150.

[70] *English Historical Documents 1660–1714*, pp. 367–8.

[71] Senior members of the parish clergy acted as surrogates in the restored church courts, as they had done before the troubles, but in doing so they were acting merely as deputies of the bishop's or archdeacon's officials, and not as elected representatives present in their own right.

offenders by the church authorities), plenary (suits begun at the instance of private individuals), and record (the probate of wills and administrations). What seems to have happened is that during the first year of the Restoration, only the last of these, probate, was commonly re-adopted; there are signs that a few instance cases were handled by the courts before July 1661, but it is unlikely that summary procedures were revived before then. As it is, it is difficult to see how the courts compelled attendance and enforced their decisions in the probate and instance cases which they handled. Demand may again provide the key—pressure from members of the laity anxious to obtain probate of a will or redress of a grievance, and pressure from officials of the church courts anxious to collect their fees. This is visible in the activity of various courts in both provinces.

The prerogative court of Canterbury conducted the probate of wills which involved property in more than one diocese in the southern province. In practice, it also handled the wills of many gentlemen and merchants whose executors preferred to go through what had become the most prestigious probate court in the land. This court had led a chequered life during the revolutionary decades, and after the death of Brent had been replaced by a secular court set up by an ordinance of 1653. This court seems to have run into difficulties in the first quarter of 1660,[72] but soon after the king's return the ecclesiastical court was restored when William Mericke, the deprived judge of the court, was re-appointed.[73] There is no discernible break between the records of the two courts, though the use of English that characterizes the Commonwealth records gives way to Latin again in June and July.[74] The early restoration of ecclesiastical control over this court is of interest, but the fact that there was an existing official anxious to regain his place probably influenced events. In the northern province, the exchequer court of York seems to have had a shadowy existence handling probate during the Interregnum. This court also revived rapidly after the king's

[72] *Prerogative Court of Canterbury Wills*, op. cit., xi, xiv-xvii; P.R.O., Probate 12/37 *passim*.

[73] Probate 6/36 f.104, but cf. ff.73-9.

[74] Ibid., and Probate 8/54 ff.79-81, 135 seqq.

return, though again one may note that there was a surviving official, the commissary, and a registrar nominated by Charles I who were anxious to restore the court to full working order as soon as possible.[75]

The first request for probate came before the consistory court of Canterbury, a diocesan court as opposed to the provincial Prerogative court, on 24 July 1660, only ten days after the officials of the court had been appointed.[76] Business soon built up, and in the second half of 1660 the court was handling almost as many cases each month as it had done immediately before its demise (in 1646).[77] Similarly, the archdeacon of Canterbury's court was active from early September 1660, within three weeks of the collation of the new archdeacon.[78] It is significant that quite a few of the inventories endorsed by the archdeacon at this time had been taken much earlier in the year; one is even dated April 1658.[79] This suggests that the centralized probate system of the Commonwealth was too expensive for those who were responsible for the probate of goods of little value, and that the return of the local archdeacon's court was greeted with relief.

The return of plenary or instance procedures may generally have been delayed until the courts' corrective powers had been restored, for until then the most serious threat at their disposal to ensure attenance was a sentence of contumacy. There may have been one or two exceptions to this rule. The Court of Arches handled about three dozen cases between November 1660 and July 1661,[80] though it is not clear from the surviving records whether the court tried to enforce its authority during that period; records of the sentences of the court do not survive before December 1661. At York, too, instance procedures

[75] Till, 'Ecclesiastical Courts of York', pp. 2-3, 113.

[76] *Z. 26,* f.3; Kent Recd. Off., *P.R.C.* 22/19 ff.94-5.

[77] Ibid. ff.83-94, 95-102.

[78] *P.R.C.* 16/265/A/H.

[79] *P.R.C.* 11/17/77; the court may have adopted a peripatetic role on occasions—cf. the endorsement 'apud Lond.' on 11/17/83 and the erasure on 11/17/50.

[80] Court of Arches Act Book *A2* ff.1-15. Some of the suits were described as 'appeals', but this must have been a circumlocution: the grievances were usually of a recent date, and few other church courts were actively handling instance suits at this stage.

were revived before the passage of the Ecclesiastical Causes Act.[81] Perhaps the officials of these courts squared their consciences by speculating that instance cases normally took several months to reach a conclusion, and that by the time the sentence was given Parliament would have restored the full authority of the courts. Even so, it is difficult to see how the courts secured the attendance of defendants and witnesses before July 1661 if they were reluctant to come.

What was probably a more typical pattern of events may be traced in three courts in the dioceses of Canterbury and Winchester. The instance act book of the consistory court of Canterbury records two brief sessions before the act was passed. On 15 July and 6 October 1660, the commissary-general and registrar exhibited their patents—the first time those of the chapter, the second those of the archbishop. However, it was not until 10 October 1661 that the first instance suit was heard.[82] This was the first of many cases of non-payment of tithes: between October 1661 and March 1663 (when the court books halt for a while) the 140 tithe cases dominated the business of the court.[83] The instance act book of the archdeacon of Canterbury records two sessions, on 1 September 1660 and 18 September 1661, at which surrogates were appointed, but the first suits were not handled until 24 September 1661. Here too, non-payment of tithes soon came to dominate the court's business.[84] The consistory court of Winchester did not hold its first meeting until 5 October 1661, but on that day it heard the first of many suits brought by incumbents and lay farmers against parishioners who had not paid their tithes.[85] It is possible that some of these cases

[81] Till, 'Ecclesiastical Courts of York', p. 5.

[82] The patents, now duly confirmed by the dean and chapter, were exhibited a third time on 4 September 1661: Cant. Cath. Chap. Arch., *Z.2.4*, ff.133-4.

[83] *Z.2.4*, ff.135-94; there were also a dozen cases of disputed wills or administrations, seven cases of defamation, and two for non-payment of salary.

[84] Cant. Cath. Chap. Arch., *Y.6.13*, ff.245-60 and *Y.6.14*, ff.1-38; again disputes over wills, defamation suits, and one dilapidations case occurred. Some incumbents seem to have divided their tithes suits between the archbishop's and the archdeacon's courts: H. Hannington, J. Penny, R. Marsh, and S. Pownell—*Y.6.13*, ff.248, 249, 251 and *Y.6.14*, f.7, and *Z.2.4*, ff.136, 141, 139, 141.

[85] Consistory Court Book, ff.3-70; nine incumbents and four lay farmers sued in the first year, though other business was handled. York consistory court was also dominated by tithe cases in these years—Till, 'Ecclesiastical Courts of York', pp. 10, 71, 73.

stemmed from personal animosity to the clergy; it is noticeable that four of the first seven tithes suits heard in Canterbury consistory court were brought by clergymen who had been sequestered in the 1640s and restored in 1660.[86] But on the whole it was probably poverty or perversity which accounted for non-payment. Many of the clerical plaintiffs (and presumably most of the laymen suing for tithes) had been in possession of the livings for several years,[87] and what we are probably witnessing are old offences being brought to the ecclesiastical courts as soon as their corrective powers were restored.

The third type of procedure may have taken much longer to restore than the other two. Summary procedure, prosecutions by the church authorities themselves, was usually the result of information or of presentments, and although information may have become increasingly available from officials or incumbents,[88] visitation presentments probably did not appear in many dioceses until 1662 or even later.[89] At least half of the Restoration bench and quite a few archdeacons did not conduct their first visitation until 1662. Bishops Sanderson and Cosin visited in July;[90] Morley, Hacket, Henchman, Skinner, Wren, and Ironside seem to have visited in late August or September,[91] Archbishop Frewen in September and October, Bishops King, Reynolds and Roberts in October,

[86] R. Dixon, R. Marsh, J. Penny and S. Pownall—*Z.2.4,* ff.135-41; *Walk. Rev.*, pp. 215, 222, 223, Hasted, iii, 360, and Lambeth MS. 1126, p. 20.

[87] E.g. J. Reading, F. Drayton, S. Creswell, J. Crawford, R. Burton, J. Brown, A. Bradley: *Z.2.4,* ff.146, 152, 154, 161, 173, 175, 178, and 'Process of Re-establishment', pp. 384, 387-9. There is little correlation between parishes in *Cal. Rev.* and parishes containing tithe defaulters.

[88] The archdeacon of Canterbury was proceeding against parishioners who would not pay parish rates from late 1661, presumably on information, Cant. Cath. Chap. Arch., *X.7.2,* ff.87 seqq. and *X.7.3,* ff.46 seqq.

[89] For episcopal and archidiaconal visitations in Sarum diocese in September 1661, see Whiteman, 'Re-establishment', p. 121.

[90] Clarendon MS. 77, f.157; *Mercurius Publicus* (1662), no. 29, 17-24 July p. 462; Tanner MS. 48, ff.12, 19.

[91] Clarendon MSS. 77, ff.305-7, 339-40, and 73, f.217; Clarendon MS. 77, f.274; *Kingdom's Intelligencer* (1662), no. 39, 22-29 Sept., p. 649; Tanner MS. 48, f.42 and *Mercurius Publicus* (1662), no. 39, 25 Sept.-2 Oct., p. 658; W. M. Palmer, *Episcopal Visitation Returns for Cambridgeshire* (Cambridge, 1930), pp. 92, 96, 98; *Mercurius Publicus,* no. 39, p. 658.

and Ward in December.[92] Archbishop Juxon did not conduct his diocesan and metropolitical visitation until 1663.[93] Some archdeacons, too, seem to have made their first visitations late in 1662, the archdeacons of Canterbury and London in September and the archdeacon of Lincoln in November, for instance.[94]

Why were visitations delayed so long? One reason may have been that bishops were awaiting the appearance of a standard book of visitation articles. In June 1661, Convocation had set up a committee of bishops to compose such a volume, and in March 1662 the results of their deliberations had been accepted unanimously, and passed on to Archbishop Juxon for his consideration. After that, nothing more was heard of them. By June, Bishop Skinner was clearly impatient for the arrival of the approved articles.[95] What seems to have happened in the end is that the bishops took matters into their own hands, and in most cases used copies of the articles produced by the committee earlier in the year. Seven bishops used virtually identical articles in their dioceses (Bath and Wells, Chichester, Exeter, Hereford, Lincoln, Peterborough, and Winchester);[96] three used articles with slight variations from these (Oxford, St. David's and Llandaff);[97] and five used sets clearly modelled on the same original articles but modified in a few clauses to suit the whim of the individual bishop (Durham, Coventry and Lichfield, Norwich, Worcester, and Gloucester).[98] Two facts make it seem

[92] University of York, Borthwick Institute of Historical Research, *R.VIa. 25b; A Sermon Preached at Lewis in the Diocess of Chichester, By the Lord Bp. of Chichester At his Visitation Held there, Octob. 8 1662* (London, 1663); *Mercurius Publicus* (1662), nos. 43-4, 23-30 Oct. and 30 Oct.-6 Nov., pp. 695-6, 724-5; ibid., no. 42, 16-23 Oct., p. 692; ibid., no. 51, 18-25 Dec., pp. 827-8.

[93] Cant. Cath. Chap. Arch. *Z.7.4,* and Lamb. Pal. Lib., Juxon Register, f.118, *VX IB/5/2 and* VC IA/1/1.

[94] *X.7.2* ff.102 *seqq., X 7.3,* ff. 74 *seqq.,* and see p. 135 n.88; T.W. Davids, *Annals of Evangelical Nonconformity in the County of Essex* (London, 1863), pp. 344, 360, 411, 415, 416, 432, 444, 462, 504, 506, 509; Whiteman, 'Re-establishment', p. 121, n.2.

[95] E. Cardwell, *Synodalia* (Oxford, 2 vols., 1842), ii, 646-7, 666 *seqq.*; Tanner MS. 48, f.14.

[96] All visitation articles are listed in Appendix 7.

[97] Oxford differs from the standard set in titles 1 (articles 4, 7), 2(art.1), 4(art. 1), and 7(art.7); St. David's and Llandaff in titles 1 (arts. 1, 8), 3 (1, 15), 4(2-6, 8-12, 16), 6(3), and 7 (3-8).

[98] For some of the changes, see next paragraph. Nicholson altered the order as well as the content. Hacket's, though much altered, contain several similarities to the standard set, e.g. standard 3(1), Lichfield 2(1, 2).

probable that the set of articles used in one form or another by at least fifteen bishops was the same as that approved by Convocation. First of all, five of the bishops on the committee used the standard set or their own versions of them (Bath and Wells, Lincoln, Oxford, Durham, and Gloucester). Of the other two members of the committee, Wren preferred to use a slightly amended version of the articles he had used before the civil wars, while Henchman's articles seem to be a hybrid of Wren's and the standard set.[99] Secondly, some of the articles in the standard set seem to have been composed with the particular circumstances of the Restoration in mind; the questions on the condition of the church, yard and glebe and on the qualifications of the incumbent are more solicitous than comparable articles used in the 1630s.[100]

Another reason for delay may have been that bishops were waiting for a clear definition of orthodoxy, and this was not given them until the Act of Uniformity was passed in May 1662. Even then, the leaders of the church were surprisingly inactive. With a little effort from Juxon or his deputy Sheldon, the standard set of articles accepted by Convocation in March 1662 could have been modified to incorporate the provisions of the Bartholomew Act. Issued to all diocesans, this would have proved an excellent means, as part of a thorough visitation perhaps the only sure means, of detecting nonconformity among their flocks. In practice, however, nothing was done. It cannot be argued that there was insufficient time, for at least nine bishops on their own initiative managed to find time to introduce references to the act's tests of conformity into their articles.[101] Moreover, four of the sets modified in this way were among the first to appear in the summer of 1662.[102]

[99] Wren's earlier articles—Tanner MS. 68, ff.63 seqq., and Brit. Lib., *E.* 238 (2). Henchman's 3(4–7) are almost identical to standard 3(10, 11, 15, 16) and there are other parallels; but most of his articles seem to stem from Wren's earlier sets. The bishops of Carlisle, St. Asaph, Bristol, and Canterbury also wrote their own articles.

[100] Titles 1 (*passim*), 3 (art. 1). The standard set was often used in succeeding years—cf. Bodl. Lib., *C.8.22. Linc.*, nos. 2, 4, 8, 9, 12, 13, 17, 21, 26, 27, 32, 33.

[101] See below, p. 144. New prayer book—Norwich, Gloucester, Ely, Sarum, Bristol, Carlisle, and Canterbury; subscriptions— Coventry and Lichfield, Ely, Carlisle; ordination—Peterborough.

[102] Durham, Ely, Sarum (dated 2 July 1662)—see above, and Peterborough—see below p. 150.

In the absence of a clear lead from Canterbury, the episcopal visitations of 1662 were characterized by considerable variation. Wren refurbished his old artillery, adding yet more questions for his visitation of Ely diocese immediately after St. Bartholomew's Day.[103] Over the county boundary, the visitation took place two months later, and the articles employed by Reynolds were a decidedly diluted version of the standard set. As befitted both bishop and diocese, Reynolds's articles were distinctly Low-Church: there was no reference to the need for episcopal ordination, no reference to Presbyterians or separatists as such, a less stringent question about the use of the Prayer Book, and even a hint of parish discipline.[104] In the north-east in the previous July, Cosin had contrived to make the standard articles more inquisitorial and High-Church. His emphasis on the quality of the church ornaments and robes is reminiscent of that of Laud and Neile on the beauty of holiness; the specific inclusion of Presbyterians in Cosin's list of possible nonconformists runs contrary to the moderation of the standard set which omits any reference to Presbyterians.[105] Bishop Gauden, on the other hand, gave his articles a liberal tone by referring to 'Ministers of the Gospel' and 'these British Reformed Churches'. He even went so far as to state that certain rites and ceremonies enjoined in the Prayer Book were 'declared to be not any necessary parts of Divine Worship, but onely things of Decency, Order, and Edification, tending to the Peace and Uniformity of the Church'.[106] Bishop Nicholson, author of a popular work on catechising, took the opportunity to expand the standard set's single question on this subject into a much larger, more searching one.[107]

The success of the visitation system rested largely on the accuracy of the presentments made by the churchwardens in each parish, and here too there may have been difficulties. In the diocese of Winchester many churchwardens failed to

[103] Compare 1636 titles 2 (art. 6), 3 (7, 12) with 1662 2(5), 3(9, 15); also note articles added in 1662 - 3 (1, 8, 10), 6(8).

[104] See titles 3 and 4.

[105] See titles 1 (4, 6, 7) and 4 (1) of the Durham articles of 1662.

[106] See title 3 (arts. 9, 6, 7) of the Worcester articles of 1662.

[107] See title 1 (art. 11) of the Gloucester articles of 1662, and W. Nicholson, *A plain, but full exposition of the catechisme* (London, 1655).

attend the first visitations, though it is hard to tell now whether this was due to religious scruple or simply the rusty condition of the visitation machine.[108] However, there is at least one case where a group of churchwardens refused to take the oath usually administered at a visitation. Probably set on by a local Parliamentarian, the churchwardens of three parishes in Lincolnshire refused the oath on the grounds that some of the articles asked questions about the work of the wardens themselves, and that by answering them they might incriminate themselves; this, they argued was contrary to the Ecclesiastical Causes Act of 1661 which had abolished the oath *ex officio*. The chancellor of Lincoln excommunicated the wardens, but they were not without support; it was rumoured that 'the factious partie there and ellswhere have made a perse to oppose the Ecclesiastical Courts', and with the help of some able lawyers (including two who had held high office under Cromwell) they sought a prohibition against the trial. It was an interesting attempt, for as the chancellor's counsel pointed out, if the statute of 1661 was interpreted as covering visitation oaths, 'then a very great part of Ecclesiasticall Jurisdiction . . . as allwaies was used . . . is taken away . . . for crimes cannot bee punished till they bee known, and the ordinary way to know them is by the Churchwardens praesentments upon their oaths'.[109] What was as serious from the authorities' point of view was a more passive form of resistance, collusion between like-minded wardens and clergymen to conceal nonconformity or partial conformity from the visitor.[110] In some areas the uncanonical reports of apparitors or the personal inspections of rural deans (where they existed) may have acted as a check upon churchwardens' returns, but it is difficult to gauge how soon these officials would be in a position to know what was going on in every parish.[111]

Perhaps one should not be too pessimistic about the

[108] There is hardly any correlation between parishes whose churchwardens were prosecuted for non-appearance (Consistory Court Book 128, ff.1 *seqq.*) and parishes whose ministers were ejected in 1662 (*Cal. Rev.*). Non-attendance by wardens was not, of course, new in 1662, but may have been worse than in the 1630s, or in some cases later.

[109] Harleian MS. 3794, ff. 114-20.

[110] See chapter VIII for some examples from Canterbury diocese.

[111] Whiteman, 'Re-establishment', p. 125.

wardens' presentments. Clearly the visitations of 1662-3 provided a great deal of valuable information for the bishops. From the letters which Morley sent to Clarendon during his visitation of Winchester diocese in late August and early September 1662, it is evident that Morley was learning much about his new diocese.[112] Juxon's visitation of 1663 probably furnished much of the information for the invaluable survey of the diocese prepared for the new archbishop a few months later.[113] Furthermore, Dr. Whiteman has found that presentments made in three dioceses in 1662—Exeter, Salisbury, and Lincoln—'throw much light on the state of the parishes at that time'. Refusal to attend church or to have children baptized, and failure to provide surplices, Prayer Books, utensils, and other furnishings were often detected. In the diocese of Exeter in 1663 'at least 144 persons were cited into the vicar-general's consistory court for nonconformity of some kind, of whom eighty-five were excommunicated and some probably later imprisoned'.[114] The renewed efficiency of the visitation system in this diocese was also demonstrated by the way in which the number of presentments in the consistory court rose in the periods just after a visitation had been held, and fell in the interim years.[115]

Mention of excommunication raises another interesting question, how soon after July 1661 was this weapon readopted? The consistory court at York issued its first excommunication on 14 November 1661, but it was clearly moving cautiously: it specified that the first excommunications were not to be read aloud, and the first writ of *significavit* (seeking the help of the secular arm) was not obtained until November 1662.[116] At Winchester the first excommunication seems to have been that recorded in the consistory instance act book on 18 January 1662, and in succeeding months at least ten more were pronounced, all for non-payment of tithes.[117] At Canterbury the first excommunication schedule dates from March 1662, and from then until December 1662 over eighty ex-

[112] Clarendon MSS. 77, ff. 305-7, 339-40, and 73, f.217.
[113] Lambeth MS. 1126; cf. chapter VIII below.
[114] Whiteman, 'Re-establishment', p. 123.
[115] Whiteman, 'The Episcopate of Seth Ward', pp. 132-5.
[116] Till, 'Ecclesiastical Courts of York', pp. 5, 11-12.
[117] Consistory Court Book 126, ff.14 (cf. f.8), 43, 65-6, 75, 96, 99.

communications were pronounced, by far the most common causes being non-appearance in court and non-payment of tithes.[118] Non-appearance was the perennial blight of the church courts, but like non-payment of tithes it was not necessarily a sign of Puritan scruples. If we compare the reasons for excommunications specified in the excommunication schedules of 1662 with those given in the schedules of 1622 or 1632, we find that non-appearance was as prevalent before the civil wars as after, and that non-payment of tithes and defamation about as common.[119] To judge from these schedules (which admittedly do not tell the whole story), the church seems to have been using excommunication as often in the 1660s as it had before the troubles: the yearly average for the twenty years before 1640 was almost exactly the same as for the period March 1662 to December 1670. The total number of excommunications in the year after Juxon's visitation of 1663 was in fact the highest for any year since 1631, and also proved to be the highest for any year up until 1689. It was in the 1670s and to a lesser extent the 1680s, that the average number of excommunications began to fall off.[120] It seems fairly clear that the revival of the church courts after the Restoration was short-lived, and that with the passage of the Act of Toleration in 1689 and a series of Stamp Duty Acts thereafter, these courts were to fall deeper into decline.[121]

One final aspect of episcopal recovery may be treated—the revival of confirmation. Several bishops seem to have used the opportunities provided by the large gatherings that greeted them on their first visitations to carry out confirmations on a large scale. From as far apart as Durham, the Isle of Wight, East Anglia, Bristol, Oxfordshire, and Wiltshire came reports of large-scale confirmations.[122] On his visit to the Isle of

[118] Lamb. Pal. Lib., *VC III/2/3* ff.1-12.

[119] *VC III/2/1* and */2/2*.

[120] Based on an analysis of *VC III/2/1-4*.

[121] Three studies throw much light on the history of the church courts between the Restoration and the Revolution of 1688/9: Whiteman, 'The Episcopate of Seth Ward', esp. chapters 3, 4, 6 and 8; Till, 'Ecclesiastical Courts of York', *passim*; and J. Potter, 'The Ecclesiastical Courts in the Diocese of Canterbury 1603-1663' (London M. Phil. thesis, 1973), chapter V.

[122] *Mercurius Publicus* (1662), nos. 32, 7-14 Aug., p. 532; 36, 4-11 Sept., p. 605; nos. 43, 44, 47, 23-30 Oct., 30 Oct.-6 Nov., 20-27 Nov., pp. 696, 725, 765, no. 39, 25 Sept.-2 Oct., pp. 658 (2), 645.

Wight, Bishop Morley confirmed 'neere a 1000 of all sorts, and amongst them all the Gentry male and female young and old of the whole Iland'; at other points on his route he confirmed '5 or 600 if not more' and 'between 2 and 300'.[123] Bishop Reynolds confirmed 600 at Bury St. Edmunds and as many at Ipswich; Hacket confirmed 500 in troublesome Coventry, and Ironside 200 to 400 a day at various places in his diocese; at Dorchester, Skinner could not finish until 'Candle-lighting'.[124] All the reports stressed that the gentry were prominent on these occasions, and that old as well as young were confirmed.[125] The bishops must have been delighted. Undeterred by fatigue and hoarseness after his labour on the Isle of Wight, Morley insisted on finishing the visitation in person, it being 'necessary I goe my self in regard of confirmation, which I see the people flock to with great devotion'.[126]

In her study of the re-establishment of the Church of England in four dioceses, Dr. Whiteman concluded that not until 1663 was episcopal administration 'in full working order and the re-establishment of the church a reality in most parishes throughout the land'.[127] The evidence adduced in this chapter serves to reinforce that conclusion. In particular, it seems unlikely that the church's traditional methods of enquiry and correction were functioning properly before the second half of 1662, if then. There is one important conclusion to be drawn from this: the leaders of the church were in no position to take the lead against Puritanism in the early years of the Restoration. Circumscribed by the moderation of royal policy, weakened by the disunity of their own views, and hampered by various difficulties in reconstructing their administrations, the Restoration bench played an insignificant part in the campaign against Puritanism waged by the Anglican laity. The church authorities even had difficulty in enforcing the Act of Uniformity in the summer of 1662.

[123] Clarendon MS. 73, f.217.
[124] *Mercurius Publicus* (1662), nos. 43, p. 696; 32, p. 534; 39, p. 658 (2).
[125] Previous notes, and on ages no. 47, p. 765 and Clarendon MS. 73, f.217.
[126] Ibid.
[127] Whiteman, 'Re-establishment', p. 111.

VII

PREPARATIONS FOR THE EJECTIONS OF ST. BARTHOLOMEW'S DAY

By the closing months of 1661 the time for moderate counsels had passed. In Ireland the bishops had already begun to harass dissident elements, and the remaining bastion of Presbyterian government in Scotland was about to fall to the powerful forces of reaction. In England the Cavaliers were busy framing their measures to extirpate Puritanism. Many of their actions were petty, but two measures were of great significance: the Corporation Act passed in December 1661 and the Act of Uniformity passed in May 1662. Both acts were designed to remove from positions of influence those men whose loyalty to the crown and the traditional forms of church government was in doubt, and thus to ensure 'the preservation of the Publique Peace both in Church and State'. Both acts also demanded subscription to two declarations and the performance of certain religious tests.[1]

It cannot be denied that Charles was in favour of passing the Corporation Act; it was the only article of the 'Clarendon Code' which he did welcome. In his eyes the electoral advantages to be gained from interfering in the corporations outweighed the disadvantages of the accompanying persecution.[2] By contrast, he fought a long and dour rearguard action against the intolerance of the Act of Uniformity, delaying the first bill, submitting provisos to the second to weaken its impact, and even after accepting it seeking some means of suspending it or mitigating its effects.[3]

There was another striking contrast between the Corporation and Uniformity Acts: while the former allowed up to fifteen months for the enforcement of the act in about

[1] 13 Car. II, St. II, c. 1; 14 Car. II, c. 4; *Statutes*, v, 321, 322, 366.

[2] J. H. Sacret, 'The Restoration Government and Municipal Corporations', *Eng. Hist. Rev.*, xlv (1930), 232–59.

[3] Abernathy, 'English Presbyterians', pp. 82–6.

two hundred corporations, the latter allowed just fourteen weeks (from 19 May to 24 August) for its enforcement upon many thousands of clergymen and teachers scattered widely over England and Wales. The reason for the shortness of the period was almost certainly the Cavaliers' spiteful desire to eject Puritan clergy before their tithes fell due.[4] But this piece of meanness was to rebound on their own heads.

During the fourteen weeks permitted by the act, every dignitary, fellow, incumbent, curate and teacher had to perform three tests. By the last Sunday before St. Bartholomew's Day, that is by 17 August, he had to read Morning and Evening Prayer from the newly revised Prayer Book, and at the same time make a public declaration of 'unfeigned assent and consent' to all that it contained. Secondly, by 24 August, he had to subscribe two declarations before the ordinary of the diocese or the vice-chancellor of the university: 'that it is not lawfull upon any pretence whatsoever to take Arms against the King', and 'that there lyes no Obligation on me or any other person from the Oath commonly called the Solemn League and Covenant'. Thirdly, if he held a cure and had not received episcopal ordination, he had to obtain it speedily.[5]

The enforcement of the act presented the bishops with several technical problems. How should they set about ensuring that all clergymen had read the new Prayer Book by 17 August? What was the best means of collecting subscriptions to the two declarations? What forms of ordination should be used for those ministers who had already received a Presbyterian ordination? What forms of law should be used to cancel the title of a nonconformist and, if necessary, remove him bodily from his living? The Upper House of Convocation had studied the provisional bill months before it was passed,[6] but no later discussions can be traced. Nor are there any signs of advice or instructions being circulated by the archbishops or their deputies.[7] Thus the individual bishops had to contend

[4] For the different dates considered for the enforcement of the act, see C. A. Swainson, *The Parliamentary History of the Act of Uniformity* (London, 1875), pp. 11-12, 32-3, 44, 47.

[5] *Statutes,* v, 365-7.

[6] E. Cardwell, *Synodalia* (Oxford, 2 vols., 1842), ii, 662.

[7] Fragments of correspondence between Sheldon and Bp. Skinner survive in Tanner

with a failure of church leadership as well as the practical difficulties created by the act.

The confusion which surrounded the implementation of the act is well illustrated by the first test: not only did the new Prayer Book fail to reach many incumbents by 17 August, but also the bishops could not possibly have known who had and who had not made the appropriate public declaration by that date. The final draft of the revised Book of Common Prayer had been approved by Convocation in December 1661 and by the king in council on 24 February 1662; the 'Convocation Book' ran into some criticism in Parliament but after a few alterations was soon accepted there too. Printing, however, was delayed until the uniformity bill, to which the new Prayer Book was annexed, received the royal assent in mid May.[8] Publication was further delayed by the system which gave one press a monopoly of printing the Prayer Book, and by the fact that the king's printers took great care with the first impression.[9] As a result, the first copies do not seem to have been available until about 6 August, only eleven days before the dead-line.

During June and July, tension rose among the clergy, for the non-appearance of the Prayer Book not only denied Puritan incumbents the opportunity to judge its contents, but also threatened the more conformable clergy with ejection. On 9 July, Dean Honywood wrote from Lincoln to William Sancroft, Cosin's secretary, who had been involved in the revision of the Prayer Book: 'Wee long to see the Common Prayer-Books, which must be read before S. Bartholomew, the penalty being so great. And we doubt, whether reading the old would serve, if that come to places too late'. By 30 July Honywood had received from Sancroft a transcript of the differences between old and new editions, and with the aid of this he modified an old Prayer Book, intending to use this if the new edition did not reach him in time.[10] This device seems

MS. 48, ff. 14, 25, 42.

[8] G. J. Cuming, 'The Prayer Book in Convocation, November 1661', *Journal of Ecclesiastical History*, viii (1957), 182; Bosher, pp. 249–50; Swainson, op. cit., pp. 22, 25, 70–5.

[9] *S.P.* 44/18, p. 33 (and cf. Burnet, i, 328); pirate editions were printed but were seized on Charles's command: ibid., and 44/3, p. 81.

[10] Tanner MS. 48, ff. 17, 21.

to have been resorted to by many other ministers, who either sent to London or made a special journey there in order to obtain a list of the alterations.[11]

On 6 August, an advertisement in *Mercurius Publicus* announced that the new Prayer Book was at last ready, 'perfectly and exactly printed'.[12] Three famous diarists recorded its first appearance, Pepys in London on 10 August, Josselin in Essex on the 16th, and Evelyn in Kent on the 17th.[13] A copy even reached Durham before the dead-line, though it was likely that Sancroft was sent one of the first copies off the press owing to his involvement in the revision.[14] Others, closer to London, were less fortunate. The bishop of Peterborough had not received a copy by 17 August, and so, evoking a clause in the act giving the 'ordinary of the place' some discretionary powers, he issued a certificate indemnifying his cathedral clergy against the consequences of non-performance.[15] Dean Honywood had still not received a copy on 23 August, and as an extra precaution he too indemnified himself.[16] Even closer to London the books may have not been circulating in time; Calamy claimed to have written testimony that 'in Middlesex very few places receiv'd the Common Prayer Book, till a Week, a Fortnight, three Weeks, or a Month after'.[17]

Further confusion seems to have arisen over whether a mere declaration of assent and consent was enough, or whether Morning and Evening Prayer had to be read as well. The dean and chapter of Durham did not think they were 'oblig'd by the Act to read prayers in the Cathedral' as well as giving their assent, but their bishop felt it was necessary 'to read prayers

[11] Kennett, *Register,* p. 837; Burnet, loc. cit. E. Calamy (*Defence of Moderate Conformity,* London, 3 vols., 1703-5, Pt. II, 100-1) said the transcripts were often erroneous.

[12] No. 31, 31 July-7 August, p. 514.

[13] *The Diary of Samuel Pepys,* iii, 161; *The Diary of Ralph Josselin,* p. 140; *The Diary of John Evelyn,* ed. E. S. de Beer (Oxford, 6 vols., 1955), iii, 331.

[14] Tanner MS. 48, f.38.

[15] Kennett, *Register,* p. 743, and cf. *Life of Adam Martindale,* ed. R. Parkinson (Chetham Society, iv, 1845), pp. 163-5. For a Lords' proviso anticipating printing delays, cf. Swainson, op. cit., p. 44.

[16] J. H. Srawley, *Michael Honywood, Dean of Lincoln (1660-81)*, Lincoln Minister Pamphlets, no. 5 (1950), p. 7.

[17] *Defence of Moderate Conformity,* op. cit., Pt. II, 100.

himself upon that occasion'.[18] Others may have been less scrupulous, and simply read out the declaration without having first seen the book, trusting that this would obviate their failure to read prayers as the act stated. Burnet was 'informed by some of the bishops' that 'too many' consented implicitly to a book they had never seen; Calamy goes further: 'of the 7000 Ministers in England who kept their Livings, few except those who were in or near London, could possibly have a sight of the Book with its Alterations, till after they had declar'd their Assent and Consent to it'.[19]

This test proved an administrative fiasco. Few, if any, bishops can have been in a position to know how many of their parish clergy had obtained a copy of the new book (or amended the old with a list of alterations), read it, and made the statutory declaration. A stickler such as Sheldon, or an enthusiast such as Cosin who visited in July, might have known which of their ministers were using the *old* Prayer Book in the summer of 1662,[20] but as far as the law was concerned this was irrelevant. The only sure way of knowing was to conduct a visitation between 17 and 24 August, and as we saw in the last chapter this was not commonly done.

Some bishops may have placed more emphasis on the second test, the subscription of the declarations denouncing rebellion and abjuring the Covenant. This test had to be performed before the bishop, and by a process of elimination each bishop should have been able to deduce which parishes had ministers who had not subscribed. The ordinary method of collecting subscriptions seems to have been to encourage the clergy to visit the bishop or his chancellor and sign a subscription book. In mid June it was reported from Lambeth that the clergy were coming in 'cheerfully' to perform the test and in mid July came news from Durham that 'Ministers come daily for there certificates, that they have renounced Anti-Christ the covenant and give the Secretary as I think what they please'.[21] (The fee could be quite heavy: Archbishop Frewen

[18] Tanner MS. 49, f.38; and cf. *Kingdom's Intelligencer* (1662), no. 35, 25 Aug-1 Sept., pp. 575-6.

[19] Burnet, loc. cit.; E. Calamy, *An Abridgement of Mr. Baxter's History of his Life and Times* (London, 1702), p. 502.

[20] *S.P.* 29/32, f.225 and *Cal. Rev.*, p. 35; Tanner MS. 48, f.19.

[21] *Kingdomes Intelligencer* (1662), no. 24, 16-23 June, p. 400 (and cf. *Mercurius*

claimed that his chancellor had orders 'not to exceed 5*s*. in ffees from any man; which falls far short of the Prince Palatines 16'.)[22] An alternative or supplementary method of collecting subscriptions was for the chancellor to perambulate the diocese, probably stopping at the major towns, or visiting aged or ailing ministers who could not travel to see the bishop.[23] In the diocese of Norwich (which had the refinement of printed subscription forms), the subscriptions are to some extent grouped geographically, which may reflect the adoption of a similar practice there.[24] In the larger dioceses, there were almost certainly two or more subscription books in use at the same time, and perhaps more than one subscription centre as well. It is noticeable that the subscription books preserved at Lambeth contain a much higher proportion of the incumbents of Canterbury diocese living near there than of the clergy of East Kent who one may suppose went to Canterbury to subscribe.[25]

The process of collecting signatures, from schoolmasters as well as ministers, predictably reached a peak in mid-August. Juxon's surviving subscription books contain only sixty-three signatures in July, but in the first three weeks of August there were 222 subscriptions. In the diocese of London's books, less than a hundred subscriptions were made in July, as opposed to three hundred in August; 184 were made in the last week before the dead-line. The figures for Norwich are even more striking: after a weekly total of about seventy in late July and early August, 592 subscriptions were received in the last two weeks; in three days, 13-15 August, 393 people subscribed.[26] This sudden upsurge of activity brings home two points very

Publicus, no. 37, 11-18 Sept., p. 614 on Exeter subscriptions); Tanner MS. 48, f.19. Cf. Winchester subscriptions before Morley at Hampton Court—Clarendon MS. 77, f.307.

[22] Clarendon MS. 77, f.222.

[23] E.g. York—ibid., and Sarum, Clarendon MS. 77, f.298. Cf. *J.L.*, xi, 573-7, for an interesting sequel.

[24] E. H. Carter, *The Norwich Subscription Books* (London, 1937), pp. 21-2.

[25] Lamb. Pal. Lib., *VC 1/1/2-3*; London may have had three books in use in July: Guildhall Library, MSS. 9539 A/2, 9539/C, and Bodl. Lib., MS. Rawlinson B.375.

[26] As previous note, and E. H. Carter, op. cit., pp. 23-4. For a similar pattern at York, see University of York, Borthwick Institute of Historical Research, Subscription Book 6, ff. 1-18. In some areas—e.g. Exeter and Lichfield dioceses—subscriptions appear to have continued after Bartholomew: Tanner MS. 48, f.48; *Sir Thomas Browne's Works,* ed. A. Wilkin (London, 4 vols., 1835-6), i, 30.

clearly. First of all, it must have taken considerable hard work at the last moment to produce a list of those parishes whose incumbents had not conformed, especially where there was more than one book or subscription centre in use. It may well have been some time after the dead-line before a completely clear picture emerged. Secondly, the test must in most cases have been a completely mechanical act performed before a lay official: the book was signed or the printed form filled in, the fee was paid, and that was that. No attempt at a deeper enquiry into the subscriber's views was made; in view of the pressure of numbers this was probably impractical. But it may be suggested that the automatic nature of the test and the absence of deeper enquiry made it easier for some clergymen, who had little intention of conforming to Anglican ritual in full, to remain within the church. One bishop who came into contact with his clergy when they were subscribing found 'very many' who 'for their worldly interest will subscribe anything . . . I have discovered such palpable hypocrisy . . . as I thought could not possibly have been found in men that pretend to godlines or tenderness of conscience'.[27] Chancellor Clarendon also observed that 'many who did subscribe had the same Malignity to the Church, and to the Government of it' as those who refused to subscribe and were ejected.[28] This situation was not just the result of hasty enforcement of the act; it was also the result of an oversight in its drafting. The Corporation Act had allowed commissioners to eject a burgess who had made the appropriate declarations if they doubted his sincerity in making them,[29] but the Act of Uniformity contained no such clause, so that even where a bishop like Sanderson detected 'hollow-hearted' subscribers he was powerless to eject them. One might argue (with Clarendon) that those partial conformists who remained inside the church 'did more Harm, than if They had continued in their Inconformity' and joined their more intransigent brethren outside it. Certainly the declarations were a less effective means of separating the sheep from the goats than the Cavaliers had hoped.

[27] Clarendon MS. 77, f.157.
[28] Clarendon, *Life,* ii, 306.
[29] *Statutes,* v, 322.

The third proof of orthodoxy, episcopal ordination, also proved to be a double-edged weapon. First of all, it presented the bishops with fresh head-aches. How could they discover what form of ordination their clergy had received? A visitation was the obvious answer, but few seem to have been inclined to conduct one at that time. Should the absence of Ember days between late May and September deter a bishop from holding an ordination, and should he if necessary raise men to the diaconate and the priesthood on the same day? A few bishops (Frewen, Sheldon, and Laney, for example) held an ordination ceremony a few days before St. Bartholomew's Day in order to allow conformable clergy to obtain episcopal ordination in time,[30] but others do not seem to have bothered.[31] There was also the controversial question of what form re-ordination should take.[32] Some bishops may have adopted a moderate line in order to encourage as many as possible to conform: Cosin is said to have offered to re-ordain Richard Frankland 'conditionally with such Words as these; If thou hast not been ordained, I ordain thee'.[33] But at least one other bishop demanded that Presbyterians repudiate their previous orders before he would ordain them.[34]

The third test also made the serious mistake of equating episcopal ordination with orthodoxy. It was a sign of the hardening attitude of some of the Puritan clergy that at least 420 of the ministers ejected in the early years of the Restoration had been episcopally ordained before the civil wars.[35] Many in episcopal orders had been in trouble with the church courts during the 1630s, and it was often the very same

[30] Frewen's was the first ordination of his archiepiscopate; from the records of the ceremony (Borthwick Institute of Historical Research, *R.I.AB.6*, ff.360–2) we cannot say how many of the thirty-seven deacons and forty-four priests were 'intruders' and how many new clergy. But both Sheldon and Laney stated that their services were for incumbents anxious to obtain episcopal ordination: *Kingdomes Intelligencer* (1662), nos. 33, 11–18 Aug., p. 546; 34, 18–25 Aug., p. 558, and *Articles of Visitation . . . within the Diocess of Peterborough*, p. 13.

[31] Juxon and Morley, for example. Juxon gave twenty-two men letters dismissory in late July and August, Lamb. Pal. Lib., *VC 1A/1/1*, ff.126–32, but only three of these were 'intruders' ('Process of Re-establishment', pp. 311, 387, 389). Morley ordained on 14 September: A. J. Willis, *Winchester Ordinations 1660–1829*, op. cit., ii, 25, 101.

[32] Whiteman, 'Restoration', pp. 73–5.

[33] Whiteman, 'The Episcopate of Seth Ward', p. 201; Calamy, *Account* p. 286.

[34] M. Henry, *The Life of the Rev. Philip Henry A. M.* (London, 1825), p. 97.

[35] *Cal. Rev.*, p. lxi.

men who refused to conform to the Act of Uniformity in 1662 and were ejected.[36] Some of those appointed during the revolutionary decades may have received episcopal ordination, but this did not guarantee their conformity in 1662; at least forty-five ministers were episcopally ordained after the Restoration only to be ejected a year or so later. Thomas Warren for example, confirmed in his Hampshire rectory of Houghton by Charles in July 1660, received orders from Bishop Sydserf of Galloway in the following December; less than two years later, he was ejected for nonconformity.[37] Bearing in mind the liberal interpretation of ordination adopted by bishops such as Reynolds, Gauden, and others,[38] it can readily be seen that episcopal ordination was by no means a proof of complete orthodoxy.

There were other means of detecting nonconformity than the three tests envisaged in the act. Chancellors and archdeacons had probably learnt the location of the leading Puritans in their areas, either by reputation or by prosecutions in secular courts for failure to use the old Prayer Book.[39] In those cases where a minister publicly announced his intention of not conforming, where he talked to the bishop but still refused to subscribe, or where he preached a farewell sermon on 17 August, the ordinary was also forewarned.[40] But these supplementary methods were not infallible: where a Puritan incumbent did not draw attenton to himself, his intractability may well have gone unnoticed. For the practical difficulties surrounding the performance of the statute's tests were so great that they may actually have helped to conceal potential nonconformity from the authorities.

Certainly, there are strong indications that on St. Bartholomew's Day the bishops were unaware of the extent of nonconformity in their dioceses. On 28 August, Morley wrote to Clarendon from Hampshire: 'Ther are not above 8 in all

[36] E.g. R. Byfield, *Cal. Rev.*, pp. 96-7; see also R. A. Marchant, *The Puritans and the Church Courts in the Diocese of York* (London, 1960), pp. 225-6, 234-5, 246, 249, 257, 260-1, 269, 274, 276, 277, 280, 285, 289.

[37] *Cal. Rev.*, pp. lxi, 511-12.

[38] See above p. 130.

[39] For these prosecutions, see chapter IX below.

[40] *Rel. Baxt.*, Lib. I, Pt. II, para. 278; Platt, Stileman, and Whitaker talked to Morley but did not conform, Clarendon MS. 77, f.307; farewell sermons, below pp. 155-6.

this County and the Ile of Wight for ought I heare yet that have not subscribed', and at the same time he named four in Surrey who had not subscribed. Ten days later, he was still computing the total of nonconformists in his diocese at twelve, although the total actually ejected in 1662 we now know to have been nearly fifty.[41] Bishop Croft of Hereford reported on 8 September that he had 'prevail'd with all the considerable persons in my diocese' except one Anabaptist; even allowing for Croft's liberal tendencies and the use of the word 'considerable' it is a little surprising to discover that at least seven were ejected eventually, including such not inconsiderable figures as Thomas Froysell and Richard Hawes.[42] Henchman told Clarendon on 28 August that there were twenty-four 'Recusants' in his diocese; five of these were in Berkshire, so presumably the rest were in Wiltshire. In fact, about forty nonconformists were ejected in Sarum diocese, thirteen in Berkshire and twenty-seven in Wiltshire.[43] Henchman was aware of ten more who (he thought) had simply been negligent; but only one of the incumbents ejected in his diocese is known to have conformed later,[44] which suggests that Henchman was unaware of the inconformability of several he took to be merely careless.

The newspapers also published figures that are much lower than modern research would suggest. In August and September it was reported that there had been only three or four ejections in Northamptonshire and nearby counties, whereas *Calamy Revised* suggests thirty-one in Northants alone; only six in Lincolnshire, while Matthews' figure is twenty-six. There were said to be very few nonconformists in Wiltshire, Cheshire, Norfolk, and Dorset, but there were probably between twenty-five and thirty ejections in each of these counties.[45] The editors of these papers often received

[41] Clarendon MSS. 77, f.307; 73, f.217; the ejected are listed in 'Process of Re-establishment', pp. 342-5.

[42] Tanner MS. 48, f.41; *Cal. Rev.*, pp. 215, 253; 31, 125, 191, 487, 515.

[43] Clarendon MS. 77, f.298; *Cal. Rev.*, pp. 20, 72, 113, 117, 130, 208-9, 230, 293-4, 390, 408, 448, 520, 543; 23, 60, 88, 107-8, 151, 155, 190, 218, 232, 247-8, 279, 280, 282-3(2?), 301, 309, 343, 373, 389, 418, 427, 452, 467-8, 470, 516(2), 550.

[44] *Cal. Rev.*, p. 408.

[45] *Mercurius Publicus* (1662), nos. 34, 21-28 Aug., p. 577; 36, 4-11 Sept., p. 606; 39, 25 Sept.-2 Oct., p. 645; 36, p. 598; and 35, 28 Aug-4 Sept., pp. 590, 591; *Cal. Rev.*, pp. xii-xiii.

reliable and full information on church matters from Anglican leaders at this time,[46] and there can be little doubt that these reports reflected the opinion of the ecclesiastical authorities in late August and September.

There are other indications that the bishops did not know who to eject on 24 August. The pages of Calamy's 'Account' and of *Calamy Revised* contain many examples of incumbents who continued to minister in their old livings—or sometimes in new ones—for several months after they should have been ejected.[47] One may also note the length of time that it took bishops and other ecclesiastical patrons to replace Puritans in Bartholomew livings: some were replaced quickly, but others not for weeks or even months, as will be shown in the next chapter.

The culmination of the activity described in this chapter was the ejection of those who had not conformed, and even here there seems to have been some doubt as to what should be done. No machinery for ejection was laid down in the act or suggested by the archbishops. One bishop, Seth Ward of Exeter, had the initiative to cite non-subscribers into court where he pronounced an official sentence of deprivation on them;[48] but other bishops seem to have hoped that the nonconformists would remove themselves from their livings at the appropriate moment. Indeed some bishops seem to have allowed nonconformists a period of grace of a few weeks in the hope that they might yet be brought to conform, Hacket in Lichfield and Croft in Hereford, for example.[49] Morley told the chancellor that he would not be 'hasty' in removing nonconformists 'but give them some time to come in and conferr with me'—an offer which he repeated at each step of his visitation in late August and September.[50] Thus even at this stage of the proceedings and at a time when there was growing fear of revolt,[51] the bishops were not acting in

[46] See above pp. 111, 147, and below p. 155.

[47] E.g. Calamy, *Account*, p. 789; Calamy, *Continuation*, ii, 884, and i, 509; *Cal. Rev.*, pp. 158, 338, 357, 371, 428.

[48] Whiteman, 'The Episcopate of Seth Ward', p. 102. Sheldon and Hall tried to ensure that the nonconformists they knew were removed by 24 August, see next chapter, and *Life of Adam Martindale*, op. cit., pp. 165–6.

[49] Calamy, *Account*, pp. 850, 354, and *Sir Thomas Browne's Works*, loc. cit.

[50] Clarendon MSS. 77, f.306; 73, f.217.

[51] Bosher, p. 259; Clarendon MS. 77, f.340.

concert. It was undoubtedly fortunate for them that the large majority of nonconformists felt honour-bound to resign their livings peacefully, and that only a minority persisted in serving their cures after 24 August, for the authorities were singularly ill-prepared to cope with a substantial campaign of passive resistance by Puritan incumbents.

In time, the bishops came to know their clergy, and the remainder of the obstinate nonconformists were deprived. But this still left the partial conformists, those who had obtained ordination from a sympathetic bishop, those who had subscribed but would shed the surplice and ignore the Prayer Book whenever they could. Their presence in the post-Bartholomew church was the direct result of the Cavaliers' over-anxiety and the shortcomings of their Act of Uniformity.

VIII

THE CHARACTER OF THE PARISH CLERGY AFTER THE EJECTIONS OF AUGUST 1662

The leaders of the church appear to have been confident that they could soon fill the livings made vacant by the Act of Uniformity. In July and August, the deans of Canterbury and St. Paul's told each other of the preparations being made by their chapters: 'make noe doubt but that wee shall quickly find able men to fill them upp', wrote Turner of the livings in his chapter's gift.[1] Similarly, a report published in a newspaper on 25 August described the way in which Bartholomew livings in the London area had been filled straight away with divines most 'eminent for their Learning and good conversation', thanks to the 'care and prudence of the most worthy Diocesan' (Bishop Sheldon).[2] However, a survey of presentations to Bartholomew livings in three dioceses—Canterbury, Winchester, and this time London as well—suggests that ecclesiastical patrons did not always act as promptly as prevailing conditions would seem to have dictated. The laity, too, with a few exceptions, seems to have been rather slow. It will also be seen, in the second half of the chapter, that the replacements were not always as orthodox or as learned as had been anticipated.

For various reasons, it is difficult to give an accurate figure for the number of weeks taken to replace ejected incumbents. In the first place, we rarely know the exact date on which a nonconformist left his cure. Episcopal policy clearly varied on this point.[3] In a few cases, the ministers themselves have left us a clue—a farewell sermon, a reference in a will, or an entry in

[1] Tanner MSS. 48, ff.23, 26; 145, f.96.

[2] *Kingdomes Intelligencer* (1662), no. 34, 18-25 Aug., p. 562; cf. Secretary Nicholas's comment, *S.P.* 44/2, p. 34, and a later account by one of Sheldon's chaplains, *Bishop Parker's History of his own Time,* trans. T. Newlin (London, 1727), pp. 33-4.

[3] Above, pp. 153-4.

the parish register, such as the following (under 23 August 1662); 'ultimo die praedicandi ministri moraliter morientis Geo: Latham. Postquam compleverit plusquam Annos 13 in divinis administrationibus in Ecclesia hujus Hunton . . . Isaiah 26.19 Thy dead men shall live'.[4] But many other nonconformists did not draw attention to themselves in this way, perhaps in the hope that an indulgence might be declared at the very last moment.[5] Another point to be taken into account is that some bishops—Sheldon in London, and Henchman in Salisbury—seem to have put preachers or readers into Bartholomew livings until a permanent replacement could be appointed. It was one of Sheldon's readers, put into St. Matthew, Friday Street, who was greeted by 'a great many young [people] knotting together and crying out "porridge" often and seditiously in the Church' ('porridge' was a nickname for the Book of Common Prayer).[6] The very temporary nature of such posts, however, means that few records have survived to tell us how common this interim measure was.[7] A further problem is that in a few instances, above all chapelries and perpetual curacies, we do not know the exact date on which the ejected minister's successor was appointed. For the purposes of this analysis, however, 24 August has been taken as the starting-point and the date of institution of the next incumbent as the later limit; where the institution of the replacement or the licensing of the curate has not survived, these livings have been left out of the calculations.

The attitudes and achievements of the bishops in our three

[4] For farewell sermons in Canterbury and Winchester dioceses, see Kennett, *Register*, p. 743; Calamy, *Continuation*, pp. 509, 551; *Cal. Rev.*, p. 316. For Byfield's will and Latham's register, see *Cal. Rev.*, pp. 97, 316. Cf. arrangements paid to pay tithes or money in August 1662, ibid., pp. 382, 502–3, and Calamy, *Continuation*, p. 511.

[5] For the currency of such hopes see *The Diary of Samuel Pepys*, iii, 161; *The Diary of Ralph Josselin*, pp. 140–1; *Life of Adam Martindale*, op. cit., pp. 166–7; *The Diary of the Rev. Henry Newcome*, ed. T. Heywood (Chetham Society, xviii, 1849), pp. 113–14.

[6] Ibid., pp. 115–16, *The Diary of Samuel Pepys*, iii, 178; Clarendon MS. 77, f.298.

[7] No signs survive at Canterbury or Winchester, unless the slight increase in the number of preaching licences issued by Juxon just before Bartholomew is related to this, Lamb. Pal. Lib. *VC1A/1/1*, ff.124–32.

dioceses seem to have varied. At first, Bishop Morley said that he was in no hurry to replace nonconformists.[8] In the event, offended perhaps by the nonconformists' refusal to talk to him, he acted fairly quickly to replace those obstinate Puritans who were in livings in his gift.[9] Of the three bishops under discussion, Morley has the best record, due partly to the small number of livings involved, and partly to the promptness of his visitation, which was conducted between 26 August and 27 September.[10] It is perhaps significant that he did not fill two livings in his gift but outside the diocese of Winchester until 25 October and 10 December, and a third not until even later.[11] Bishop Sheldon faced greater problems in that more ministers were ejected from his diocese (approximately 130) than from any other in 1662,[12] but as far as can be seen he had not computed 'the Number of that faction' accurately enough to be able to supply all of the Bartholomew livings in his gift at once, especially not in Essex. The attitude of Archbishop Juxon towards nonconformity remains a mystery; at least two Puritans regarded him as a moderate, but a contemporary churchmen remembered hearing Juxon say that the best way to govern the Puritans was 'by straight Rain'.[13] In the event, Juxon made several appointments quite quickly, but there were some surprising delays, for example in replacing Nicholas Thoroughgood at Monkton. Juxon must surely have known of his nonconformity, for in July 1662 Thoroughgood had been prosecuted by a secular court for not using the Prayer Book, and on 22 August he had preached a farewell sermon; however, a successor was not collated until 5 January 1663.[14]

[8] Clarendon MS. 77, f.307.

[9] For the figures in the following paragraphs, see Table 1 which is based on 'Process of Re-establishment', pp. 340–52.

[10] Hants Recd. Off. *B/1/A 4 34*, and London Record Office, *DW/VB.1631, 1662, 1664*.

[11] Patney and East Knoyle rectories, Wilts.: *Cal. Rev.* pp. 343, 232, and *Lib. Inst.*; for the third see below p. 162.

[12] Comparable figures of 1662 ejections by counties are given in *Cal. Rev.* pp. xii–xiii.

[13] *Rel. Baxt.*, Lib. I, Pt. II, para. 425; Calamy, *Continuation*, p. 477; L. Womock, *Two Letters Containing a further Justification of the Church of England Against the Dissenters* (London, 1682), p. 58.

[14] Calamy, *Continuation*, p. 551.

The performances of the cathedral chapters in these three dioceses were as varied as those of their bishops. The dean and chapter of Winchester had filled their sole Bartholomew vacancy within a month, perhaps urged on by Bishop Morley who on his visitation in early September had found Romsey—the living in question—to be 'the woorst place I have come to'.[15] St. Paul's must have been one of the best prepared chapters in the country, for by 29 August at least four of their Bartholomew livings had been filled, and by 9 September another four. Nonetheless, a further seven livings in their gift in this diocese were left vacant for periods ranging up to several months. Canterbury chapter had to fill only four Bartholomew livings in its diocese, but did not move as quickly as Dean Turner had anticipated. Although Tenterden had been held for eight years by a Presbyterian known to be 'a great seducer', and Faversham by a minister who had been in trouble with the civil authorities in February 1662, the chapter did not fill these livings until mid November and early December respectively.[16]

Clearly a sense of urgency was felt by some of the bishops and chapters involved, but no more than a beginning to the process of replacement was made in the first weeks. The average time taken by the bishops and chapters in appointing to livings in their own dioceses was nearly seven weeks.

A few lay patrons were also able to present new ministers within days of Bartholomew, for example the king. Charles was in a position to do this because Secretary Nicholas had written to the bishops requesting urgent information on the number of royal livings in their dioceses made void by the act.[17] The number of royal presentations recorded on the Patent Rolls in the five weeks after 24 August rose to fifty-five, compared to a monthly average of sixteen in the preceding months.[18] Most lay patrons, however, and some corporate bodies such as colleges and hospitals were manifestly not ready to act quickly. The average length of time taken by laymen and

[15] Clarendon MS. 73, f.217.

[16] *Cal. Rev.* pp. 253, 535; Lambeth MS. 1126, p. 38; *S.P.* 29/50 f.22.

[17] References to this letter may be found in Clarendon MSS. 73, f.217; 77, f.298; and Tanner MS. 48, ff.41, 45.

[18] Based on an analysis of the Patent Rolls *C.* 66/3004, 3021, 3068.

TABLE 1:

	Institutions by the end of							*After*
	2 wks.	*1 mth.*	*2 mths.*	*3 mths.*	*4 mths.*	*5 mths.*	*6 mths.*	*6 mths.*
Canterbury								
Abp.	3	2	6	1	3	1	1	
D. & Ch. of Cant.				2	1	1		
Other churchmen		1				2	2	
Others	1		1	1	2	1		1
Winchester								
Bp.	2	3						
D. & Ch. of Winch.		1						
Other churchmen			2				1	
Others	1	2	2	7	5		4	6
London								
Bp.	2	3	5	1	1	1		
D. & Ch. of St. Paul's	5	3	1	2	2			2
Other churchmen	1	1	1			1?	2	1
Others	4	7	12	11	9	5	14	16

Note 'Other churchmen' = bishops and chapters of other dioceses, or lesser churchmen within the diocese. 'Others' = the king, laymen, institutions, colleges, schools, and hospitals.

colleges in our three dioceses was over four months.

Dr. Whiteman has examined the process of replacing nonconformist ministers in the diocese of Exeter. Her survey shows that laymen constituted easily the largest group of patrons, controlling thirty-two of the fifty-five livings for which an accurate interval can be given.[19] That forty-six of the fifty-five livings were filled within six months of Bartholomew, and of those twelve or thirteen in the first four weeks, does indeed suggest 'efficient co-operation between the bishop and his diocesan officials and the many patrons who suddenly found themselves bound to make a new presentation'.[20] In some respects this is a better record than that of the other three dioceses under discussion here.

[19] Whiteman, 'The Episcopate of Seth Ward', pp. 106–7.
[20] Ibid., p. 107.

For various reasons one would have anticipated that in the diocese of Canterbury there would have been a comparable, if not a greater, swiftness in substituting orthodox for unorthodox ministers. Canterbury was a more accessible diocese, the great majority of its livings being in East Kent, and the bulk of its peculiars grouped together not far from Lambeth Palace.[21] Secondly, nearly two-thirds of the livings in the diocese of Canterbury were in the hands of ecclesiastical patrons; of the thirty-three replacements where an approximate interval can be given, twenty-six were made by churchmen. Above all, Canterbury was the first see in England, and its ordinary or his officials should have set an example to other dioceses. However, in Canterbury diocese, only seven institutions were made in the first month. Progress thereafter did not improve: nearly half of the Bartholomew livings were still vacant after three months, and even in the new year a quarter had not been filled, due largely to the slowness of ecclesiastical patrons. In the diocese of Winchester, there was not such a clerical predominance; only eight of the thirty-six Bartholomew replacements which we can date approximately were the responsibility of ecclesiastical patrons. Inspired perhaps by Bishop Morley, the patrons of this diocese made a good start, filling a quarter of the vacancies within a month. Their efforts soon faded: there were still sixteen livings vacant after three months, and eleven of these were not filled until 1663. Winchester College, for example, left the important parishes of Portsea and Portsmouth unattended until January and December 1663; the dean and canons of Windsor did not fill Hartley Wespall until February 1663; and St. John's College, Cambridge, did not replace Creswick at Freshwater, Isle of Wight, until the same month, though Morley had silenced Creswick personally on his visitation the previous September.[22] The pattern in the diocese of London resembles that of Winchester. Of the 113 Bartholomew replacements we can date, only a third were in the gift of churchmen. The bishop and chapter gave a good lead, and a total of twenty-six institutions were made in the first month. In succeeding

[21] In the deaneries of Shoreham (West Kent), the Arches (London), and Croydon (East Surrey).

[22] Calamy, *Continuation*, p. 509.

months, the totals dropped, and after three months there were still fifty-four livings without a permanent incumbent. Even after six months there were still nineteen livings without a new minister.

It took on average just under three months to fill a Bartholomew living in the diocese of Winchester, just over three months in Canterbury, and over four months in London. By seventeenth century standards this may have been quite rapid, but in the particular circumstances of August 1662 it is arguable that these intervals were longer than discretion permitted. It may be true that the fear of unrest which had spread in August began to abate when it was realized that most nonconformists were prepared to leave their livings quietly, but the closing months of 1662 were still full of rumours of plots by disaffected nonconformists.[23] There was also a new cause of concern: ejected ministers were setting up separate churches in their former parishes and taking their flocks with them.[24] Yet another element of uncertainty was added when Charles at last decided to risk issuing a declaration of indulgence. On 26 December he announced that he would ask Parliament to pass an act which would enable him 'to exercise, with a more universal Satisfaction, that Power of Dispensing, which we conceive to be inherent in us'.[25] The hopes of Puritan incumbents ejected four months earlier must have begun to revive at this news, especially those ministers whose former livings had yet to be filled.[26] So stately had been the progress of replacing the ejected that at the moment the declaration was issued three-eighths of the Bartholomew livings in the diocese of London, nearly a third of those in the diocese of Winchester, and almost a quarter of those in Canterbury had not been filled. Why did these delays occur?

The answer almost certainly varies from living to living, but some general factors may be suggested. As has already been

[23] *S.P.* 29/56–65 *passim.*

[24] For ejected incumbents soon conventicling in their old parishes in Canterbury diocese, see Lambeth MS. 1126 pp. 4 (Durand), 6 (Johnson), 20 and 22 (Davis), 36 (Goodridge), 38 (How), 56 (Latham), and 64 (Maynard).

[25] Kennett, *Register,* p. 850.

[26] Though Baxter says that it was the Independents whose hopes were raised highest by the proposed indulgence: *Rel. Baxt.*, Lib. I, Pt. II, paras. 418–19.

pointed out, the time allowed by Parliament for the enforcement of the act was inadequate, and many patrons must have had little or no warning of the need to make a fresh presentation until 24 August arrived. Secondly, there is no evidence that the archbishop or his deputy anticipated any problems in replacing Puritan clergy; consequently no advice was given as to how such problems could be surmounted.

One such problem was the complex pattern of patronage. Many of the greatest patrons in the land—the king, a few members of the nobility, the colleges of Oxford and Cambridge, not to mention several bishops and chapters—had acquired advowsons that were scattered widely over England and Wales.[27] and it cannot have been easy for them to discover how many appointments they had to make in the limited time available. Even churchmen had difficulty. The dean and canons of Windsor, whose livings stretched to south-west England, north Wales and Kent, were slow to nominate clergy in at least four dioceses.[28] Bishop Morley was another to run into difficulty; on 6 December 1662, Archbishop Frewen wrote to Sheldon: 'I not knowing where to finde our Brother of Winton, tell him I pray, when you next meete, that sorry I am to hear that his Prerogative at Newcastle stands still empty; it being a very populous towne, to say noe more'.[29] Sheldon may have acted as a clearing-house for such information,[30] but of a more organized campaign to persuade local diocesans to inform absentee patrons of vacancies in their gift there is no sign.

Delays due to distance cannot, however, be used to explain the slowness of those who lived in or near the livings of which they were patron. In some of these cases, delays must have been due to the patron's reluctance to see the old minister leave, or to his desire to appoint exactly the right replacement. Calamy records various instances of efforts being made by ecclesiastical and lay patrons to persuade certain incumbents

[27] *The Clergyman's Intelligencer: or a compleat Alphabetical List of all the Patrons in England and Wales* (London, 1745), *passim*.

[28] Ibid.; the three dioceses covered by Table 1, and Exeter, Whiteman, 'The Episcopate of Seth Ward', pp. 108–9.

[29] Tanner MS. 48, f.69.

[30] Cf. ibid., f.42.

to conform.[31] Joseph Osborne, vicar of Benenden, Kent, was so loved by his parishioners that the patron, his brother, and the dean of Rochester all urged him to conform, though in vain.[32] If such persuasion failed, various devices seem to have been adopted to soften the blow of ejection and to secure a suitable replacement. Nearly fifty of the ejected were given chaplaincies or similar posts in the households of the nobility and gentry.[33] Some patrons gave the departing minister a generous grant or insisted on the new incumbent giving his predecessor specified financial support[34] (a move reminiscent of the fifths granted the sequestered clergy in the 1640s). Sometimes the old minister was given the choice of his successor, or resigned the living to a near relative or assistant.[35] Some of the new incumbents were so moderate that they formed a firm friendship with their predecessors, even to the extent of listening to their sermons.[36] Occasionally, there is even some doubt as to the orthodoxy of the replacement, as in the case of the new minister appointed by Thomas Digges, patron of Chilham, Kent. The replacement, Robert Cumberland, was a young man who matriculated at Oxford in 1658, was not ordained and instituted until December 1662, and in a confidential report prepared a year later was described quite simply as 'A Presbyterian'.[37] Arrangements such as these must have taken the patrons some time to make.

In this context, the record of the earl of Warwick in appointing to eleven Bartholomew livings in Essex is of interest. The earl himself had been a Parliamentarian in the civil wars, and his wife Mary was a very devout woman who

[31] Calamy, *Continuation*, pp. 757 (Thos. Forward); 318 (J. Herring); and 427-8 (Thos. More).

[32] Ibid., p. 538.

[33] *Cal. Rev.*, p. lvi.

[34] Calamy, *Continuation*, pp. 282 (J. Burgess); 291-2 (Nathan Jacob); 243 (Alex. Hodge); and see below p. 164.

[35] *Cal. Rev.*, p. 234 (J. Greensmith); Calamy, *Continuation*, p. 646, and Kennett, *Register*, p. 894 (Walter Hornby); *Cal. Rev.*, p. 281 (J. Hubbard); Calamy, *Continuation*, p. 225, and *Cal. Rev.*, p. 293 (Robt. Jago II); ibid., p. 387 (J. Petter); Calamy, *Continuation*, pp. 424-5 (Tim. Sacheverell); *Cal. Rev.*, p. 512 (Jonas Waterhouse).

[36] *Cal. Rev.*, pp. 153 (J. Crump), 411 (J. Richardson), 429 (Chris. Scott), 520 (Sam. Wells).

[37] *Alum. Oxon.*; Lamb. Pal. Lib., Archbishop Juxon's Register; Lambeth MS. 1126, p. 10.

clearly felt much sympathy for the ejected Puritans.[38] None of the eleven ejected ministers was replaced speedily: the earliest institutions resulting from the earl's presentations came nearly two months after Bartholomew, three more followed in December, and the final six came in February and March 1663.[39] The length of time taken was probably due in large part to the arrangements he chose to make. In two cases, the ejected ministers received generous financial rewards, and in another three relatives of the ejected were appointed to replace them.[40] Of the eleven incumbents appointed, three had probably been conformist incumbents in the Commonwealth church, and eight had possibly been fellows or students of the Puritan universities in the 1650s.[41] At least three of them had received orders in 1660 from Irish or Scottish bishops,[42] although ordination by English bishops was becoming increasingly available. It must have taken Warwick, and other patrons of a Puritan hue, some time to find exactly the right replacements. Meanwhile, there was very little that the church authorities could do to make them act more speedily.

There may have been other reasons for the delays in replacing ejected nonconformists, such as a shortage of episcopally ordained clergy.[43] But whatever the reasons, the church authorities do seem to have permitted many livings in their own gift to remain vacant for a longer period of time than was wise. At the same time, they seem to have failed to

[38] *The Complete Peerage*, ed. Vicary Gibbs *et al.* (London, 12 vols., 1910–59), xii, Pt. II, 414–15; *Dict. Nat. Biog. sub.* Mary Rich.

[39] 'Process of Re-establishment', pp. 347–51 for the following livings, all in Essex: Moreton, High Ongar, Barnston, Childerditch, Braintree, Rayleigh, Felsted, Hawkswell, Ashingdon, Little Leighs, and Prittlewell.

[40] *Cal. Rev.*, p. 317 (J. Lavender) and p. 385 (Thos. Peck); John Benson's son (ibid., p. 49), Thomas Peck's son (ibid., p. 385) and Abraham Caley's nephew Samuel Bull (ibid., p. 99).

[41] Rd. Mitchell (*Alum. Cant.*); Sam. Bull (*Transactions of the Essex Archaeological Society*, new ser., xxi, 1933–7, p. 80): J. Forward (*Cal. Rev.*, p. 208). Forward and Robt. Carr, J. Smith, J. Idle, Dan Joyner, J. Benson, Wm. Alchorne (*Alum. Cant.*), and S. Peck (*Alum. Oxon.*).

[42] Smith, Idle, and Joyner (*Alum. Cant.*)

[43] Bishops may have been reluctant to create a pool of conformable clergy by ordaining extra priests just before August 1662, since by canon law the bishop was liable to maintain any minister he had ordained who had no living to go to; E. Gibson, *Codex Iuris Ecclesiastici Anglicani* (Oxford, 2 vols., 1761), i, 140.

make some lay patrons aware of the urgency of the need to replace nonconformist incumbents. It was suggested in the last chapter that the church was fortunate in late August 1662 that the great majority of the Puritan clergy were such loyal subjects. It would again seem to have been fortunate in the closing months of that year that the Puritans did not attempt to take advantage of the many pulpits which were allowed to remain vacant until the time of the royal declaration of December 1662.

In August 1662 Dean Turner had anticipated that there would be no shortage of 'fitt', able men to take the places of the 'Deserters', and one description of the replacements called them 'most eminent for their Learning'.[44] The learning of the replacements does not, however, seem to have been noticably greater than that of the ejected in our two dioceses, in so far as this can be judged by the degrees which these ministers had obtained. Of the eighty-four ejected in these dioceses, fifty-seven had acquired a B.A., an M.A., or at least matriculated; of the eighty-two replacements, fifty-three had a lesser degree or had matriculated. A larger number of the replacements had acquired a higher degree, eleven as opposed to the ejected's three; but in fairness it should be pointed out that six of the eleven were honorary degrees conferred on them by the king after the Restoration.[45] In at least one other diocese, the standard of learning of the ejected may have been slightly higher than that of their successors.[46]

Other figures throw an interesting light on the orthodoxy and fitness of the replacements. At least fourteen of the forty replacements in Canterbury diocese and eleven of the forty-two in Winchester had previously held livings in the Cromwellian church.[47] Indeed, the figures may well have been

[44] Above p. 155.

[45] For full details, see 'Process of Re-establishment', pp. 354–5. These totals include replacements of uncertain date and their predecessors (listed ibid., pp. 340–5) who for obvious reasons have been omitted from previous calculations about speed of replacement.

[46] Exeter diocese, ejected and replacements 1660–2: Whiteman, 'The Episcopate of Seth Ward', pp. 110–11.

[47] Full details of the replacements described in this and the next paragraph are given in 'Process of Re-establishment', pp. 355–7, 384–407.

higher, for there are two categories of replacement whose earlier careers are not easily traced, non-graduates, and those who had worked in other dioceses and then moved to Canterbury or Winchester after the Restoration; some of these may also have served the church in some capacity in the 1650s. A further six of the replacements in Canterbury diocese, and a further twelve in Winchester had graduated from a university which had been under a Puritan regime for all or part of their time there. It may seem unfair to classify these students alongside the Cromwellian clergy as Commonwealth conformists, but there are good reasons for doing so. During the 1640s and 1650s the more conservative members of the universities were purged, and their places were filled by prominent and learned Puritans. The atmosphere which prevailed during the Interregnum naturally reflected these changes, and vice-chancellors and heads of colleges laid particular stress on prayers, preaching, piety, and the teaching of true religion. Furthermore, there were also certain tests to be performed by members of the universities, even if these were enforced erratically.[48] It would be surprising if the formative years of university life, the contact with leading Puritans, and the use of the Directory in college services did not leave a marked imprint on the opinions of many who later became parish clergy under the restored house of Stuart.

It was by comparison a surprisingly small proportion of Bartholomew replacements in these two dioceses who had held themselves strictly aloof from the Puritan church. Only six members of the sequestered clergy took charge of a Bartholomew living in these two dioceses, even though there were many of their fellow sufferers still active. Perhaps the majority of the sequestered clergy had been rewarded for their loyalty to king and church in the first two years of the

[48] This picture is drawn from: C. H. Cooper, *Annals of Cambridge* (Cambridge, 5 vols., 1842-53), iii, 370, 375-9, 439-42; *Cambridge University Transactions during the Puritan controversies of the 16th and 17th Centuries,* ed. J. Heywood and T. Wright (London, 2 vols, 1854), ii, 457-8, 463, 508, 530-8; J. B. Mullinger, *The University of Cambridge* (Cambridge, 3 vols., 1873-1911), iii, 208-9, 273-392 *passim.*, 484-8, 546-7; *The Register of the Visitors of the University of Oxford from A.D. 1647 to A.D. 1658*, ed. M. Burrows (Camden Society, new series, xxix, 1881), 1, li, xcviii, 22, 274, 329; C. E. Mallet, *A History of the University of Oxford* (London, 3 vols., 1924-7), ii, 371-86, 389, 391-7.

Restoration, and were now reluctant to take on a new living or exchange an old one, especially if it meant taking over a troublesome parish or making a financial sacrifice.

The question naturally arises as to why over a half—and possibly more—of the replacements in these two dioceses were to some extent tainted with conformity during the Interregnum. Clearly most patrons would not have chosen Commonwealth conformists had they not believed that the new men were going to be more orthodox than the old. It is also true that all of the replacements should have made a declaration of conformity under the terms of the Act of Uniformity (though some of the limitations of this statute and of its enforcement have been touched upon). Nevertheless, the high proportion of Commonwealth conformists among Bartholomew replacements requires some explanation, and the most convincing one would seem to be that the replacements represented a typical cross-section of the parish clergy of these dioceses after 1662. For upon examination the post-Bartholomew clergy can be seen to have contained a very small proportion of ministers who had held aloof from the Puritan church, and a very large proportion who had served continuously from the revolutionary decades through to 1663 or beyond, or conformed in some other way during the Interregnum.

The character of the post-Bartholomew clergy in the dioceses of Canterbury and Winchester has been assessed through an examination of the earlier careers of all ministers holding livings in these dioceses in the year 1663. The visitations of Juxon and Morley in 1663–4 (supplemented in the case of Canterbury by a valuable manuscript 'catalogue' prepared in 1663) have provided the names of the clergy,[49] while pre-war records,[50] Parliamentary and Protectorate records,[51] Restoration addresses,[52] and the better county histories (quoting manuscripts and monumental inscriptions

[49] Cant. Cath. Chap. Arch., *Z.7.4;* Hants Recd. Off., *B/1/A.4.34;* London Record Office, *DW/VB 1631, 1662, 1664;* Lambeth MS. 1126.

[50] Hants Recd. Off., *B/1/A.3.33;* Institution and Composition Books in the P.R.O.

[51] Listed conveniently by J. Houston, *Catalogue of Ecclesiastical Records of the Commonwealth 1643-1660 in the Lambeth Palace Library* (Farnborough, 1968), pp. 198, 1-71.

[52] E.g. *To the Kings most Excellent Majesty, The most humble, and joyfull Address*

that are not always now available)[53] have augmented the information available from more recent biographical aids[54] on the previous careers of these ministers. In many cases, it has not proved possible to trace the previous history of incumbents, and in others no more than a likely link has been found; moreover, of necessity our concern has been with numbers rather than consciences. Nevertheless, some conclusions may be drawn with reasonable confidence.

The proportion of Bartholomew replacements who had in some measure conformed during the 1650s was seen to be about half in the two dioceses under discussion. This is a very similar proportion to that of the whole clergy of these dioceses in 1663 who had bowed the knee during the previous decade. In the diocese of Canterbury there were about 400 churches and chapels at this time,[55] and of these as many as 183 were filled in 1663 by ministers who had served cures or attended university while the Puritans were in power. About twenty-seven cures were occupied by ministers who had been appointed before the outbreak of the civil wars and apparently held office continuously until 1663.[56] About sixty-eight were filled by minsters who had been appointed between 1642 and 1660 to the cures they still held in 1663.[57] A further fifty-six were occupied by clergymen who had conformed during the later 1640s or 1650s, but had not served the same livings continuously from then until 1663, having exchanged their old cure for a new one after the Restoration. Finally, about thirty-two cures were served by graduates who attended university at

of divers Rectors, Vicars, and others of the Clergy in the County of Surrey (Brit. Lib., *C. 112. h. 4.* no. 76).

[53] Hasted; O. Manning and W. Bray, *The History and Antiquities of the County of Surrey* (London, 3 vols., 1808–14).

[54] *Alum. Oxon.*, *Alum. Cant.*, *Walk. Rev.*, and *Cal. Rev.*

[55] Based on a count of cures in Lambeth MS. 1126.

[56] Full details of the ministers described in this paragraph and the next are given in 'Process of Re-establishment', pp. 383–403. Two alterations have been made since the thesis was completed: Jas. Cowes (who attended Puritan Cambridge before being appointed rector of Luddenham, Kent) has been added to Part 4(a) of App. 1, chap. VII; Sam. Bluden or Blundell (who appears as curate of Sutton, Hants., both in 1642 and 1663) has been added to Part 2(b).

[57] Since Parliament was interfering with some royal and ecclesiastical patronage as early as 1642 (W. A. Shaw, *History of the English Church*, op. cit., ii, 180–2, 184; J. Houston, op. cit., p. 1), that year has been taken as the starting-point and December 1659 as the closing-point for the appointment of clergy in this category.

some time during the 1650s. Some ministers cannot be placed in a particular category with a great deal of confidence, but on the other side it should be remembered that if we knew more of the Commonwealth clergy (especially of the careers of non-graduates, of those who moved around the country, and of those who held more than one living in the 1650s), then the final figures might well be higher than those presented here. As it is, there are several livings where there is no clear indication of who held them in the late 1650s, and it is quite possible that the first men to be found serving or being instituted to these livings after the Restoration had in fact been in possession for some time.[58]

That Canterbury was not an exceptional diocese in the scale of its Commonwealth conformity is suggested by the figures for Winchester. Of approximately 440 churches and chapels in that diocese, as many as 224 were served in 1663 by Commonwealth conformists. About thirty-two were filled by ministers appointed before 1642 who had 'kept in all the times'; another 111 by incumbents appointed between 1642 and 1660 who conformed at the Restoration sufficiently to be still in the same livings in 1663–4; a further forty-four by incumbents who had probably served in the Interregnum church but not continuously in the same cure until 1663; and a possible thirty-seven by graduates of the purged universities who obtained livings after the Restoration. As in the diocese of Canterbury, only the silence of the sources prevents us from tracing more minsters who had probably conformed during the 1650s.[59] Nevertheless, even if the proportion of Commonwealth conformists in the post-Bartholomew church was only 45 per cent in the diocese of Canterbury and 50 per cent in that of Winchester, this does suggest that over England and Wales at large the total number of such incumbents must have been very high.

It must be stressed that the majority of those incumbents

[58] E.g. the livings of Canterbury All Saints and St. Mary Magdalen (rectories), Bethersden, Charing, Ewell (vicarages), and many others in Kent and elsewhere. See also above p. 129.

[59] The following were instituted to livings after June 1660 but may have already been in possession: Rd. White (Basingstoke, vicarage), Chris. Cosier (Caterington, v.), Rd. Pocock (Colmer, rectory), Nath. Crawford (Ellesfield, r.), Wm. Birstall (Eversley, r.), Edw. Cage (Faringdon, r.), and many others.

who served in both Cromwellian and Restoration churches were generally quite conformable after 1662. They were obviously more orthodox or more flexible than those 'intruders' who balked at performing the tests of conformity laid down in the Act of Uniformity. On the other hand, there is evidence that a minority, perhaps a sizable minority, of Commonwealth conformists still in office after 1662 could not forget their formative years. Clarendon observed that 'many who did subscribe had the same Malignity to the Church, and to the Government of it' as those who were ejected, and that these partial conformists did more harm inside the church than they would have done outside.[60] Archbishop Sheldon made the same point when replying to the complaint that the door of conformity had been too narrow in 1662: had he known that so many ministers inclined to Puritanism would conform, he 'would have made it straiter'.[61]

For the diocese of Canterbury, we are in a particularly fortunate position to judge the orthodoxy of the clergy in 1663. In that year a very valuable document was prepared (for Sheldon, soon after his elevation to the primacy), entitled 'A catalogue of all the benefices and promotions within the diocese and jurisdiction of Canterbury With the State of every particular Parish as it stood at October 1663'.[62] This manuscript contains many thumb-nail sketches of parishes and individual incumbents, especially those in Kent. The comments on the incumbents are obviously the result of a fairly thorough investigation, perhaps conducted during Juxon's visitation earlier in the year, and they have the additional virtue of being completely candid, so much so that it was later decided to cross out some of the most derogatory remarks.[63]

The 'catalogue' expresses disquiet about some incumbents who had been appointed before the troubles and had then stayed in their livings through all the changes in church government. Edward Aldey, rector of St. Andrew's,

[60] Clarendon, *Life*, ii, 306.

[61] Quoted in W. G. Simon, *Restoration Episcopate* (1965), p. 135 (no source given).

[62] Lambeth MS. 1126.

[63] Ibid., pp. 2, 10, 12, 16, *et passim*.

Canterbury, from 1624 to 1673, was adjudged 'A soft man, of weake resolutions, and heretofore a little inclining to Presbyt:'; his parish was 'full of Sectaries and Schismatiques'.[64] John Sackett, rector of Great Mongeham since 1628 was described as a Presbyterian in 1663, and his brother Stephen, the long-serving vicar of two livings in Kent was little better—'of wary principles', the 'catalogue' says.[65]

More outspoken criticism was reserved for those appointed during the revolutionary decades who were still serving cures in 1663. Nicholas Dingley, rector of Kingston after the sequestration of a canon of Canterbury, was termed 'A pure Presbyterian'; Samuel Creswell was noted simply as a 'Conforming Intruder' but the absence of a surplice in his parish church may indicate partial conformity; Robert Clarke was 'Somewhat suspected, because he hath kept in for 17 yeares together during all the troubles and changes'.[66] Samuel Jemmett was dismissed with the scathing remark 'A Covetous fatt Presbyterian Conformist'; his living was worth £200 a year.[67]

Even incumbents appointed after the Restoration, and indeed after Black Bartholomew, had their orthodoxy called into question. Thomas Perne, a graduate of Puritan Cambridge, then appointed to two livings near Dover after the Restoration, was 'a person whose principles are doubted'.[68] Robert Cumberland, successor to an ejected Puritan at Chilham, was termed 'Presbyterian' in 1663; his church contained 'No font; No surplice'.[69] Others appointed after August 1662, though not to Bartholomew livings, may also have caused concern, for instance, William Osborne, junior. His father (rector of East Langdon 1641-74) was regarded as a Presbyterian by the authors of the 'catalogue', and the report on his son (rector of Fordwich from 1663) was also disquieting: 'A person favouring Presbytery; the Towne a pretty bigge place, And the Inhabitants and minister a like principled for

[64] Lambeth MS. 1126, p. 1.

[65] Ibid., pp. 16, 1, and cf. pp. 24, 56 (Ross and Cunningham).

[66] Ibid., pp. 11, 34, 37 and cf. p. 26 (Ansell).

[67] Ibid., p. 51; other 'Conforming Intruders' held livings worth at least £80—J. Webb, T. Carter, J. Cowes, Leversidge. Ibid., pp. 6, 26, 52, 64.

[68] Ibid., p. 20(2), and cf. pp. 16, 17, 24, 52 (Walton, Lodowick, Spencer, Cowes).

[69] Ibid., p. 10, and cf. p. 16 (Ibbot) and *Cal. Rev.*, pp. 92-3 (T. Hammond).

the most part'.[70]

Nor was this problem confined to Canterbury diocese. Other dioceses also had incumbents who, having been apointed before the civil wars and 'kept in all the times', did not conform in full after 1662, for instance John Angier at Denton (near Manchester), William Mew in Gloucestershire, and Ralph Josselin in Essex.[71] Other dioceses also had 'intruders' who continued to pose a threat to Anglican uniformity after 1662, Henry Swift in Yorkshire, Nicholas Kenrick in Northmptonshire, and Samuel Hardy in Dorset and Hampshire.[72] One should also remember that even after 1662 the more determined partial conformists could often find loop-holes in the facade of Anglican uniformity. Donatives or peculiars outside episcopal jurisdiction harboured half-conformists, as in the case of Josselin's neighbour at White Colne, John Bigley, and others.[73] 'Vacant, dark, and neglected' places provided other opportunities, the vicarage of Shap on the Westmorland moors, the 'obscure' chapel of Longridge in Lancashire, even a church in Suffolk neglected by a pluralist vicar.[74] Then again, lay patrons sometimes encouraged partial conformity: Lady Jackson (sister of Sir George Booth) encouraged that 'Picture of an old Puritan' Nathan Denton to continue preaching at a Derbyshire church though he had not conformed in August 1662.[75] Even ecclesiastical patrons sometimes showed their reluctance to waste the abilities of moderate Puritans; one may cite Bishop Reynolds's treatment of Candler, and Archdeacon Palmer's attitude to Kenrick,[76] as well as the actions of latitudinarian figures such as Laney and Wilkins in later years. It is also

[70] Lambeth MS. 1126, pp. 17, 2, and cf. p.1 (Stockar).

[71] Calamy, *Account*, pp. 395, 332; A. Macfarlane, *The Family Life of Ralph Josselin* (Cambridge, 1970), pp. 28-30, and *The Diary of Ralph Josselin*, pp. 141, 143, 146, 156, 159-62, 169, 178.

[72] J. Addy, *The Archdeacon and Ecclesiastical Discipline in Yorkshire 1598-1714 Clergy and the Churchwardens* (St. Anthony's Hall Publications No. 24, York, 1963), pp. 14, 27-8; Calamy, *Continuation*, p. 645; Calamy, *Account*, pp. 281-2.

[73] Ibid., p. 309 (and *Continuation*, p. 483) and cf. pp. 281, 774 (Hardy, Fownes) and *Cal. Rev.*, pp. 71, 157 (Brecknock, Daranda).

[74] Kennett, *Register*, p. 755; *Cal. Rev.*, p. 156 (Dalton); Calamy, *Account*, pp. 412 (T. Smith), and 292 (and *Dict. Nat. Biog.*, Stockton).

[75] Calamy, *Continuation*, pp. 950-1, and cf. p. 881 (Wyar).

[76] Calamy, *Account*, p. 315; *Continuation*, p. 645.

noteworthy that in 1665 Archbishop Sheldon felt it necessary to urge bishops to ensure that pluralists kept orthodox and conformable curates.[77]

One of the hallmarks of continuing adherence to Puritan ideals was a dislike of the surplice, as is shown by the behaviour of partial conformists such as Josselin and Swift.[78] On this subject, the 'catalogue' provides us with some very interesting information. As late as October 1663, at least twenty-six parishes in the diocese of Canterbury were denoted as having no surplice, and in several cases no font either.[79] Nor was this the result of poverty or negligence. Against the parish of St. Peter's, Sandwich (which lost two Puritan ministers) was put the note 'Noe Surplice, nor any will be indured'; at Alkham, the churchwardens were 'unwilling to provide' a surplice.[80] Moreover, in the majority of cases where a minister had no surplice, some indication of an earlier conformity to the Puritan regime can be traced today.[81] Indeed, there may well have been other parishes without a surplice in 1663; the silence of the 'catalogue' on many parishes may reflect a reliance on the evidence of churchwardens who, as at Sandwich and Alkham, were anxious to prevent the return of the hated vestment.

It cannot, in fact, have been easy to obtain frank reports on Puritan parishes where 'Inhabitants and minster' were 'a like principled for the most part'. 'Little knowne' is the honest remark against the rector of Barfryston, though he had been there eleven years, and still had no surplice in 1663.[82] Under normal circumstances, the officials of a diocese could rely upon the body of information built up by their predecessors, but the face of the parish clergy had been transformed beyond recognition by the upheavals of the revolutionary decades and then by the ejections of 1660 and 1662. In the dioceses of Canterbury and Winchester, well over half of the clergy

[77] Wilkins, *Concilia* (London, 1731), iv, 582.

[78] *The Diary of Ralph Josselin,* pp. 169, 178, and A. Macfarlane, loc. cit.; J. Addy, op. cit., p. 14.

[79] Lambeth MS. 1126, pp. 9, 10 (3 cases), 11, 12, 15, 16 (2 cases), 17 (2), 18, 20 (3), 22 (2), 23, 24, 28, 31, 32, 33, 34, 38, 47; no font, pp. 9, 10, 16, 17.

[80] Ibid., pp. 17, 20.

[81] 'Process of Re-establishment', p. 373, n. 3.

[82] Lambeth MS. 1126, p. 15; P.R.O., Composition Books.

serving in 1663 had held their livings for less than three years.[83] Under normal circumstances, visitations proved to be a major source of information on the clergy, but again the ecclesiastical authorities made their own task more difficult by delaying their first visitations until late 1662 or 1663. It was probably several years before the authorities knew which of their clergy were keeping the promises made in 1662 and which were not.

If we turn to examine the other extreme of the clergy in 1663, those of unimpeachable orthodoxy, we find that their numbers were probably very small. Only twenty-nine of the 400 churches and chapels in Canterbury diocese and forty of the 440 cures in Winchester were served by sequestered clergy who had remained strictly aloof from the Interregnum church.[84] (Even if we include those sequestered ministers who had conformed sufficiently to be serving at the time of the Restoration, the total for Canterbury diocese would be only three higher, and that for Winchester only one larger.)[85] While the ranks of the sequestered clergy may safely be said to have contained some of the most implacable opponents of Puritanism, their ability to form the vanguard of a 'Laudian' campaign at parish level was limited by various factors. Many of them were now very old; an extreme example is Richard Fawkner, rector of Yarmouth, Isle of Wight, from 1615, ejected about 1643 for senile debility and insufficiency, but restored in 1660 and still there at the time of Morley's visitation in 1663.[86] Others of the sequestered clergy restored to parish livings were also canons or prebendaries, and as such were preoccupied with other matters.[87] The cases of John Reading and Samuel Pownall also suggest that the orthodoxy even of the sequestered clergy was occasionally not above suspicion. According to the Anglican martyrologist Walker,

[83] This estimate is reached by deducting those appointed before 1660 and those restored to livings in 1660 from the total number of clergy.

[84] 'Process of Re-establishment', pp. 404–7; most of these ministers had returned to the livings from which they had been driven, but a few had taken on additional livings or moved to new ones by 1663.

[85] Ibid., pp. 376, 387, 397–8.

[86] *Walk. Rev.* p. 183; cf. the comments on Miles Barnes and Samuel Pownall in Kent, Lambeth MS. 1126, pp. 25, 20.

[87] A total of seven in our two dioceses—'Process of Re-establishment', p. 377.

Reading was at one time esteemed by Puritans as a strict Calvinist, though this did not prevent him from being ejected from his vicarage at Dover for opposing Parliament; he seems to have conformed in his second living and to have added another living in 1660 rather than return to Dover.[88] The 'catalogue' made the rather sour comment on him: 'well enough knowne to be no extraordinary man' (though it was later seen fit to cross this through).[89] That Reading, a canon of Canterbury since July 1660, had failed to provide surplices for his two parishes by 1663 is a surprising reflection on one who should have been a pillar of the restored Anglican church.[90] Pownall also had no surplice in 1663, and his report is little better than Reading's—an 'indifferent good person'.[91]

The sequestered clergy were not, of course, the only men who had suffered for their king and church. A certain number of the new ministers appointed in the first three years of the Restoration were men of proven loyalty to the Stuart cause. Peter Mews had been a captain in the royal army, sustained several wounds including the loss of one eye, and then worked as a Royalist agent and again as a soldier under the Duke of York; in 1663 he was rector of South Warnborough in Hampshire.[92] Another Hampshire incumbent, Charles Appleford,[93] had also served in the royal army, while Paul Knell, of St. Dunstan's Canterbury, had been a chaplain in the same army, and had preached against Parliament in 1647 and 1648.[94] Edward Wilsford had been an active Royalist in the 1640s, and had organized the gentry of Kent to meet Charles II in 1660.[95] Other ministers newly appointed to livings in the diocese of Canterbury we know from the 'catalogue' to have been recommended by leading Anglican churchmen or by loyal gentry. David Terry was described as a 'good honest

[88] J. Walker, *An Attempt towards recovering an Account of the Numbers and Sufferings of the Clergy of the Church of England* (London, 1714), pp. 8, 343; *Walk. Rev.*, p. 224.

[89] Lambeth MS. 1126, p. 10.

[90] Ibid., pp. 10, 20.

[91] Ibid., p. 20.

[92] *Dict. Nat. Biog.* and S. H. Cassan, *The Lives of the Bishops of Winchester* (London, 2 vols., 1827), ii, 189, 193.

[93] *S.P.* 29/7, f.65.

[94] *S.P.* 29/6, f.30 and *Walk. Rev.*, p. 221.

[95] *S.P.* 29/12, f.32; *Walk. Rev.*, p. 228.

playne man lately put in by your Grace [Sheldon], at the recommendation of Dr. Casaubon'; Lucius Seymour was recommended by a Captain Buffkin.[96] A certain number of the clergy appointed after the Restoration in the diocese of Winchester may also have been recommended in this way, for instance, Abraham Allen, whose petition and testimonial were among the first to be handled by the Sheldon-Earle-Morley 'committee' in 1660.[97] However, the total number of incumbents in 1663 who had been sequestered, who had a royalist background, or are known to have been recommended for their orthodoxy by a reliable referee, was, on the evidence at present available for our two dioceses, not nearly as high as the number of those who had held livings or attended universities during the Interregnum.

It is remarkable, in fact, how few of the incumbents listed in the 'catalogue' were prized very highly for their orthodoxy or their 'parts'. It is true that the 'catalogue' did commend the abilities and views of some incumbents: Henry Cussen was a man 'of right principles', Richard Whitlock was 'orthodox', and William Lovelace was 'of good parts and Principles'.[98] Many others were thought to be 'right for the church',[99] but very few were commended in glowing terms: the new vicar of Charing was very orthodox and a good, diligent preacher and catechizer; Robert Boys was a 'person very right'; Peter Pury (rector of Knowlton continuously from 1639 to 1663) was 'much commended for his parts and life'.[100] One or two were even thought to be too earnest: Moses Lee was good, sound but 'thought by some to be too busily zealous for the Church'; John Cooper had 'zealous principles for the Church if he knew how to governe them to the best advantage'.[101] The discretion of other incumbents was also questionable.[102] The abiding impression left by the 'catalogue' is that although there were a few whose loyalty to the church was in doubt and at the other extreme a few of above average zeal or ability, the great

[96] Lambeth MS. 1126, pp. 14, 43.

[97] See above, p. 54.

[98] Lambeth MS. 1126, pp. 29, 35, 3..

[99] Ibid., pp. 7 (2), 13, 14, 28, 31, 32, 33, *et passim.*

[100] Ibid., pp. 36, 29, 16.

[101] Ibid., pp. 35, 36.

[102] Ibid., pp. 6, 16, 18, 31 (Young, Whiston, Dicus, Marsh).

majority of incumbents were regarded simply as being 'conformable enough' and 'of parts sufficient' for their livings.

The evidence provided by this chapter enables us to throw new light on certain aspects of the Restoration church settlement. First of all, it allows us to put the ejections of 1662 in a better perspective: far more Commonwealth clergy conformed to the Restoration settlement, at least outwardly, than were ejected for nonconformity. Against the forty ejected in Canterbury diocese, we should place the hundred Commonwealth conformists who decided to continue serving in the church, against the forty-four ejected in Winchester, the 140 who remained.[103] Secondly, the suggestion that the episcopal church was re-established from below must surely have doubt cast upon it: the large measure of continuity with the Puritan church of the Interregnum, the relatively small numbers of active or zealous episcopalian clergy in the parishes, the delays in the reintroduction of some features of Anglican worship, and other signs of partial conformity in 1663 all point to the opposite conclusion. Uniformity was imposed from above, by the Cavalier House of Commons, and it was not achieved as easily as they had hoped in 1662.

[103] The figures are taken from 'Process of Re-establishment', pp. 340–5 and 384–400. The disparity would be even greater if we added graduates of the Puritan universities, or made allowance for a number of incumbents whose earlier careers are not clear but who may well have served in the Interregnum church.

IX

THE ROLE OF THE GENTRY IN THE RESTORATION CHURCH SETTLEMENT

In March 1662, Charles told the members of the Cavalier Parliament that he had heard how zealous for the church they were, how 'very solicitous and even jealous that there was not Expedition enough used' in reaching a final settlement of ecclesiastical affairs.[1] Later generations of historians have embroidered this theme: Macaulay with typical hyperbole described the Cavaliers as being 'more zealous for royalty than the King, more zealous for episcopacy than the Bishops'.[2] Of late, there has been a tendency to modify this picture. David Ogg suggested that the harshness of the Cavaliers towards non-conformity derived not so much from Anglican zeal as from the fear of rebellion which was fed by the daily reports of plotting and conventicling.[3] It has also been shown that the Cavalier House of Commons was by no means uniformly hostile to the Puritans: the number of moderates who voted against the Cavaliers' most intolerant measures was much higher than the four dozen M.P.s of demonstrably Puritan background.[4]

However, there remain too many examples of persecuting intent for us to doubt that the Cavalier House of Commons as a whole was 'very zealous for the Church'. Indeed, such was their sense of urgency that they pushed aside the king's own views and his other, more pressing business in their campaign to impose Anglican worship on all his subjects. In the preambles to the acts which constitute the 'Clarendon Code'

[1] Clarendon, *Life*, ii, 285.

[2] *History of England from the Accession of James II by Lord Macaulay*, ed. C. H. Firth (London, 6 vols., 1913-15), i, 156.

[3] *England in the Reign of Charles II* (Oxford, 2 vols., 1934), i, 208; many of these reports were groundless or exaggerated.

[4] D. T. Witcombe, *Charles II and the Cavalier House of Commons 1663-1674* (Manchester, 1966), pp. 4-5, 9, 19, 37; D. R. Lacey, *Dissent and Parliamentary Politics in England, 1661-1689* (New Jersey, 1969), chap. 4, and App. 2.

we can see the driving forces behind their campaign: their hatred of what Puritanism had done in the past, their fear of what it could still do in the future, and their reliance on the episcopal Church of England as a bulwark against the 'poisonous principles of schism and rebellion'.[5] It is fair to say, with Ogg, that the Cavaliers were anxious to stamp out sedition, but this concern should not be placed in antithesis to their support for the Anglican church; the two were complementary. Through its prayers and its sermons, its patronage, tithes, and leases of church land, the episcopal church furnished theoretical and practical support for the social supremacy of crown and gentry. The gentry in their turn attacked those forces which challenged the ecclesiastical hierarchy and the existing order of society.

While a good deal of attention has been paid to the Cavaliers' demonstrations of zeal in Parliament, comparatively little has been given to similar exhibitions in the counties. The balance obviously needs redressing: the Cavalier Parliament was in session for only eighteen months of the first five years of its existence,[6] and it cannot be doubted that individual members were strongly influenced by what they saw and heard in their home counties in the intervening periods. Many M.P.s also held office in the counties. In some cases their appointment as a J.P. or a deputy lieutenant may have been a gesture of courtesy, but many M.P.s undoubtedly took these duties seriously. If we take the counties which made up the dioceses of Canterbury, Rochester, and Winchester, we find that a dozen members for Hampshire constituences, a dozen M.P.s for Surrey, and eight Kentish M.P.s were all active on the bench in their respective counties.[7] Furthermore,

[5] *Statutes*, v, 575; cf. 516.

[6] *J.L.*, xi, 240-701.

[7] St. John of Basing, Humph. Benett, J. Bulkely, Rd. Goddard, Laur. Hyde, Giles Hungerford, S. Wm. Leavis, S. J. Norton, Rd. Norton, Wm. Oglander, S. J. Trott, S. Hen. Worsely; S. Thos. Bludworth, Edw. Bish, S. Edm. Bowyer, Ad. Browne, S. Nich. Carew, Geo. Evelyn, S. Wm. Howard, Rog. James, Geo. Moore, Arth. and S. Rd. Onslow, Edw. Thurland; Robt. Barnham, S. Fran. Clerke, S. Edw. Hales, S. Nort. Knatchbull, S. Edw. Masters, S. Thos. Peyton, S. J. Tufton, S. Fran. Vincent: *Return Members of Parliament, Part 1, Parliaments of England 1213-1702* (London, 1878), pp. 527-8; 529; 524, 532. Hants Recd. Off., 'Quarter Sessions 1649 to 1658 and 1659 to 1672, Summary of Orders . . . etc, by J. S. Furley', p. 101. 'Surrey Quarter Sessions Records, Order Books, and Sessions Rolls, 1659-1661', '1661-1663',

four members from Kent and three from Hampshire served as deputy lieutenants in those counties.[8] Even on temporary commissions, M.P.s were well represented: members for Kentish constituencies comprised nearly half of the body of commissioners who enforced the Corporation Act in that county.[9] These figures would in fact be higher if we included those gentlemen who resided in our three dioceses but served seats elsewhere. Seven men who served as J.P.s in their home county of Surrey held seats in other counties. Sir George Sondes was member for a borough in Devon, but he was active as a J.P., as a deputy lieutenant, and as a Corporation Act commissioner in his home county of Kent.[10] There is no reason to doubt that this pattern of office-holding was repeated throughout the country.

It may be useful, therefore, to ask how far the collective zeal of the Cavalier Commons was inspired by the observations of individual M.P.s in their constituencies or home counties. At the same time we may examine the ways in which the actions of the gentry at local level influenced the course and eventual shape of the church settlement. In this chapter, four aspects of gentry activity in the south-east will be examined: their work in the militia, their involvement in the enforcement of the Corporation Act, their prosecution of Puritan incumbents, and their relations with the restored bishops, deans and chapters.

One of the recurring themes in the state papers and news-papers of the early months of the Restoration is the eagerness of the gentry to join the militia.[11] The government naturally took advantage of this situation: one set of instructions stipulated that there should be one officer for every fifty men

'1663-1666', *Surrey Records*, vi, vii, viii, (1934, 1935, 1938), *passim*. Kent Recd. Off., *Q/S.B.8; Q/S.B.9; Q/SO E.1; Q/SO W.2.*

[8] Hales, Knatchbull, Peyton, Tufton; Bennett, S. J. and Rd. Norton. *Twysden Lieutenancy Papers 1583-1668,* ed. G. S. Thomson (Kent. Arch. Soc. Records Branch, x, 1926), 13, 27. Addit. MS. 21,922, f.238.

[9] Clerke, Hales, Knatchbull, Masters, Peyton, Tufton, Vincent; Wm. Lovelace, and S. Edm. Pierce. Egerton MS. 2,985, f. 66, and see below p. 185.

[10] Francis, Ld. Angier, S. Allen Brodrick, S. Rd. Browne, Ab. Cullen, S. J. Maynard, S. Walter St. John, S. Fran. Vincent: *Return Members of Parliament,* pp. 529, 520/528, 530, 531, 521, 532, and *Surrey Records,* vi, vii. Sondes: *Return Members of Parliament,* p. 521, and sources in previous notes.

[11] *S.P.* 94/44, ff.77, 98; 29/16, f.84; 29/21, f.32.

(so that as many persons of quality and influence as possible could become officers); another set ordered that volunteers should be formed into separate units (presumably because it was thought that these would be especially reliable in suppressing internal revolt).[12] New lord lieutenants, deputy lieutenants, and officers were soon appointed to replace those nominated by the Rump. The new lord lieutenant of Kent ws commissioned by 10 July, his deputies were appointed by 1 August, and the officers were named by early October.[13]

Within weeks of their appointment, the new officers were seizing suspects and hunting for arms held by disaffected persons, to the dismay of the Presbyterians in the Convention Parliament.[14] The reaction of the deputy lieutenants of Hampshire to the news of Venner's rising on 6 January 1661 was swift (as we can see from the letter-book of Richard Norton, M.P. for that county and one of the local deputy lieutenants). They wrote to their lord lieutenant, describing the numbers of 'unlawfull assemblies . . . under pretence of Worshipping God'; they appointed a rendezvous at which the companies would muster to disperse any rebels; and they issued warrants to search the house of all suspected persons for arms, stating their intention to fill the jails if necessary.[15] Their zeal continued unabated throughout 1661.[16]

The religious element in militia activity at this time can be seen clearly in some of the declarations then drawn up. One addressed to Charles in May 1661 by the officers of the Devon militia condemned all principles and practices which ran contrary to monarchy and episcopacy, adding pointedly that as Caesar had been rendered his due, they hoped that God would be rendered his in the form of a revived Church of England, 'the second built more glorious upon the Foundations of the First'. Similar addresses thanking the king for 'that

[12] *S.P.* 29/26, f.77; 29/8, f.188.

[13] *Twysden Lieutenancy Papers,* op. cit., pp. 11-13; *Parliamentary Intelligencer* (1660), no. 41, 1-8 October, pp. 647-8.

[14] *J.C.*, viii, 175, 184, 187-8, 207-8; *S.P.* 29/18, f.75; 29/23, f.87; *Mercurius Publicus* (1661), nos. 2, 10-17 Jan., p. 31; and 4, 24-31 Jan., pp. 52, 53, 62, 63-4.

[15] Addit. MS. 21,922, ff.245-6; cf. J. R. Westerr., *The English Militia in the Eighteenth Century* (London, 1965), pp. 33-4.

[16] *Mercurius Publicus* (1661), nos. 13, 28 March-4 April, p. 194; 45, 31 Oct.-7 Nov., p. 696.

great Work of reestablishing Episcopacy' and swearing to defend the 'State Civil and Ecclesiastical establisht by Law' were sent from this part of the country at other stages of 1661.[17] There were also special musters with a religious quality. At various places, 29 May 1661—a day of thanksgiving commemorating the king's birthday and his return to England—was marked by a muster and a sermon. At Winchester, the deputy lieutenants and troops were entertained by the prebendaries in the close after the service; both there and at Sandwich the opportunity was taken to burn the Covenant ceremonially.[18] On other occasions the militia turned out to greet a new bishop and conduct him to his lodgings.[19] An item in Norwich chapter's accounts reminds us of an even closer link between church and militia: 'Expenses about Trophies for this Church-company, and for soldiers pay and ammunition'— £61. 6*s.* 11*d.* In 1663 when an attempt was made to seize Dublin castle and there were rumours of further trouble, the bishop of Chester, his chapter, and several clergymen each provided one horse for the militia.[20]

As a result of the new Militia Act passed in May 1662, the militia was to some extent re-organized. But most of the officers appear to have been re-appointed, and certainly their energy did not flag.[21] During the unsettled months of late 1662, the militia gave martial displays in different parts of the country in order to deter dissidents. On his visitation of Lincoln diocese in July, Bishop Sanderson was met by trained bands who fired volleys in his honour.[22] On the eve of St. Bartholomew's Day, the deputy lieutenants of Hampshire arrested two men who had been active supporters of the Commonwealth in Winchester, examined others, intercepted

[17] Ibid., nos. 21, 23-30 May, pp. 325-6: 32, 8-15 August, p. 500; and 18, 2-9 May, pp. 282-3.

[18] *Kingdomes Intelligencer* (1661), nos. 24, 10-17 June, pp. 360-1; 23, 3-10 June, p. 355; see also *Mercurius Publicus* (1661), no. 22, 30 May-6 June, p. 337.

[19] Morley—ibid., no. 37, 12-19 Sept., pp. 588-91; Frewen—Clarendon MS. 77, f.222.

[20] Tanner MS. 134, f.139; J. R. Western, op. cit., pp. 24-5.

[21] *Twysden Lieutenancy Papers*, op. cit., pp. 37-9; for activity in Kent and on the Isle of Wight in June and July, cf. *S.P.* 29/56, f.48, and *Mercurius Publicus* (1662), no. 29, 17-24 July, p. 463.

[22] Ibid., p. 462; for a muster in Nottinghamshire on 19 Aug., see ibid., no. 35, 28 Aug.-4 Sept., p. 584.

the post, and discovered arms in Southampton.[23] Bishop Morley was met by the militia at various points of his visitation in late August and early September; he reported to Clarendon that the militia officers were 'much troubled' by rumours of a proposed indulgence for nonconformists.[24] Another bishop, Roberts of Bangor, was accompanied on his visitation by 'divers worthy, noble and loyall Gentry' including the High Sheriff; one man even combined the role of bishop and lord-lieutenant—at the same time that he was ejecting and replacing Puritan clergy, Bishop Cosin of Durham was also issuing warrants for the arrest of suspects and ensuring that his militia was well officered.[25]

Compared to the apathy of the early seventeenth century or the slackness which had set in by the 1670s,[26] the spirit of the militia was particularly high in the first years of the Restoration. It is surely no accident that this period of ardent gentry interest in the militia coincided with the years in which the 'Clarendon Code' was passed and enforced. On an individual basis many deputy-lieutenants who had grappled with plots and 'Seditious Sectaryes' in their localities were elected to serve as M.P.s in the Cavalier Parliament. Other M.P.s who were not themselves in the militia must surely have been impressed by what they saw and heard in the counties, and by the need (as the Hampshire deputy-lieutenants put it) to make the people 'more conformeable, and . . . better Christians, and Subjects'.[27]

Nowhere was the need greater than in the corporations. Throughout 1662 commissioners appointed by the king under the powers granted him by the Corporation Act were busy ejecting aldermen whose loyalty to the crown and the traditional forms of the church was in doubt. The com-

[23] Addit. MS. 21,922, ff.251-8, 260; for Woodward, cf. B. C. Turner, *Winchester Cathedral Record* (1960), pp. 16-17; for Ellis, cf. *Cal. Rev.*, p. 182.

[24] Clarendon MSS. 77, f.340; 73, f.217; *Mercurius Publicus* (1662), no. 36, 4-11 Sept., p. 605.

[25] Ibid., no. 42, 16-23 October, p. 692; *S.P.* 29/61, f.55; G. S. Thomson, 'The Bishops of Durham and the Office of Lord Lieutenant in the Seventeenth Century', *Eng. Hist. Rev.*, xl (1925), 360-1.

[26] T. G. Barnes, *Somerset 1625-40* (London, 1961), pp. 250, 271; J. R. Western, op. cit., pp. 26-9. For other activity in late 1662, cf. *S.P.* 29/61, f.119; *S.P.* 29/62, f.14, and *Mercurius Publicus* (1662), nos. 39 (pp. 643-4), 45 (p. 733), 48 (pp. 775-6), 49 (p. 797).

[27] Addit. MS. 21,922, f.257.

missions were 'nearly always composed of the leading royalist county gentry of the several counties'; in Kent, four-fifths of the commission were drawn from long established county families, and only one of them (the recorder of Canterbury, Francis Lovelace) actually held office in a Parliamentary borough.[28] The three Kentishmen who were most active on the commission—Sir Thomas Peyton, Sir Edward Hales, and Sir John Tufton—had all been Royalists during the Interregnum; Peyton's manor-house in east Kent had been the centre of Kentish conspiracies against the Commonwealth.[29] Like most of their fellow commissioners, they had played a major part in local government at the Restoration, as J.P.s and in the militia, and like quite a few of them also, they had become tenants of the restored church.[30] Such men were likely to have had little sympathy with the vestiges of Puritan and Parliamentarian influence in the boroughs of their county.

One of the most interesting features of the enforcement of the Corporation Act in Kent is the correlation between the ejections of magistrates and ministers. The commissioners did most of their work between 12 and 29 August 1662,[31] at the same time that several Puritan ministers were forced to leave livings in those boroughs. At Maidstone, for example, six jurats and fourteen councillors were removed on the 12th, and two ministers on the 24th.[32] At Sandwich on the 22nd almost all the old jurats and officers were removed, only days before the ejection of one of the town's ministers took effect.[33] At Dover, one of the incumbents was ejected on the 24th, and three jurats and seventeen councillors on the 25th.[34]

For those predisposed to finding a link between Puritanism and 'corrupt' magistrates there were many opportunities to be proved right. It was the 'constant observation' of the Corporation Act commissioners in Devon that 'in those places

[28] J. H. Sacret, 'The Restoration Government and Municipal Corporations', *Eng. Hist. Rev.*, xlv (1930), 251-2; A. M. Everitt, *The Community of Kent and the Great Rebellion 1640-1660* (Leicester, 1966), p. 322; M. V. Jones, 'The Political History of the Parliamentary Boroughs of Kent, 1642-1662' (London Ph.D. thesis, 1967), p. 220.

[29] Ibid., p. 500; A. M. Everitt, op. cit., pp. 279-80, 283, 303.

[30] Sources as on pp. 180-1 above; and below pp. 197-9.

[31] M. V. Jones, op. cit., p. 223.

[32] Ibid., pp. 223-4, and *Cal. Rev.*, pp. 153, 524.

[33] M.V. Jones, op. cit., pp. 227-8, and *Cal. Rev.*, p. 516.

[34] M. V. Jones, op. cit., pp. 228-9, and Hasted, iv, 119.

where the most factious Ministers had planted themselves they found the Magistracy and People most infected', at Exeter, Dartmouth, Plymouth, Torrington, and Tiverton, for instance. The commissioners not only removed 'corrupt' magistrates, but also decided to levy a fine of one shilling on all who did not go to church, the money thus raised to be given to the poor.[35] The mayor of Reading ejected by the commissioners was probably a relative of a Puritan minister in that town, and was himself alleged to have obstructed the reintroduction of the Prayer Book in Reading, and to have given help to Anabaptists.[36] At Norwich, some aldermen tendered the oaths specified in the Corporation Act went to consult the most eminent of the city's divines before making their decision.[37] At Coventry, Lord Northampton had just finished dismantling the town's fortifications and enforcing the Corporation Act (removing twelve men) when a scurrilous letter was thrown into his lodgings. The letter, he told the king, contained 'the whole spirit of Pagan Presbytery, without the least tincture or mixture of Anabaptists or Quakers Schisme'; by it the king could see that it was the Presbyterians that were 'your onely implacable enemies' because they still 'adored' the Covenant. Northampton also pointed out that the ministers in the two churches in Coventry, John Bryan and Obadiah Grew, were 'transendent in two most excellent qualities ignorance and obstinance', as well as in a third—'dissaffection to the present government both in churche and state'.[38] The bishop of the diocese wrote to Clarendon bemoaning the fact that the two 'seditious preachers of Coventry' were going to stay in the city and that the 'silly people' did not seem to want new ministers appointed.[39] Not far away at Leicester the removal of some non-subscribers by the Corporation Act commissioners led to an attack upon the church on the day when the new mayor was to be elected. The intruders 'abused the Utensils' and stole the surplice, and by such deeds shewed themselves to be 'the right spawn of the Good Old Cause', to

[35] *Mercurius Publicus* (1662), no. 36, 4-11 Sept., p. 601.
[36] Sacret, art. cit., 253.
[37] *Mercurius Publicus* (1662), no. 26, 26 June-3 July p. 406.
[38] Clarendon MS. 77, f.236.
[39] Ibid., f.274.

quote a contemporary newspaper.[40]

By 1663 dissident magistrates and clergymen had been removed from positions of authority but not from the milieu in which they had been active for many years. In some cases, it had proved difficult to find suitable replacements for the ejected aldermen, and in the Parliamentary boroughs of Kent the waning zeal of some of the new aldermen and councillors seems to have allowed the ejected magistrates to regain part of their former influence after 1662.[41] Similarly, there was nothing to stop ejected ministers from staying in their former parishes, and we can tell that the state of the towns was still a cause of concern to J.P.s and church authorities. In the 'catalogue' prepared for the archbishop in 1663, the report on Sandwich was disturbing: the mayor and jurats were not completely reliable, the town was full of sectaries, there was no surplice 'nor any will be indured', and one of the incumbents lately put in preached 'after the Presbyterian modell'. Maidstone was badly infected by Presbyterians and fanatics, while Dover had Quakers, Anabaptists, and an ejected minister holding conventicles.[42]

Together the Corporation Act and the Act of Uniformity had promised much, but it was soon realized that they had not done enough. Many individual M.P.s must have discovered for themselves what conditions were like in the corporations, through their work as commissioners or J.P.s or simply through intercourse with fellow gentry and churchmen. Herein must surely lie the origins of the Conventicle Acts and the Five Miles Act.

The third aspect of the gentry's behaviour to be considered is their prosecution of Puritan clergy, particularly in the period before the Act of Uniformity was passed. Dr. Bosher has suggested that the 'staunch churchmanship' of the Cavalier squires appointed to the bench after the Restoration led to a campaign of persecution from as early as September 1660. The latitude granted by the October declaration (for example in the use of the Prayer Book) does not appear 'to have damped the churchly zeal of the Justices'. Dr. Bosher has

[40] *Kingdomes Intelligencer* (1662), no. 40, 29 Sept.-6 Oct., pp. 665-6.
[41] Sacret, art. cit., 253-5; M. V. Jones, op. cit., pp. 234-9.
[42] Lambeth MS. 1126, pp. 17, 43, 21-2, and see below, p. 196.

discovered one Nottinghamshire J.P., Peniston Whalley, who expressed the view that the king might have granted Puritans an indulgence from the laws of the land as far as he was concerned, but he did not mean that the J.P.s should do the same; Whalley therefore charged the jury to present all incumbents who did not read the Book of Common Prayer. It seems possible, says Dr. Bosher, that the 'campaign was secretly encouraged' by government instructions telling J.P.s to restore the use of the Anglican liturgy 'according to the laws in being'. Persecution of Puritan incumbents was also practiced in another way: grand juries (chosen from the local gentry) laid charges at the local assizes, which resulted in the prosecution of Puritan clergy before the judges on assize.[43] There is evidence for both types of persecution, at quarter sessions and in the charges of the grand juries, but the evidence is incomplete, and should be treated cautiously.

The 'outbreak of prosecutions throughout England' by zealous J.P.s, for example, should not be exaggerated. The quarter sessions records for the early years of the Restoration in the counties of Kent and Hampshire contain not one example of an incumbent being prosecuted for not reading the Prayer Book or for a similar offence.[44] In Surrey, the situation seems to have been different: in 1660 one vicar was indicted for not reading the Book of Common Prayer, and in the closing months of 1661 another nine were charged with failing to use the Prayer Book as ordered in the Acts of Uniformity 5/6 Edward VI and 1 Elizabeth.[45] Furthermore, one minister was arrested and jailed for alleged forcible entry into the church of which he had been incumbent from 1656.[46] But even these prosecutions seem to have had comparatively little effect. The vicar of Farnham jailed for forcible entry recovered considerable legal damages against the justice who ejected him, and, according to Calamy, returned to preach there until August 1662.[47] Of those indicted on charges of not using the Prayer Book only one conformed, while at least eight

[43] Bosher, pp. 200–4.

[44] Kent Recd. Off., *Q/S.B.8, Q/S.B.9, Q/SO E.1., Q/SO W.2;* Hants Recd. Off. *Q.0/4, Q.I.*

[45] *Surrey Records,* vi, 38–9; vii, 110, 112, 149.

[46] Ibid., vi, 127.

[47] Calamy, *Account,* p. 669; *Cal. Rev.,* p. 464.

of the other nine remained in office until their ejection on St. Bartholomew's Day,[48] a pattern which seems to have been repeated among those prosecuted in other counties.[49]

There also seems to be no warrant at all for the idea that in September and October 1660 the government secretly ordered the J.P.s to ensure that the Book of Common Prayer was read. No such instructions have been found, and the notion that there ever were any is not a contemporary one. It seems to have originated in the early eighteenth century when the historian White Kennett made an unwarrantable assumption from a chance remark in a contemporary pamphlet—William Annand's *Panem quotidianum,* printed in London in 1661. In his preface, Annand, a Commonwealth conformist, said that he had been summoned by the local magistrates to deliver a sermon and read prayers at one of their meetings at Bedford early in October 1660; he had hastened to dust off his Prayer Book and obey their oders. The summons to attend this meeting 'for the publick reading of the Liturgy of the Church of England' was mistaken by Kennett for a general order to all Bedfordshire incumbents to use the Prayer Book, and he speculated that in doing this the justices were acting under instructions from the court.

But this cannot have been the case. We can see from a later remark of Annand's that the use of the Prayer Book was still a subject of controversy: he warned the J.P.s that he would be 'assaulted' for 'yielding obedience to your Honours commands in this particular'.[50] It would also have been completely contrary to the tenor of government policy and to the explicit wording of the Worcester House declaration for the government to have issued the instructions envisaged by Kennett.[51] Furthermore, Charles and Hyde often intervened to protect Puritan parish clergy from harassment by over-zealous officials. As Baxter pointed out, the victims of such attacks were 'commonly delivered' when the Presbyterians sought the

[48] *Surrey Records,* vi, 38-9: compare ibid., vii, 110, 112, 149, and *Cal. Rev.*, pp. 391, 408, 347, 134-5, 143-4, 45, 104, 16; the ninth—Bartholomew Clark—is not in *Cal. Rev.* himself, but see Wm. Batho, p. 36.

[49] Ibid., pp. 8, 25, 42, 53-4, 60, 193, 217, 302, 345, 353-4, 373, 414, 418, 480, 495, 527, 549.

[50] Kennett, *Register,* pp. 271, 308-9; W. Annand, op. cit., preface.

[51] See above pp. 8-9, 40; *English Historical Documents 1660-1714*, pp. 369-70.

help of the court.[52] Nor can it be accepted that Peniston Whalley's gloss on the October Declaration in any way confirms Kennett's assumption. A copy of what may have been the original printed version of Whalley's charge to the jury (to present all incumbents who did not use the Prayer Book) is to be found in the state paper collection with certain passages marked, which may suggest that its author had run into trouble for impugning the declaration.[53] Certainly another edition of Whalley's charge omits the whole section in which he had urged the jury to ignore the indulgence granted by the king in October 1660.[54]

It is not being suggested that there were *no* prosecutions of Puritan incumbents at quarter sessions. For the period October 1660 to August 1662 over the country as a whole, A. G. Matthews found evidence for about thirty such prosecutions, usually for not reading the Book of Common Prayer; further research in sessions records may reveal many more cases. But in our dioceses of Canterbury and Winchester few such cases can be traced, and it may be that such prosecutions were fairly localized. It must be more than coincidence that one third of the cases found by Matthews were in Nottinghamshire, the county in which Whalley officiated.[55] Pressure may also have been applied by threats rather than legal charges,[56] but as far as actual prosecutions are concerned, the evidence so far is limited and does not justify the picture of a far-reaching national 'campaign' by 'militant' magistrates drawn by Dr. Bosher.

A similar conclusion may be drawn from an examination of the grand juries' presentments to the judges on assize—the other form of persecution of parish clergy who did not use the Prayer Book or administer the sacrament. The type of assize record that has survived varies considerably from circuit to circuit, as the records of the dioceses of Canterbury and Winchester

[52] *Rel. Baxt.*, Lib. I, Pt. II, para. 132.

[53] *S.P.* 29/34, f. 79.

[54] Bosher, p. 203, n.1.

[55] *Cal. Rev.*, pp. 8, 17, 147, 193, 198, 291, 305, 372, 402, 414, 495, 527 (Nottinghamshire); 53–4, 345, 353–4, 373, 549 (Derbyshire); 113–14 (Leicestershire); 25 (Staffordshire); 60 (Bedfordshire); 91, 217, 480 (Hertfordshire); 418 (Wiltshire); 166, 221, 472 (Middlesex); 42, 302, 396, 407 (Sussex).

[56] See above pp. 43 and 188 (vicar of Farnham).

demonstrate. Hampshire was on the large western circuit, for which no minute books, indictments, depositions, or pleadings for the early 1660s have survived. The only informative document that survives is a bail book for the period 1654–67 which tells us rather inadequately that in the seven counties on the large western circuit over thirty clergymen were bailed to prosecute their traverse (that is to deny the charges against them, presumably charges connected with the Prayer Book) in the assizes held in the autumn of 1661 and in the autumn and winter sessions of 1662 immediately following St. Bartholomew's Day.[57] Surrey, together with Kent and three other counties, was part of the south-eastern circuit; again there are no minute books, depositions, or pleadings, but instead of a bail-book there are clear records of indictments including several charges against incumbents for not using the Prayer Book. If we extract from these materials those cases which affected incumbents in our two dioceses, the total reads as follows: in Hampshire two Puritan incumbents were bound to prosecute their traverse, on charges of not reading the Prayer Book, at the autumn assizes of 1661, and a further five endured a similar fate at the autumn assizes of 1662; in Kent, three Puritan incumbents were indicted in 1661 on charges of not reading the Prayer Book, and one minister faced a second charge of 'pernitiosus et perverse opinionis contempnens Religionem'.[58]

Even if the incompleteness of the records is taken into account,[59] there is no sign of a national surge of assize prosecutions. A. G. Matthews used many (though not all) of the surviving assize records, and also drew on other sources such as the diaries of some of the accused. But over the whole of England and Wales, he could detect only nine assize prosecutions in 1660, fifteen initial prosecutions in 1661, and thirty initial prosecutions in 1662.[60] It is perhaps significant

[57] P.R.O.,Assizes 24/1; for their names and backgrounds, see *Cal. Rev.*, pp. 57–8, 66, 116–17, 121–2, 146–7, 169, 197, 281–2, 285, 304, 311, 426, 451, 452, 492, 523 (Devon); 52, 296, 325, 353, 381, 422 (Somerset); 341, 411–12, 488–9, 499, 515, 519, 551 (Hampshire); 37, 373–4 (Cornwall); 494 (Dorset); 155, 452 (Wiltshire).

[58] Assizes 24/1, ff.94, 100, 106–7 (my foliation); Assizes 35/102, pt. 9, ff.36–8; 35/103, pt. 9 ff.9–10.

[59] The forty indictments mentioned in a report of March 1662 (see below pp. 193–4) are not to be found among existing records.

[60] *Cal. Rev.*, pp. 1, 121, 143, 196–7, 203–4, 257, 304, 406–7, (420?), and 461–2

that the only newspaper reports of assize proceedings against Puritans come from counties on the western circuit, which accounts for nearly two-thirds of the known assize prosecutions of Puritan clergy in the years 1660 to 1662.[61] As in the case of quarter sessions prosecutions, a pattern of localized harassment may emerge.

The true significance of these assize prosecutions lies not in their numbers, but in other aspects—the nature of the allegations, the comments made by the gentry and squires on the grand juries, the actions of the assize judges, and the possible effect of these charges on the Puritan clergy as a group. The charges made against three Kentish incumbents in 1661 were that they had omitted to use the prayers and divine services in the Book of Common Prayer to the detriment of uniformity and in contempt of the king's laws. The insistence on uniformity is noteworthy, since in two cases these charges were made *before* the first bill of uniformity of 1661 had been formulated.[62] The uniformity and the king's laws to which the charges referred were those of Edward VI and Elizabeth, and in their insistence that these laws were valid and had to be enforced the members of the grand jury were expressing the same view as Whalley—the law was above the king's declaration exempting parish clergy from the need to read the Prayer Book. The further charge against Ephraim Bothell, vicar of Hawkhurst, of holding perverse opinions that ran contrary to those of the Church of England as expressed in the Prayer Book,[63] is revealing in a different way, for it shows laymen presuming to decide on doctrinal matters. Perhaps the absence of the church courts' corrective powers was their excuse for this encroachment on ecclesiastical preserves. Certainly one of the clergymen indicted thought that the charges against him were of dubious validity: Nicholas Thoroughgood insisted that he could not be compelled to

(1660); 267-8, 285, 325, 350, 353, 366-7, 381, 411-12, 422, 431, 445, 451-2, 452, 487-8, 494 (1661); 37, 52, 54-5, 57-8, 66, 116-17, 121-2, 146-7, 155, 169, 197, 198-9, 281-2, 290, 296, 304, 311, 341, 362, 373-4, 426, 451, 452, 488-9, 492, 508, 515, 519, 523, 551 (possibly 293, 521) (1662).

[61] See previous note and below pp. 193-4.

[62] Assizes 35/102, pt. 9, ff. 36, 38; the charges were made in March 1661.

[63] Assizes 35/102, pt. 9, f.37.

reply to the charge since the indictment was not sufficient in law.[64]

Although prosecutions for not reading the Prayer Book seem to have been the most common, as in Kent and Hampshire, other charges were made by the grand juries. One Shropshire minister was accused of saying that he would never read the Prayer Book service or administer the sacrament; three incumbents of Staffordshire were accused of not having read 'the book containing the proclamation'—perhaps the one which announced the Restoration; others in the Midlands and North faced more serious charges of seditious words, seditious prayers, or of speaking or preaching against the Prayer Book.[65]

The assizes provided other opportunities for loyal churchmen to express their views. The grand jury of the assize held at Winchester in September 1660 asked the judge to convey their thanks to the king 'for His care in settling Religion according to the Government of the Church' established in the reigns of Elizabeth, James, and Charles 'of ever-blessed Memory'; this form of government 'they unanimously declared, was by Episcopacy'.[66] Similarly, the presentment of the grand inquest at the Devon assizes in April 1661 asked the judges to thank the king for appointing such an eminent and pious bishop, and to bring to his attention the need to enforce the payment of church rates, the observance of the Sabbath, and the prosecution of recusants. The second clause of the presentment is the most interesting:

> Whereas his Majestie's most Candid Indulgence in his Declaration hath not produced the much expected Conformity in divine Service: therefore that some fit expedient may be found to reduce all the Clergy of this Kingdome to the Liturgie, and the same Administration of the Sacraments'[67]

A year later the 'loyal Grand Jury' at Exeter 'formed at least forty Indictments against some eminent Non conformists of

[64] Assizes 35/103, pt. 10, f.86.

[65] *Cal. Rev.*, pp. 1, 121, 362, 451-2 (cf. *Tudor and Stuart Proclamations*, i, no. 3196); 267-8; 54-5, 487-8, 445, 198-9, 420, 431. In several cases, the charges were found to be not proven.

[66] *Parliamentary Intelligencer* (1660), no. 38, 10-17 Sept., pp. 607-8.

[67] *Mercurius Publicus* (1661), no. 15, 11-18 April, pp. 228-9.

the Ministry, for not reading Common-prayer, as by Law they ought'. At the same time, the grand jury complained of the 'sedition and rebellion' taught by some ministers 'justly ejected' in 1660 and now 'travelling about' the country; urged penalties against those who did not attend their parish churches but ran abroad 'to hear factious Ministers'; and presented disaffected persons who had not taken the oath of allegiance but were still in office (petty constables, high constables, and others).[68] These statements in April 1661 and March 1662 not only reflect the gentry's dislike of the Worcester House declaration, but also anticipate the severe tone of the preambles to the acts which constitute the 'Clarendon Code'.

The measures taken by the assize judges seem by contrast very moderate. One or two of the judges may have been more liberal than most of their contemporaries,[69] or perhaps in the heat of the moment they were simply more impartial. Their usual judgement seems to have been to bind those accused of not using the Prayer Book by a surety to appear and prosecute their traverse at the next assizes,[70] a neutral course and one which could be accommodated to any decisions made by Parliament in the meanwhile. In general, though the evidence is far from complete, the accused were not ejected from their livings (the province of ecclesiastical jurisdiction), nor imprisoned or fined, nor as far as is known constrained to read the Book of Common Prayer in their ministrations. The ultimate significance of assize prosecutions lies perhaps not in the number of ejections or 'resignations' which followed, but in the fact that the Puritan clergy were given yet another indication of the feelings of the Anglican gentry towards them. On top of the activity of the militia and the work of the Corporation Act commissioners, there came the harassment by J.P.s and Grand Juries who were anticipating, indeed trying to accelerate, the settlement of the church in the old way. The Act of Uniformity merely confirmed what the Puritan clergy already knew, that there were certain members of the gentry

[68] *Mercurius Publcus* (1662), no. 12, 20-7 March, pp. 189-90.

[69] A. F. Havighurst, 'The Judiciary and Politics in the Reign of Charles II', *Law Quarterly Review*, lxvi (1950), 63-4, 71-2.

[70] E.g. Assizes 24/1 ff.94, 100.

intent on hounding them out of office unless they resumed the old ritual.

It was seen that the number of prosecutions of Puritan clergy in the diocese of Canterbury was small. Nevertheless, the invaluable 'catalogue' of 1663 makes it abundantly clear that the presence of staunchly Anglican magistrates was regarded as a great blessing by the church authorities of that diocese. The 'catalogue' contains many references to the leading members of the laity and analyses their attitude to the church. Captains Newman and Petitt of the parish of St. John's in Thanet were 'both freinds of the Church'; Captains Rooke and Crips at Monkton were 'honest gent. and Justices of Peace', and so on.[71] Not all the comments were favourable: Mr. Fowle was the only gentlemanly person in the parish of Sandhurst, but he was 'not right'; Mr. Diggs (who presented the 'Presbyterian' Cumberland to a Bartholomew living in December 1662) was 'melancholy' and 'cracked'; it was noted also that the mayor and jurats of Sandwich were only 'so so affected'.[72]

It is quite obvious that the authors of the 'catalogue' drew a close link between attendance at church and the presence of some representative of the landed classes in the parish. The earl of Thanet lived in the parish of Hothfield which was very conformable; the parishioners of Mersham came well to church 'by the discretion of the Incumbent, and the Helpe of Sir Norton Knatchbull who lives in the Parish'.[73] In other parishes the lack of a 'freind of the Church' and the meanness of the inhabitants were blamed for the high level of non-conformity. Tenterden was 'A corporate town and not one

[71] Lambeth MS.1126, pp. 6, 36, for these and another captain (Tuck). The frequency of military titles (probably militia ones) is of interest, though many other 'freinds of the Church' held no such title.

[72] Ibid., pp. 38, 10, 17.

[73] Ibid., pp. 37, 30; cf. pp. 32, 36, 42, 55, 56 (Shaddoxherst, Charing, Lenham, Bexley, Penshurst). One could cite cases of poor attendance despite the presence of gentlemen (pp. 9, 17, 35, 37, 51, Beaksbourne, Northbourne, Bethersden and Biddenden, High Halden, and Faversham); also there are examples of good attendance though no person of rank lived in the parish (pp. 3, 8, 13, 25, Milton, Whitstable, Stourmouth, Hastinglegh, and many others). But the authors of the 'catalogue' were clearly convinced by the social formula: gentry equals attendance (cf. pp. 16, 20, 38, Gt. Mongeham, Alkham and Beauxfield, Newenden)-a fitting belief for the county which produced Filmer's 'Patriarcha' with its emphasis on the guiding influence of the gentry.

honest Justice in it'; at Cranbrook there was 'Noe justice nor gentlemen in the parish' and despite the zeal of the incumbent attendance was pitiful.[74] No persons of note lived in the parish of St. Laurence in Thanet which was 'full of Presbyterians of whom the Leader is Johnson the late Minister put out for Non-Conformity'.[75] Even worse, at Benenden the lord of the manor was one of the many Presbyterians in the parish.[76] In cases such as these, the 'catalogue' seems to have had singularly little confidence in the ability of the revived church courts to enforce conformity; instead it carefully detailed the whereabouts of the nearest reliable J.P., or 'freind of the Church'. Under Ashford it records 'Sir Norton Knatchbull a neere Justice, a good freind to the Church'; under Tenterden it notes that Richard Hulse lived nearby 'but hath no power there' to help the incumbent who was daily affronted.[77] At least three of the church's friends were also M.P.s for Kentish constituencies,[78] and if they were as alive as the church authorities were to the number of conventicles being held and the number of ejected Puritan clergy still active in their former parishes, then the drafting of the later articles of the 'Clarendon Code' need occasion little surprise.[79]

A common front against nonconformity was not the only interest shared by the church and the gentry. There was also land, and if the picture presented by bishops and chapters contains but a shadow of the truth, then the restored church adopted a generous leasing policy towards the gentry. Old tenants who had become purchasers in their own defence were charged a reduced fine on their new leases in 1660; other tenants who had been ousted in the revolutionary decades were often restored, again with an abatement of fine in consideration of their sufferings.[80] Tenants in some dioceses were

[74] Ibid., pp. 38, 36.

[75] Ibid., p. 6, and cf. pp. 20, 22, for a similar situation in two parishes near Dover.

[76] Ibid., p. 35.

[77] Ibid., pp. 32, 38.

[78] Hales, Knatchbull, and Peyton.

[79] The 'catalogue' noted the rifeness of nonconformity in places where ejected ministers were still active: Lambeth MS. 1126, pp. 4, 6, 20, 22, 36, 38, 64 (and *Cal. Rev.*, pp. 173, 299-300, 158-9, 226, 253, 346); for other active leaders of nonconformity in 1663 who were probably not beneficed in 1662, see pp. 35, 37-8, 43, 55.

[80] Above pp. 101-3, and Tanner MSS. 141, f.169; 147, f.53; 150, f.24.

allowed to make their own assessment of the estate to be leased, and this valuation was accepted even when the reverend landlords knew that the real value was much higher.[81]

Not all of the church's tenants were well born. The dean and chapter of Canterbury leased a large number of properties to tradesmen and widows—tenements, shops, and messuages in the cathedral city. The chapter of Rochester leased many small properties in Dartford to the families of sailors, at minimal rents and fines.[82] But for the more substantial properties of the church—manors, woods, sizeable estates leased as one unit—large fines were set; fines over £1,000 were quite common, and many others were well over £100.[83] Generally speaking, such sums could be afforded only by the nobility and the richer squires and gentry, though the leasehold tenants of Canterbury chapter did include a sprinkling of London merchants.

That the church in Kent drew its more important tenants from the landed classes could be demonstrated simply by listing the titles and addresses of its lessees. But here a more specific relationship has been sought by comparing the tenants of the church with those gentlemen who held certain offices in Kent in the opening years of the Restoration. The list of tenants has been compiled from the estate records of the archbishop of Canterbury, and the chapters of Canterbury and Rochester; the officers studied were members of the Cavalier House of Commons, Corporation Act commissioners, deputy lieutenants, sheriffs, and J.P.s.[84] Within the limitations imposed by the evidence, the comparison applies

[81] Tanner MSS. 130, f.69; 144, ff.8, 153.

[82] *Z.26* and *Z.27 passim;* Tanner MS. 147, f.10.

[83] In the period Sept. 1660 to Nov. 1661, nine of the chapter of Winchester's tenants paid fines of over £1,000 (the highest was £2,500), and many others paid fines over £100, Traffles's 'Abstracte'.

[84] The evidence for office-holding has been cited above, pp. 180-1, though it is supplemented here by the commission of the peace for 1665 (Kent Recd. Off., *Q/JC. 10*) and *Public Record Office Lists and Indexes No. XI. List of Sheriffs for England and Wales* (reprinted New York, 1963), p. 70. The evidence for landholding is drawn largely from Lambeth Palace Library, *Auditor Phelips's Account of the Revenue of the Archbishoprick of Canterbury 1663/4* (hereafter cited as *Phelips*); Cant. Cath. Chap. Arch. Registers *Z.26* and *Z.27;* and Kent Recd. Off., *DRc/Els.* 3 (abstract of chapter of Rochester leases).

mainly to the years 1661-5. Two further points should be remembered. The office-holders are drawn from the whole county, but the tenants do not include those of the bishop of Rochester whose estate records have not survived; almost certainly some office-holders held land from him. Secondly, estates were not the only properties which the church leased to the gentry, for example individual incumbents leased tithes to the laity; the numbers that follow would probably be higher if these somewhat elusive leases could also be included.[85]

The comparison reveals that at least nine, and possibly ten, of Kent's M.P.s were tenants of the church—both of the knights of the shire and seven (or eight) of the sixteen M.P.s representing Kentish boroughs in the Cavalier Parliament. At least two M.P.s serving constituencies outside Kent were also tenants.[86] Eleven of the nineteen commissioners who took part in the enforcement of the Corporation Act in Kent were tenants of the church,[87] as were ten of the thirteen deputy-lieutenants in 1662.[88] The sheriff of Kent in 1662/3 held land from the archbishop, and the sheriff for 1665/6 later held land from the dean and chapter of Rochester.[89]

A simple correlation of those named on the commission of the peace of 1665 with tenants of the archbishop or chapters produces a figure of about thirty-three tenants among over 100 justices.[90] But since many of those named on the

[85] *Z.26*, ff.105-9, 229-31, for some of these leases.

[86] S. Thos. Peyton, *Z.26*, f.74, *Z.27*, f.96; S. J. Tufton, Cant. Cath. Chap. Arch., Domestic Economy 91, f.4. Phin. Andrewes, *Phelips*, p. 5; Robt. Barnham, *Z.26*, f.79; S. Fran. Clerke, *DRc/Els.* 3, f.34, and */Ele.* 119/1A; S. Edw. Hales, *Z.26*, ff. 37-40, 188; S. Nort. Knatchbull, ibid., ff.29, 229; Fran. Lovelace, ibid., ff.167-8; Edw. Masters, ibid., ff.8, 225. The John Harvey who was M.P. for Hythe may have been a tenant of the chapter of Rochester: *DRc/Els.* 3, f.24. S. Wm. Killigrew, *Phelips*, p. 3; S. Geo. Sondes, ibid., p. 14.

[87] Peyton, Tufton, Clerke, Hales, Knatchbull, Lovelace, Sondes as above; S. Ant. Aucher, *Phelips*, p. 7, *Z.26*, ff.42, 74, 88, 121; S. Edw. Filmer, *DRc/Els.* 3, f.33; S. Wm. Hugessen, Domestic Economy 91, f.4; S. Rog. Twysden, ibid., f.4.

[88] Aucher, Barnham, Hales, Knatchbull, Peyton, Sondes, Tufton, and Twysden as above; Thos., Ld. Culpepper, *Z.26*, ff.76, 211, 244; S. Wm. Swan, *DRc/Els.* 3, f.33.

[89] Nich. Toke, *Phelips*, p. 12; S. Humph. Miller, *DRc/Els.* 3, f.30.

[90] Aucher, Barnham, Clerke, Culpepper, Filmer, Hales, Hugessen, Knatchbull, Masters, Peyton, Sondes, Swan, Tufton, and Twysden as above; Rd. Allen, *DRc/Els.* 3, f.33; S. J. Banks, ibid., f.29; S. Arn. Brames, *Phelips*, p. 12; Geo. Curtois, *DRc/Els.* 3, f. 30; Rd. Duke, *Z.26*, ff.95-7; Ld. Finch, Domestic Economy 91, f.4; Thos. Fludd, *Phelips*, p. 10; Wm. Hamond, ibid., p. 13; Cranmer Harris, ibid., p. 13; S. J. Hendon, *Z.26*, f.162, *Z.27*, f.57; Thos. Hooper, *DRc/Els.* 3, f.32; J. Horsmonden, ibid., f.26; Rd. Marsh, *Z.27*, f.282; Rd. Masters, *Phelips*, pp. 1, 6, 8; S.

commission were courtiers or lawyers who had no other links with the county, while others were inactive for one reason or another,[91] a more realistic comparison would be between those justices who were active on the bench and the tenants of the church in Kent. The sessions papers and order books for the years 1661-4 supply the names of sixty-two J.P.s who seem to have played some part in local administration and justice,[92] and it is possible that twenty-three of these were tenants of the church. The number would almost certainly be higher if we could include the tenants of the bishop of Rochester: in the eastern divison (where ecclesiastical records are very full) about half of the active J.P.s can be shown to have been church tenants, but in the western division (where the records are defective) less than a third can be demonstrated to have held lands from this source.[93]

This survey is by way of being an exploratory venture. The records do not overlap neatly, either chronologically or geographically, and some of the connections which have been drawn are tentative. But within these limitations there does seem to be a significant correlation between office-holding gentry and the tenants of the church. A considerable proportion of those gentlemen who served in Parliament or in their home county had a common interest with the leaders of the episcopal church in preserving its hierarchy and its endowments. As a further illustration of this, we may look briefly at the views of one of these men.

Sir George Sondes was one of those Kentishmen who in the early 1640s had wished to reduce the bishops 'to their pristine function of taking care of the churches'. However, he had soon been alienated by the railing spirit of the Puritans, and had been dismissed from the bench in 1642. He was a great believer in a

J. Mennes, *DRc/Arb.* 1, f.11; S. E. Monyns, *Phelips,* p. 7; Geo. Newman, *Phelips,* p. 1; S. Hen. Palmer, *Z.26,* ff.45-6, *Z.27,* f.68; Duke of Richmond, *DRc/Els.* 3, f.33.

[91] E.g. Clarendon, Albemarle; Finch, Bridgeman, and other crown lawyers. The earls of Southampton and Winchelsea had links with Kent, but were busy elsewhere.

[92] Kent Recd. Off., *Q/S.B.8; Q/S.B.9; Q/SO E.1; Q/SO W.2.*

[93] The figures are twelve out of twenty-five and eleven out of thirty-seven. In the east, Aucher, Brames, Hugessen, Hales, Knatchbull, Rd. Masters, Edw. Masters, Monyns, Newman, Peyton, Sandys; also Lovelace (not on 1665 commission, but cf. *Q/SO E.1,* f.50). In the west, Allen, Banks, Barnham, Clerke, Duke, Fludd, Horsmonden, Swan, Tufton, and Twysden; also Ste. Alcock (not on 1665 commission, but cf. *Q/SO W.2,* f.85, and *DRc/FRb.* 13, f.9).

hierarchical society, and was 'ever for order and government, both in church and state. Parity speaks nothing but confusion and ruin. God is the God of order and therefore of His own courtiers He hath degrees'. For Sondes, it was not only right that there should be hierarchy in the church, but also necessary that the bishops should have a 'certainty of maintenance'.[94] For him, the estates of the church were an essential support of the church's hierarchy and hence of good order and government in society at large. After the Restoration, Sondes took a lease of tithes from the archbishop, was restored to the commission of the peace, was elected to the Cavalier Parliament, and became a deputy lieutenant.

Other bonds between church and gentry were re-forged at the Restoration. Two of the new canons of Canterbury were drawn from well-established Kentish families, John Aucher, and Peter Hardres. The officials appointed by the restored bishops and chapters included many members of the local gentry.[95] But perhaps the most important bonds were those described in previous paragraphs—the friendship, the similarity of outlook, and the financial ties. All of these were renewed soon after the Restoration, and in some ways they may have been even stronger than before; for the events of the revolutionary decades may have made both sides more aware of the identity of their interests.

The more one examines the Restoration church settlement, the more difficult it is to escape the conclusion that the most important single influence upon its shape was the zeal of the gentry for the episcopal Church of England, both in the counties and at Westminster. It was this more than anything else which forced Charles to abandon first the idea of comprehension and then the possibility of a royal indulgence. It was probably this factor too which undermined the morale of the Puritan clergy, so that in August 1662 well over a thousand ministers, despairing of a royal indulgence and surrounded by a gentry which for some time had shown its hostility towards

[94] *The Harleian Miscellany,* ed. T. Park (London, 10 vols., 1808-13), x, 40, 33; A. M. Everitt, op. cit., p. 122.

[95] Hants Recd. Off., *Liber Decimus Quartus Briani Winton;* P. M. Hembry, *The Bishops of Bath and Wells 1540-1640 Social and Economic Problems* (London, 1967), pp. 46-8; *Z.26,* ff.101-4, *Z.27,* ff.38-9.

them, left their livings quietly and resignedly. A newspaper report on the ejection of one nonconformist in Somerset gave no credit to the episcopal authorities for the ejection, or for the rapid institution of a successor. Praise was reserved for the gentry of Somerset, who deserved 'thanks for their care and vigilancy in setling the Church and County according to the Laws established'.[96]

[96] *Mercurius Publicus* (1662), no. 34, 21-28 August, p. 578.

X

CLARENDON AND THE 'CLARENDON CODE'

In the nineteenth century, when the phrase 'Clarendon Code' was probably coined, there was little doubt that the chancellor had been in complete agreement with the swingeing measures associated with his name—the Corporation Act of 1661, the Act of Uniformity of 1662, the first Conventicle Act of 1664, and the Five Mile Act of 1665.[1] The most recent exposition of this view is to be found in Dr. Bosher's account of the Restoration church settlement.[2] Of late, there has been a tendency to qualify the phrase, 'the so-called Clarendon Code', to remind the student of history that these laws may have coincided with Clarendon's period of power but were not drafted or introduced into Parliament by him.[3] Some historians have gone even further. In two brief notes Professor Feiling listed the occasions on which the chancellor was to be found on the side of the Puritan rather than the Anglican angels,[4] and Professor Abernathy in a major reappraisal of Clarendon's role cast even more doubt on the chancellor's commitment to a hard line. Abernathy believes that Clarendon was a moderate, afraid that an exclusively Laudian settlement would drive the king into the 'unco-operating arms of an Anglican church party . . . thrifty, anti-court squires' who would limit his freedom to use his prerogative powers. Charles and Clarendon shared a 'fervent desire to preserve intact all remaining instances of monarchical prerogative', and it was by the exercise of the royal prerogative in

[1] I have not found the phrase in contemporary works, or in the major histories of the period written in the eighteenth century; but in 1904 G. M. Trevelyan could write that these measures were 'called in history after the . . . Earl of Clarendon' (*England under the Stuarts,* London, 1904, p. 341). Cf. J. Stoughton, *History of Religion in England*, op. cit., iii, 247-8, 364-7. Hyde was created earl of Clarendon in 1661, but for the sake of convenience he will be referred to as Clarendon throughout this chapter.

[2] Bosher, pp. 278-82 and *passim*.

[3] *English Historical Documents 1660-1714*, p. 360; cf. D. Ogg in *New Cambridge Modern History Vol. V*, ed. F. L. Carsten (Cambridge, 1964), 306.

[4] *Eng. Hist. Rev.*, xlii (1927), 407-8, and xliv (1929), 289-91.

ecclesiastical affairs that they endeavoured to secure a more comprehensive settlement or at least an indulgence for moderate Puritans.[5] More recently, Dr. Witcombe has tried to reconcile the conflicting views of Abernathy and Bosher by suggesting that Clarendon may have been a moderate in the early years, up to about 1663, but that his views changed when it became clear that a majority in the Commons were resolute opponents of toleration.[6]

It must be confessed that Clarendon has made it very difficult for us to read his mind. As chancellor he was called upon to conciliate the various factions who could be of service to the king; to this task he brought a formidable intellect and a remarkable propensity for dissimulation. In the spring of 1661, for example, he was still cultivating the impression in Baxter's mind that he was an ally of the moderate Puritans, and he was also in correspondence with the Catholic earl of St. Albans hinting that the new Parliament might be lenient towards his co-religionists. But at the very same time he was urging Orrery in Ireland and Middleton in Scotland, in terms which matched the aggressive mood of both men, to do all that they could to hasten the end of Presbyterianism in their countries.[7] This ability to be all things to all men makes it hard to see where public duty ended and private conscience began. The same applies to his public statements—speeches to Parliament, draft declarations and provisos, and writings intended for publication—in all of which we may detect a constant striving after effect which now acts as a screen to conceal his more intimate thoughts from us.

It cannot be doubted that Clarendon was a deeply religious man. During the periods of inactivity forced on him by two periods of exile, he reflected on the mysteries of the Christian faith, and wrote contemplative polemical works.[8] But

[5] Abernathy, 'English Presbyterians', p. 91 and *passim*.

[6] D. T. Witcombe, *Charles II and the Cavalier House of Commons* (Manchester, 1966), p. 211. The most recent and perceptive survey of Clarendon's career is to be found in Professor H. R. Trevor-Roper's tercentary lecture *Edward Hyde, Earl of Clarendon* (Oxford, 1975).

[7] *Rel. Baxt.*, Lib. I, Pt. II, paras. 152-6, 170; Clarendon MS. 74, ff.311, 297, 290-3.

[8] E.g. *Contemplations and reflections upon the Psalms of David*, printed in *Miscellaneous Works* (London, 1751); *Animadversions upon a Book entitled Fanaticism* (1673), and *Essays moral and entertaining* (1815).

even these do not provide us with a definitive guide to his religious standpoint, for his devotional writings seem to have contained a different emphasis from his political or historical works. In the former, he tended to dwell on the pure and unalterable essentials of saving faith, an idea he derived from the latitudinarian Tew Circle, of which he had been a member in the 1630s, and by which he was clearly still influenced in some of the polemical works written during his second exile. His political works, and in particular his history of the civil wars and his autobiography, however, were pervaded by a different notion—Religion of State, the political need for religious unity in a state.[9] Which of these influenced him most strongly during the early 1660s it is not easy at first sight to say.

In this chapter, particular weight will be placed on two sources, letters written by Clarendon to close friends, and his autobiography, and a few words about both of these may be justified. Daily contact with most of his confidants at court rendered correspondence superfluous for long periods, but there were a few occasions when this was not so, and the letters which have survived from these periods repay close attention. There are, for example, the letters written to Morley, Barwick, and Cosin in the early months of 1660 before they were all re-united in London in the spring, and those written to the duke of Ormonde after he had left London to take up the lord lieutenancy of Ireland in July 1662. The latter are of particular interest because we know that Clarendon felt it necessary to turn his more controversial comments into cypher; in one letter, Clarendon went so far as to insist that the all-powerful duke should perform the tiresome chore of decyphering himself so that not even his private secretary should see what Clarendon had said.[10] It is surely in letters such as these that we come closest to a frank statement of Clarendon's views.

Clarendon's autobiography has come in for much criticism, a certain amount of it justified. It is true that there are many factual errors in the account, as Professor Abernathy and Dr.

[9] B. H. G. Wormald, *Clarendon: Politics, History and Religion* (Cambridge, 1951), pp. 264–76, 303–7.

[10] Carte MS. 47, f.1.

Witcombe have pointed out.[11] But in fairness to the chancellor the conditions under which it was written should be borne in mind. Clarendon's autobiography was written in two stages; the first part, known as the *Life,* covered the period until 1660, and the second the *Continuation,* took the story from the Restoration to his fall in 1667. The *Continuation* was not started until 1672, at a time when Clarendon's health was poor and he had only months to live; moreover, he had only a fraction of the documents necessary for such an undertaking at his disposal.[12] One should not expect, therefore, to find unerring accuracy of detail, but rather a spirited reconstruction of what was said and done. It is in fact a tribute to the chancellor's sustained mental vigour that the accuracy of so many of the details in this lengthy work can be confirmed from other sources.

There are more serious objections to the use of the autobiography. In his lonely exile, Clarendon fell prey to two temptations—to hide the truth about the king's strong attraction to Catholicism, and to exonerate his own reputation by presenting a judicious selection of facts which would justify his every action in office. In writing his autobiography, Clarendon tells us, he was resolved to 'say Nothing on his own Behalf and for his own Vindication, that might in the least degree reflect upon his Majesty'.[13] Now Clarendon knew for a certainty that Charles leaned strongly towards Catholicism, but he could not admit this if he was to retain hope of a royal pardon and a return to England; it would have been particularly indiscreet to broadcast his suspicions in 1672, just after Charles has issued his declaration of indulgence. The decision to obscure the king's true religious sympathies, however, prevented Clarendon from giving a perfectly frank account of royal policy. Thus in the autobiography there is no trace of Charles's cynical attempts to confound the rival Protestant groups in 1660, nor of the obstinacy with which he pursued better treatment for Catholics. Instead there is the

[11] Abernathy, 'English Presbyterians', pp. 86, 89-90; D. T. Witcombe, op. cit., pp. 21, 26, 29, 43, 57.

[12] C. H. Firth, 'Clarendon's "History of the Great Rebellion" ', *Eng. Hist. Rev.*, xix (1904), 246-62, 464-83, describes the genesis of the autobiography.

[13] Clarendon, *Life*, iii, 905.

polite fiction that Charles was devoted to the faith of his martyred father; it was only when evil men (Clarendon's rivals) at court exploited Charles's compassionate nature that he appeared to deviate from this position. It must be conceded that this is a distortion of the facts, but the bias is at least consistent, and provided that it is always taken into account does not diminish the value of the account too much.

The same may be said of the other bias in the *Continuation,* the special pleading on Clarendon's own behalf. The *Continuation* is an avowed work of self-justification written to 'vindicate himself from those Aspersions and Reproaches which the Malice of his Enemies had cast upon him', to prove his innocence to his children and friends and probably to a wider audience as well.[14] The result is a work of uneven texture; long passages are devoted to refuting the charges made against him while in office, but little is said of matters in which his role was uncontroversial. Furthermore, the impartiality of the *History of the Rebellion* is much less evident in the *Continuation,* with its fulsome references to his own political perspicacity, moral rectitude, devotion to duty, and financial disinterestedness, and the persistent insinuation that those courtiers with whom he disagreed on matters of policy were disloyal, immoral, and irreligious.[15] With all its faults, however, the *Continuation* does have a certain internal logic: it consists of a picture of Clarendon as he would have liked to be remembered, as a great minister and a loyal son of the episcopal Church of England. In harsh reality, the civil wars and then the heterodox opinions of Charles II had robbed him of this accolade, but he could still dream of what might have been. His autobiographical technique was not to manufacture blatant untruths (which as a historian he knew might be exposed in later years); it was rather to suppress unhappy memories and to present a judicious selection of facts with some basis in reality. In the case of the church settlement he is clearly trying to exonerate himself in the eyes of his staunchest supporters, the clergy and laity of the Anglican church; he omits to mention many of the things he said and did as part of the king's schemes for comprehension or indulgence, but

[14] Ibid., and ii, 3.

[15] Ibid., ii, 9-12, 43-5, 49-50, 76-92, 282-3, 296-7, 359-64, 468-75.

records in detail the occasions when he urged Charles to restore the episcopal church to its old position. If he does mention some of his manoeuvres to help the Puritans, as in the summer of 1662, it is to explain that the church party did not then know 'the Engagement that was upon him'.[16] This preoccupation does, of course, cast some doubts on the accuracy of his account, but again the bias is consistent, so that measures may be taken to counter its effect. In the following pages, it has been assumed that where Clarendon chose to mention an incident there is likely to have been some basis in reality, even if it is not the full picture that has been given. No great weight has been placed upon such testimony, however, unless there is other strictly contemporary evidence to confirm its general tenor. In practice, many of his statements *are* supported by other sources, which is why, flawed as it is, the *Continuation* must not be dismissed out of hand.

One of the earliest opportunities to see Clarendon's mind at work is in the early months of 1660. The letters which he wrote to his close allies, George Morley, John Barwick, and John Cosin, in March and April 1660 leave little doubt that he was then anxious to recover as much of the old ecclesiastical order as was possible. On the subject of Morley's overtures to the moderate Presbyterians in March, he wrote to Barwick: 'I hope no Arts or Artifices are omitted to dispose them, for their own Sakes, as much as is possible to repair the Ruins they have made'.[17] It may be true that in the early months of 1660 Clarendon was prepared to countenance one or two concessions to the Puritans, and to admit that some of their moderate leaders might undergo a genuine conversion to 'Piety towards the Church',[18] but there were good reasons for this. In the first place, the situation was then so unsettled that it would have been impossible to insist on a full restoration of the episcopal church at once.[19] Secondly, Clarendon's return from exile and his continued tenure of office in the face of determined Presbyterian opposition depended solely on his

[16] Ibid., ii, 139–43, 288–306; cf. Abernathy, 'English Presbyterians', pp. 82–4, 85–6.
[17] Barwick, p. 514.
[18] Ibid., p. 515; note his concern about others who were only 'willing to appear converted' for their own ends.
[19] Chapter I above; cf. Clarendon, *Life*, ii, 280–1.

retaining the goodwill of the king; to have appeared as anything but an enthusiastic and obedient agent of royal policy would have been fatal. If Charles sought a 'meeting in the Midway' between episcopalians and Presbyterians, then Clarendon had to follow suit—at least in public. If Charles indicated that Morley should offer the Presbyterians' leaders 'present good preferments in the Church', then Clarendon had to convey that message, though in doing so he added an anxious rider of his own: 'But in my own Opinion, you should endeavour to win over those, who being recover'd will have both Reputation and Desire to merit from the Church, than be over solicitous to comply with the Pride and Passion of those, who propose extravagant Things'.[20] For Charles, these conciliatory gestures towards the Puritans represented a genuine attempt to effect a rapprochement between the two sides. But from Clarendon's correspondence it can be seen that both he and the staunch episcopalians in his circle put quite a different construction upon these moves. Clarendon clearly regarded these concessions as a means of creating what he termed a 'schism' between moderate and obdurate Presbyterians,[21] a schism which (he told Cosin) would ensure that 'the Church will be preserved in a tollerable condition, and by degrees recover what cannot be had at once'.[22] Though his energies were being channelled into working for a compromise settlement for the king, his personal resolution remained to 'repair the Ruins' of the episcopal church as far as was possible.

The summer and autumn of 1660 must have been a period of disillusion for Clarendon. He had known for some time that Charles was very sympathetic towards the condition of his Catholic subjects. He was also aware that Charles was prepared to barter religious concessions for political help; as chancellor in exile he had personally handled most of these negotiations and probably regarded them as the very stuff of diplomacy.[23] It must have come as quite a shock therefore to realize how far Charles was prepared to go in order to obtain

[20] Bosher, pp. 111-12, 140; Barwick, p. 525.
[21] Ibid., p. 514.
[22] Clarendon MS. 71, f.221.
[23] See above p. 25.

greater toleration for Catholicism. As the summer advanced and the surviving members of the Laudian church began to despair, it became increasingly obvious that Charles was not going to restore the old order, but was searching for a novel form of church government which would balance the Puritan and episcopalian elements in the church; if he succeeded, he would simultaneously strengthen his political power and increase the chances of toleration for the Catholics. Like the loyal retainer that he was, the chancellor assisted at the birth of this new model of church government. He may even have played a part in persuading some of his friends, such as Morley and Nicholas, to express their joy at its arrival (though if he tried to persuade Cosin, he clearly failed).[24] But underneath this facade, Clarendon must have been seriously disturbed. Though no letters to close friends survive from this period, there are several indications that he was chafing at the direction which royal policy was taking.

Clarendon's underlying hostility to the scheme for modified episcopacy can be gauged from a comparison of his original draft for the Worcester House declaration with the finished article. The first draft contained several sharp phrases which if not downright offensive to the Puritans were decidedly tactless. Clarendon suggested, for instance, that those Englishmen in favour of the use of ceremonies were 'we believe much Superiour in Number and Quality' to those who did not. Those who thought the Church of England was 'overburthened with Ceremonies' had obviously not attended the services of the reformed churches abroad (as Clarendon had done on occasions); they were so lacking in ceremonial as to constitute an 'absence of Devotion', nay a 'great and scandalous Indecency'. The Book of Common Prayer, he asserted, was the 'best we have seen' with very wholesome rules on different aspects of worship, and the surplice had 'for so many Ages' before the present one been accepted as a 'most decent Ornament' for the clergy.[25] Predictably the Presbyterians took exception to these and other phrases in the draft, and Charles

[24] T. H. Lister, *Life . . . of Clarendon*, op. cit., iii, 110-11; *S.P.* 77/33, f.129; W. Bates, *Works* (London, 1723), p. 725.

[25] Compare *Rel. Baxt.*, Lib. I, Pt. II, para. 105 with the final declaration in *English Historical Documents 1660-1714*, pp. 265-70.

removed them all from the final declaration.

There is another indication of Clarendon's hostility to the scheme in a letter written by George Morley just after the penultimate meeting on the Worcester House declaration. We learn from this that at that meeting Clarendon had put forward two arguments which, if adopted, would have made it very difficult if not impossible for the Presbyterians to have accepted the document. He sided with the bishops in their reluctance to accept Presbyterian ordination as being valid for the cure of souls in the restored episcopal church; and he expressed the view that incumbents who had not been legally instituted, that is by a bishop, had no right to the tithes of the living which they were serving.[26] Both notions ran counter to the king's hopes for a broadly based parish clergy, and significantly neither was pressed at the last meeting of all. This meeting provides another clue to Clarendon's attitude, for it seems clear that Charles deliberately prevented his chancellor from attending it, fearing that he might object to the further concessions which were made to the Presbyterians on that occasion. Instead Charles chose two moderate Presbyterian laymen, Holles and Annesley, to arbitrate between the Presbyterian and Anglican clergymen, and the declaration took its final and very moderate shape.[27] It is hardly surprising that Clarendon's comments on the declaration in the *Continuation* are hostile.[28]

It seems clear that Clarendon doubted the wisdom of allowing so many Puritan clergy to remain in office in the first two years of the Restoration. In the *Continuation* he gives a very one-sided description of these ministers: he accuses them of having incited the civil war, of having brought about the deaths of sequestered clergy by their harsh treatment of them, and of endeavouring 'to infuse . . . Sedition into the hearts of their several Auditories' in the early years of the Restoration.[29] This account is manifestly unfair to the great majority of the Commonwealth clergy who continued to serve after the

[26] T. H. Lister, *Life . . . of Clarendon*, op. cit., iii, 110.

[27] See above p. 20.

[28] Clarendon, *Life*, ii, 141-3; he suppresses embarrassing details (his authorship of the first draft, the 'other paper' which could have led to toleration for Catholics) and confines his comments largely to the ultimate failure of the scheme.

[29] Ibid., ii, 15, 142, 282, 305, 398.

Restoration, but it is probably an accurate reflection of Clarendon's attitude to them at the time, as can be seen from some of his public statements in 1660 and 1661. Speaking in Parliament on the occasion when the Act for Settling Ministers became law, he conceded that the measure had the virtue of gratifying 'many worthy and pious Men' who had helped to bring about the king's return, but he then went on to suggest that the act had also undoubtedly pleased 'some, who did neither contribute to His coming in, nor are yet glad that He is in. How comes it else to pass, that he receives such frequent Information of seditious Sermons, in the City and in the Country'.[30] A few weeks later (as we have just seen) he expressed the view that reordination and episcopal institution should be preconditions of the confirmation of Commonwealth clergy.[31] Again in May 1661 he made a speech that contradicted the line taken by the king. He first drew a distinction between moderate and extreme dissenters, and suggested that Parliament should prepare different remedies for their patients' different maladies. For the fanatics he had no mercy: Parliament must be prepared to take vigorous measures against the seditious preachers who were 'repeating the very Expressions and teaching the very Doctrine, they set on-foot in the Year 1640'. 'If you do not provide for the thorough quenching these Firebrands; King, Lords, and Commons, shall be their meanest Subjects, and the whole Kindled into one general Flame'.[32] Such warmth was perhaps acceptable in the wake of Venner's Rising and in view of the urgent need to settle the king's revenue and the militia. What was more significant was the treatment which Clarendon advocated for the more moderate dissenters on this occasion. In the previous September, Charles had welcomed an Act for Settling Ministers which had contained no tests of orthodoxy,[33] and in October he had issued a declaration which specifically dispensed with the need for parish clergy to take any oaths which offended their consciences. However, this was not the line

[30] *J.L.*, xi, 175.

[31] See previous paragraph.

[32] *J.L.*, xi, 242-3; cf. a similar phrase about the clergy and 1640 in Clarendon's letter to Orrery a few weeks earlier, Clarendon MS. 74, f.297.

[33] Anabaptists were excluded, but they were presumably to be identified by common fame rather than by a specific test.

taken by Clarendon in May 1661, for he urged that:

> If the present Oaths have any Terms or Expressions in them a tender Conscience honestly makes Scruple of submitting to, in God's name let other Oaths be formed in their Places . . . but still let there be a Yoke: Let there be an Oath, let there be some Law, that may be a rule to that Indulgence, that, under Pretence of Liberty of Conscience, Men may not be absolved from all the Obligations of Law and Conscience.[34]

It is a tribute to the force of Clarendon's argument or to his sympathy with the outlook of the Anglican gentry that the oath did in fact become the cardinal device of the Cavalier Parliament in all its religious legislation from 1661 to 1678, despite the king's efforts to prevent this.

The following year, 1662, should have witnessed the fulfillment of all Clarendon's hopes for the complete re-establishment of the traditional Church of England, but instead it placed him in a further quandary. From the moment in November 1661 when the king admitted that the settlement of the church had proved too hard for him and handed it over to an intolerant Parliament, Clarendon's hopes must have risen. But the king had not changed his policy, merely his tactics, and when he began a rearguard action against the severity of the bill of uniformity in the early months of 1662, Clarendon was expected to participate in the fighting. As always, the chancellor did his duty. He drafted provisos to the bill, and managed to persuade some of the bishops who were moderates such as Reynolds and Gauden, and some who were susceptible to his influence such as Morley and perhaps Sheldon, to vote for measures which were not in the best interests of the episcopal church. But his task was becoming more difficult: Cosin and a few other bishops openly opposed this tampering with the bill, and the Commons would not countenance the Lords' modifications.[35] The chancellor was finding it increasingly difficult to run with the royal hare and hunt with the Cavalier hounds.

Indeed, there are some indications that the strain of pursuing a policy which in his heart he deplored began to tell

[34] *J.L.*, xi, 242.
[35] Abernathy, 'English Presbyterians', pp. 83–4.

in the summer of 1662. A minor incident which must have occurred in late May suggests that his usual equanimity was disturbed. For some time the chancellor had been especially polite to Richard Baxter, perhaps in the hope that he might yet accept the king's offer of a bishopric, or at the least incline his fellow moderates to support royal policy. On 25 May Baxter announced publicly that he was surrendering his pulpit, and a few days later went to see Clarendon on a matter of business (to do with the New England Corporation). In so far as his duty lay in furthering royal policy, Clarendon was bound to press Baxter to re-consider his decision. But instead Clarendon berated Baxter for being proud and factious; he accused him of preaching humility but not practising it, and cited particular instances of his rudeness in the past to Dr. Earle and Bishop Morley. The author of one version of this incident suggested that 'for all his pretentiones' the chancellor was really in favour of the ejection of the Puritan clergy.[36]

During the three months which followed the passage of the Act of Uniformity, two attempts were made to prevent its enforcement—the first in early June, and the second in late August. The origins of these attempts are still shrouded in mystery. It can be shown that in late May or early June, Clarendon received a Presbyterian delegation and promised to pass their petition to the king. There is also a supposition that at the council meeting which discussed this petition on 10 June the chancellor gave a grudging approval to a scheme for a three month suspension of the act, though in the end the manoeuvre was defeated by opposition from the lawyers present. It can also be demonstrated that in August Clarendon and Albemarle, with the king's full approval, invited a few leading dissenters to petition for a royal indulgence. Again the scheme was blocked in council, this time by the solitary bishop present, Sheldon of London, with some help from the duke of York; and it is clear from Sheldon's letter to Clarendon dated 30 August that he had been surprised and upset by the chancellor's support for the scheme at the council meeting two days before.[37]

[36] *Rel. Baxt.*, Lib. I, Pt. II, para. 269; Carte MS. 31, f.532. Cf. Clarendon's speech of 19 May criticizing the 'Frowardness and Pride' of some of the Puritan clergy (*J.L.*, xi, 476).

[37] Abernathy, 'English Presbyterians', pp. 85–6.

Was Clarendon the architect of these two designs, or simply the agent of royal policy? There is a passage in the *Continuation* which almost certainly refers to the first attempt to bypass the Act of Uniformity. He states that the council met at Hampton Court (the August attempt took place at Whitehall); he says that there were bishops present (whereas there was only one bishop present on 28 August); also present was the duke of Ormonde (who left England in July); he further states that the project was a suspension of the act for three months (whereas in August the aim seems to have been dispensation for individual dissenters).[38] It seems difficult to believe that this passage is a complete tissue of lies, as far as the delineation of his own attitude to the June attempt is concerned. There are the usual traces of expiation: he is describing the incident because at the time the bishops did not understand what he was doing; the idea was not his, but the work of evil men who had too easy access to the king. However, Clarendon is quite adamant that he did his utmost to try to dissuade the king from attempting to circumvent the act. It was only when Charles 'required' him not to oppose the scheme and bade him 'think of the best Way of doing it' that he grudgingly gave way.[39] Charles was clearly in an unusually masterful mood; just how forceful he could be in overriding his chancellor in the summer of 1662 will be seen shortly in the Lady Castlemaine affair. Clarendon had to obey, though his zeal for the episcopal church 'never declined in the least Degree'.

By itself, this passage cannot be accepted as a definitive account of Clarendon's attitude towards the June attempt. There is, however, one piece of evidence which may incline us to accept its tenor. In April 1663, Clarendon wrote a cypher note to Ormonde in which he referred to 'that passion, which I expressed when we were last together with the King at Hampton Court'.[40] There can be little doubt from the context in which he then wrote, after yet another attempt to undermine the Act of Uniformity had been made against Clarendon's advice, that what had provoked him to such anger

[38] The reference to Albemarle's role in this affair may have been a mistake for their joint activity in the August attempt, or it is possible that the duke was party to both attempts.

[39] Clarendon, *Life*, ii, 299–305.

[40] Carte MS. 47, f.45.

ten months earlier was the way in which Charles had listened to councillors not noted for their enthusiasm for the revived Church of England, rather than to his senior and more orthodox advisers. Clarendon must have been particularly upset if he expected Ormonde to remember the incident ten months later.

On only one occasion does Clarendon seem to have moved a shade closer to the king's more liberal policy of his own accord, and that was late in August 1662. This was the only occasion after the Restoration on which the chancellor wrote to a close friend in terms suggesting less than absolute commitment to a hard line towards dissenters. We cannot be certain exactly what Clarendon said in defence of the indulgence project on 28 August, but the general conclusion to be drawn from two letters written shortly afterwards is that at that particular juncture he doubted the wisdom of a rigorous enforcement of the Act of Uniformity. On 1 September, he wrote to Ormonde:

> The very seveare execution of the Acte of uniformity which is resolved on, may I feare, add more fewell to the matter that was before combustible enough: But wee are in, and must now proceede with steddynesse, and so must you; and I wish I were as confident, that wee shall do so, as that you will.[41]

Morley's letter of 3 September was probably written in reply to a note sent by Clarendon just after the council meeting on the 28th. Morley expressed surprise that the chancellor 'should have such sad apprehensions, who are not naturally apt to be . . . affected with them'. He also gave various reasons for not granting an indulgence (which he was under the impression had been demanded by the Presbyterians rather than promoted by the chancellor). He urged his old friend to 'resume your old Courage and your old cheerfullness, for Certainly if we be not wanting to ourselves God will not forsake us in soe good a cause as this'.[42] It should be noted that neither letter implies that Clarendon had been converted to the more irenic views of the king, merely that he had doubts about the political and military wisdom of enforcement at that time.

[41] Ibid., f.3.
[42] Clarendon MS. 77, f.340.

Morley was clearly under the impression that the chancellor was still a staunch ally of the church party, and Clarendon's letter to Ormonde refers to his intention to 'proceede with steddynesse' rather than seek another means of circumventing the act.

What was the reason for the chancellor's temporary adoption of a more indulgent line towards the Puritans? It is difficult to be sure, but the answer would seem to be that from May to August Clarendon experienced a growing sense of isolation, and that to counter this he shifted a little closer to the king's position. Clarendon's efforts to undermine the Act of Uniformity in Parliament in March, and then in council in June, had alienated many of his natural allies among the church party and episcopate, without winning any new friends among the Puritans. In July he became even more isolated when his old friend and ally in council, Ormonde, left for Ireland.[43] What was even more disturbing was that his relations with the king were becoming very strained, and that Charles was looking elsewhere for advice. It must have come to Clarendon's attention by June, if not earlier, that a personal enemy of his, the earl of Bristol, and a potential rival, Sir Henry Bennet, had the king's ear. Bristol was touting a scheme to modify the Act of Uniformity devised by the Low-Church Bishop Gauden, while Bennet, at the king's request, drew up a memorandum in May or June on what measures should be taken next. There is a copy of this memorandum in the Clarendon state paper collection with a contemporary endorsement,[44] but such second-hand knowledge must have been galling for one who by nature preferred to lead rather than to follow.

There were other reasons for the growing tension between Charles and Clarendon at that time. The decision to sell Dunkirk to the French was taken against Clarendon's advice (or so he insists in his autobiography), but it was on to the chancellor's capable shoulders that the king thrust the burden of the final negotiations.[45] Charles and Clarendon also came

[43] Clarendon, *Life*, ii, 304–5; Carte MS. 47, f.11.

[44] Clarendon MS. 76, ff.150–3. The collection also includes copies of Gauden's letters to Bristol (Clarendon MS. 77, ff.50–3), but these appear to be later copies from Brit. Lib., Birch MS. 4104, ff.341–4.

[45] Clarendon, *Life*, ii, 383–91; Carte MS. 47, f.11; cf. index of *Calendar of*

into conflict over the king's attempt to appoint a royal mistress, Lady Castlemaine, to a position in the new queen's bedchamber. The chancellor tried to dissuade the king, pointing out how much scandal the move would cause, but in reply he received one of the most masterful, and lengthy, letters that Charles ever wrote:

> I thinke it very necessary to give you a little good councell . . . least you may thinke that by making a further stirr in the businesse you may deverte me from my resolution, which all the world shall never do . . . You know how true a frinde I have been to you . . . if you desire to have the continuance of my frindship, medle no more with this businesse.[46]

Twice in this note, written in June or July, Charles indicated that anyone who opposed this scheme or was unfriendly to his mistress would be his lifelong enemy. Clarendon was in a quandary. He could not condone Charles's behaviour, and he refused to allow his own wife to re-pay a visit by 'the Lady', much to the king's annoyance.[47] But on the other hand he could not afford to lose the king's favour, and so throughout the summer he tried to reconcile the queen to the appointment of this rival to a position in her bedchamber.[48] This pill must have tasted the more bitter in that Lady Castlemaine, a recent convert to Catholicism, was the 'fiercest solicitor' the Puritans had in their requests for an indulgence in August 1662. What difficulty Clarendon had in swallowing it can be gauged from his letters to Ormonde, usually in cypher on the subject of 'the Lady'.[49]

To add to his other worries, there were particularly insistent rumours of risings planned to coincide with St. Bartholomew's day. Although not above using such rumours for political ends if the occasion demanded, Clarendon seems to have taken the reports seriously on this occasion, as the gloomy tone of his letters to Ormonde and Morley indicates.[50] This is not altogether surprising, for even friends of toleration such as

Clarendon State Papers, ed. O. Ogle *et al.*, vol. v, *s.v.* Dunkirk.

[46] Brit. Lib., Lansdowne MS. 1236, f.128.

[47] Clarendon, *Life,* iii, 683–4.

[48] Ibid., ii, 317–40.

[49] Carte MS. 32, f.3.

[50] Carte MS. 47, ff.1, 3, and Morley's reply Clarendon MS. 77, f.340.

Bennet and Coventry occasionally believed in the reality of the threat of rebellion.[51] For Clarendon in August 1662, this threat must have delivered a final blow to his wavering self-confidence, and against his better judgement he decided to support the August indulgence attempt. After all this heart-searching, it was ironic that the attempt failed. The failure simply compounded Clarendon's misery; once again he had offended the bishops, but no compensating gains had been made for the Puritans, who at once suspected that a trick had been played on them.[52] It was at this point that Clarendon wrote his woeful letters to his friends, letters which should be seen as the product of a crisis in his fortunes rather than a shift in his basic beliefs.

As the threat of rebellion receded and Charles became less distant, some of Clarendon's self-confidence returned. On 30 September, he lost almost the last of his Anglican allies in office, when the aging secretary of state Sir Edward Nicholas was replaced by the ambitious crypto-Catholic Sir Henry Bennet. Yet Clarendon was able to put a brave front on this, and he even chid the 'good old man' for spreading the rumour that he had been removed from office against his will (which was essentially true).[53] Clarendon wrote to Ormonde that speculation about further changes in office in the near future was unfounded; the king had taken pains to show that his confidence in the chancellor was unimpaired. Clarendon was still uneasy, however; in cypher he indicated how worried he was by the king's erratic behaviour, and how sorely he missed the support of Ormonde—'that faithful bosome I had to discharge my self into'.[54]

Shortly afterwards, Clarendon fell seriously ill, and for several weeks he was unable to leave Worcester House. From mid November 1662 to mid March 1663 he did not attend the Privy Council once.[55] It is more than likely, however, that what had started as a genuine ailment was later used as an

[51] Clarendon MS. 76, ff.150-3; D. T. Witcombe, op. cit., p. 34, n. 4, p. 36.

[52] Bosher, pp. 261-2, and Carte MS. 32, f.3; Clarendon MS. 77, f.319: Bodl. Lib., MS. Rawlinson Letters 109 f.87.

[53] Carte MS. 47, ff.373, 14.

[54] Ibid., f.11.

[55] P.R.O., *P.C.* 2/56 ff.219-335; Abernathy, 'English Presbyterians', p. 87.

excuse to avoid involvement in Charles's latest attempt to breach the Act of Uniformity. This consisted of a declaration (issued on 26 December 1662) proposing that the king's prerogative power of granting indulgences to individual dissenters should be confirmed by Parliament; two months later a bill to implement the declaration was introduced into Parliament. The events of the winter of 1662-3, and in particular of March 1663, were to produce another crisis in Clarendon's fortunes, and we must pause a moment to examine them more closely.

A few years ago, Professor Abernathy discovered a draft defence of the December declaration prepared by Clarendon, probably in early March 1663. On the basis of this document, and on the evidence of some contemporary letters (not from the chancellor himself), he has argued that Clarendon was a wholehearted supporter of the king's project.[56] There are two principal objections to this argument. Statements of royal policy drafted by Clarendon in his role of chancellor are not an infallible guide to his personal opinions, for example the draft declaration prepared in August 1660. Secondly, the evidence of Clarendon's own writings suggests that he was far from being a supporter of the scheme. The account provided by the *Continuation* does contain factual errors,[57] but its essence is confirmed by cypher notes to Ormonde, and by the reports of two ambassadors then in England.

The first Clarendon knew of the proposed declaration, he told Ormonde in a lengthy cyper message, was that

> one day, when I was in great payne, Sir H. B. [Henry Bennet] came to mee and told mee that the King . . . resolved . . . to publish a declaration . . . I was surprised, having never heard a word before of such a purpose. When I had heard it, I made many objections against severall parts of it, and some doubts of the seasonableness.[58]

Clarendon's indisposition was not the real reason for his being kept in the dark until the declaration was written. During the chancellor's not infrequent bouts of illness, Charles often held

[56] Ibid., pp. 86-91; Addit. MS. 4107 ff.260-4.

[57] Clarendon places the whole incident in 1664 (another year in which he missed the start of a session through illness); for other errors see Abernathy, 'English Presbyterians', pp. 89-90.

[58] Carte MS. 47, f.24.

meetings at his bedside to discuss important business; the sale of Dunkirk, for example, had been discussed at such a meeting earlier in 1662.[59] That this was not done in December suggests that Charles anticipated opposition from Clarendon, and decided to present him with a *fait accompli*. The chancellor was piqued by the fact that another adviser was usurping his role of drafting royal declarations, but, isolated by illness and the loss of former allies, he was in no position to thwart the scheme. When Bennet returned with a slightly amended version and a message from the king that he was determined to publish the declaration at once, Clarendon bowed to the inevitable—outwardly, at least.

The next Clarendon probably knew was that the king intended to promote a bill to implement the declaration. At a meeting held at Clarendon's bedside in mid February, the bill was read through, and Charles declared that 'He hoped none of his servants, who knew his Mind as well as every Body there did, would oppose it, but either be absent or silent'. At this Clarendon and Southampton demurred, to the king's obvious annoyance.[60] The only account of this meeting which has survived is in the *Continuation*, but it does look as though Clarendon's prolonged convalescence may have been a response to the order to be silent or be absent. On 9 March, the French ambassador reported the rumour that Clarendon had stayed away from the first three weeks of the session in deference to Charles's support for the indulgence bill, this being a measure which the chancellor's conscience would not let him support.[61] By late February, the campaign to implement the declaration had run into major opposition in the Commons and some hostility in the Lords. In early March, the promoters of indulgence decided to withdraw (perhaps deeming it wiser to preserve such freedom as there was rather than provoke Parliament into a new wave of persecution). At this juncture, the debate on the bill was adjourned for a few days, and at the end of that period Clarendon made his first

[59] Abernathy, 'English Presbyterians', p. 87; Clarendon, *Life*, ii, 384, 468-70; iii, 603.

[60] Ibid., ii, 468-70.

[61] W. D. Christie, *A Life of Anthony Ashley Cooper* (London, 2 vols., 1871), i, 267, and cf. 268.

appearance in the Lords. He appeared, said the Venetian resident, by the king's order, and made a soothing speech in which he assured Parliament that the king would co-operate in matters of religion as well as of state.[62] The French ambassador reported that Clarendon secured a month's postponement of discussion of the bill (during which time it was discreetly shelved), and made what must have been a remarkable speech; 'he appeared to take no side in the matter; he managed well his master's reputation, the designs of the Parliament, and his own conscience, which he believes concerned'.[63] To reconcile these three contrasting interests was no mean feat. There is no contemporary copy of the speech, but in the *Continuation* Clarendon provides us with a version which, though probably impressionistic, corresponds closely to what the French ambassador heard at the time. Clarendon first re-assured the Lords of the king's steadfast adherence to the Protestant religion. In his opinion, the king was 'more worthy to be trusted than any Man alive' in discharging the trust of granting indulgences to tender consciences, (hardly an honest statement in view of what Clarendon knew of Charles's Catholic proclivities, but one which protected the king's 'reputation' and defended his prerogative power of dispensing). The question was not, however, was the king worthy of the trust, but was the trust worthy of the king? Would not the confirming of the king's powers of indulgence subject him to 'daily and hourly Importunities' from dissenters? (This point salved the consciences of those loyalists who did not wish to be disrespectful to the king but who objected to the principle of toleration, and it is interesting that it appears in a letter written by an M.P. in early April, claiming that the rebuttal of the king's declaration 'would keep him often from importunity'.)[64] Finally, in the heat of the debate Clarendon was provoked by some offensive remarks of Ashley's into letting fall 'some unwary Expressions', (perhaps the salving of his conscience referred to by Comminges). Ashley is alleged to have said that it was unfortunate for the king that in this debate his prerogative of indulgence 'should be supported only

[62] *Cal. St. Pap. Venetian 1661-1664*, p. 238.

[63] W. D. Christie, op. cit., i, 267-8.

[64] *Hist. MSS. Comm. Heathcote* (London, 1889), p. 77.

by such weak Men as himself, who served his Majesty at a Distance, whilst the great Officers of the Crown thought fit to oppose it; which he more wondered at, because Nobody knew more than They the King's unshakeable Firmness in his Religion'. In reply, Clarendon refuted the implication that he (and Southampton) opposed the bill because they thought the king was a Catholic sympathizer, and insisted that it was the 'Wildness and Illimitedness in the Bill' which worried him: 'it was Ship-Money in Religion, that Nobody could know the End of, or where it would rest; that if it were passed, Dr. *Goffe* or any other Apostate from the Church of England might be made a Bishop or Archbishop here, all Oaths and Statutes and Subscriptions being dispensed with'.[65]

On the surface, Clarendon had done everything that the king had asked of him on 12 March. He had re-assured Parliament, and earned Charles a breathing space of a month, in which he could either prepare a further campaign to pass the bill, or make a dignified withdrawal. It is therefore with some surprise that we learn from a note written to Ormonde a few days later that the king had been angry with him, and that this had made him very 'melancholyque'.[66] The reasons for the king's displeasure may have been threefold. It is clear from Clarendon's cypher letters to Ormonde that the promoters of the bill were blaming him for the failure of their scheme, and that the king to some extent believed them.[67] It was probably common opinion at the time that Clarendon had stayed away from the first weeks of the session deliberately, and the defection of the king's most senior and most orthodox minister had probably stiffened the resistance of the Cavaliers and the bishops to the bill. This was certainly the implication in Comminges's letters, and in Ashley's speech as recorded in the *Continuation*. Secondly, if the chancellor did lose his temper in debate and make the remarks described in his autobiography, then it is not in the least surprising that Charles was annoyed. The comparison between the bill and the ship-money collected by Charles I was decidedly tactless, and the allegation that Catholics could be made bishops would have

[65] Clarendon, *Life*, ii, 471-3.
[66] Carte MS. 47, f.91.
[67] Carte MS. 47, ff.91, 45.

created further suspicion about the king's real intentions. If Clarendon did say this on the 12th (or possibly the further debate on the 13th which both he and Ashley also attended),[68] it would indeed have given his enemies ample oportunity 'to make Glosses and Reflections . . . to his Disadvantage', and account for the king's coldness in the days following the debate. Thirdly, Charles may have blamed Clarendon for what was perhaps an unforeseen result of his intervention: the attention of Parliament was turned away from indulgence towards further persecution of the Catholic and Puritan communities. This result was not really Clarendon's fault. As one M.P. observed, had the pretensions of the Catholics not been so great, 'our countenancing the laws against them had not been so pressing'.[69] But the very success of Clarendon's speech in assuring Parliament of the king's orthodoxy and his readiness to co-operate with them in matters of religion, meant that the Commons quickly turned to consider measures against Catholic priests and Puritan conventicles.[70]

On 19 March Clarendon's hopes were raised briefly when the king ordered him to attend him alone, 'which for a good time I had not done'. At this conference, Charles spoke very freely, and the chancellor later confided to Ormonde that he might yet regain the king's complete trust. We have only a brief account of this meeting in the cypher note to Ormonde: the king was beginning to find that he had been misled by those advisers who 'weare themselves never in the right way', and was again showing Clarendon some favour after a short period in disgrace.[71] But in the *Continuation* there is a passage which is probably a highly coloured version of the occasion. It is Clarendon at his most priggish. At first the king reprimanded Clarendon for opposing royal policy, but the chancellor, unabashed and 'with the Confidence of an honest Man', presumed to lecture Charles on the ignorance of those councillors who had proposed this venture. His arguments made some impression, he thought, though the king did not change his mind, commenting merely that 'it was no Time to

[68] *J.L.*, xi, 491, 492.

[69] *Hist. MSS. Comm. Heathcote*, pp. 77-8.

[70] *Cal. St. Pap. Venetian 1661-1664*, pp. 238-9.

[71] Carte MS. 47, f.91.

speak to the Matter, which was now passed'.[72]

Encouraged by this sign of renewed confidence from the king, Clarendon tried dutifully to abate the persecuting zeal of the Cavaliers. We know that some time before 26 March he spoke against the idea of asking the king to issue a proclamation against Catholic priests, without success, and that in early April at the king's instruction he made a last effort to mitigate Parliament's severity towards the Catholics. He delivered what the Venetian resident called a 'weighty and pregnant harangue' describing the king's great debt to the Catholics for their support during the 1640s and 1650s. The Commons, however, simply replied that this was a private obligation which the king could meet privately; it must not be allowed to affect the laws of the land.[73] Comminges noticed that the chancellor's great credit with the Commons at the start of the session was now almost lost due to 'the ambiguous manner in which he has twice lately spoken'.[74] The pattern of events in the previous August was repeating itself: the chancellor was failing to achieve what the king required of him, his natural allies were alienated by the ambiguity of his behaviour, and his enemies were more hostile than ever. As Comminges put it succinctly, 'his friends lose heart, and his enemies decry him to the King'.

It was at this point, on 11 April, that Clarendon wrote a cypher note to Ormonde which provides the greatest insight not only into this affair but into his whole career as chancellor. He began by admitting ruefully that his optimism after the private meeting with the king on 19 March had been unfounded, and that he was again in disfavour, so much so that he was contemplating offering his resignation. Since Ormonde had left England in July, his life had been so unpleasant that he had hardly been able to carry on. At the moment of writing, he was being blamed for the failures of the previous weeks, in particular by Sir Henry Bennet who had 'credit enough to persuade the King that, *because I did not like what was done,* I had raised all the evil spirit that hath

[72] Clarendon, *Life,* ii, 473-4.

[73] *Hist. MSS. Comm. 7th Report,* App., Pt. 1, 484; *Cal. St. Pap. Venetian 1661-1664,* p. 241.

[74] W. D. Christie, op. cit., i, 268.

appeared upon and against it'. He was particularly concerned by the allegation that he had fostered opposition to the king's policy because he personally disliked it. He hopes that Ormonde will absolve him from such a charge:

for without doubte, I coulde as easily turne turke as act that part. On the contrary, God knows, I have taken as much paines to prevent those distempers *as if I had been the contriver of the councells.* I did, in truth, beleeve that the King had been satisfyed with my protestations in that kind, not because I made them but because he knew my nature and passion for his service could not admitt such corruption. But Sir H. Bennet and his freinds have more credit.[75]

This passage brings us as close as we are ever likely to come to understanding Clarendon's position in the early years of the Restoration. It anticipates the autobiography by ten years, both in its bitterness towards those advisers who weaned the king away from his former reliance on the chancellor, and in the ingenuousness of the self-justification. For Clarendon was deluding himself if he thought that his reservations about royal policy could be kept completely hidden from the Cavaliers in Parliament. The events of February and March 1663 suggest that the tension between king and chancellor was public knowledge, and a cause of concern to the predominantly Anglican political classes. Although Clarendon's comments to Ormonde betoken outraged innocence, it was the ambivalence of his own position, half-way between king and Parliament, which lay at the root of his difficulties.

The failure of this further attempt to undermine the Act of Uniformity cast a long shadow on Clarendon's fortunes. In late April and early May, Clarendon's fall was widely anticipated. On 29 April, the earl of Sandwich told Pepys that the chancellor was 'irrecoverably lost', and two weeks later the diarist noted that the new favourites had 'cast my Lord Chancellor upon his back, past ever getting up again'. Pepys expected that Treasurer Southampton, who had opposed the king's religious policy even more openly than Clarendon, would soon find himself in the same position.[76]

[75] Carte MS. 47, f.45 (my italics).

[76] *The Diary of Samuel Pepys,* op. cit., iv, 115, 137. For further evidence of Clarendon's decline, in the field of Parliamentary management, see D. T. Witcombe, op. cit., pp. 20–2.

With hindsight, Clarendon himself realized that although he continued to be employed by Charles on important matters of state, he 'never had the same Credit with him as He had before'. There was a further 'and a greater Mischief' which resulted from the whole episode: 'the Prejudice and Disadvantage that the Bishops underwent by their so unanimous Dislike of that Bill . . . from that Time the King never treated any of them with that Respect as he had done formerly'.[77] The only consolation for Clarendon must have been that their common exclusion from royal favour brought about a rapprochement between himself and his old friends in the episcopate, so that in the subsequent attacks upon him he could rely on the firm support of the bishops in the Lords.

The first of these attacks took place in July 1663 when the earl of Bristol tried to impeach the chancellor on charges of high treason.[78] Bristol was one of the favourites mentioned by Pepys as having discomfited the lord chancellor, and his particular bitterness against Clarendon may have been due to the idea that Clarendon was the major obstacle in the path of greater toleration for the Catholic community. Whereas most English Catholics had probably been convinced by the events of February and March that they should wait for some time before making a further attempt at toleration, Bristol made a typically hot-headed onslaught on the man whom he regarded as being responsible for the failure of past attempts. Bristol seems to have known that Clarendon had been in close touch with the English Catholics on the king's behalf, but suspected that Clarendon was pursuing a policy of divide and rule, that is playing off the different elements within the Catholic community against each other.[79] Bristol decided, therefore, to bring about Clarendon's fall, a move which would both avenge

[77] Clarendon, *Life*, ii, 473-6.

[78] *J.L.*, xi, 555-7.

[79] In his recent book on *Popery and Politics in England 1660-1688* (Cambridge, 1973), pp. 94-102, Dr. J. Miller has suggested that Clarendon may have favoured a measure of toleration for Catholics. But, as he himself points out, it is not possible to be certain: Clarendon was certainly an enemy of the over-zealous Catholics, and in the *Continuation* attributes to himself a hard line towards the Catholics in the 1660s. I incline to believe that Clarendon was opposed to toleration for Catholics (partly because Montagu and Bristol seem to have thought this); as in his relations with the Puritans, Clarendon probably disapproved of the negotiations which the king called upon him to make.

past failures and, by diverting the Cavaliers' opprobium away from the Catholics and towards Clarendon, clear the way for another attempt at toleration. The greatest problem was to prove that the chancellor had committed treason. Bristol accused Clarendon of having promoted the most unpopular moves of previous years—the Portuguese match, the sale of Dunkirk, etc., and voiced the current suspicion that Clarendon was making vast profits from office. But the burden of his charge was that the chancellor was pursuing a dastardly design to alienate the affections of the king's subjects from him by creating the impression that Charles was a Papist. Bristol seems to have imagined that by accusing Clarendon of spreading malicious rumours about the king's orthodoxy and by shifting the entire responsibility for the secret negotiations with the Catholics away from the king and on to the chancellor, he would ruin Clarendon's credit with the Cavaliers and strengthen Charles's hand in future attempts to grant an indulgence.

Although Bristol had not been in a position of sufficient confidence to be able to make really accurate charges against Clarendon, several of his accusations had a basis in truth. Clarendon had in fact supported the move to obtain a cardinal's hat for the king's kinsman and his own personal friend, d'Aubigny. Equally, he *had* been in discussion with leading English Catholics in 1662 over a new oath of allegiance which—if adopted—would have secured greater freedom of worship for those moderates prepared to take it.[80] It seems quite in character for Clarendon in a moment of exasperation or a fit of depression to have murmured in the hearing of other councillors that the king was leaning towards Catholicism, or that in replacing Secretary Nicholas by Henry Bennet the king had removed a zealous Protestant to bring into a place of high trust a concealed Papist. The notion attributed by Bristol to Clarendon's dependents that only the chancellor stood between England and reconciliation with Rome accords well with the impression given by the *Continuation* of his role in the early 1660s.[81] Some of the non-

[80] J. Miller, op. cit., pp. 95-6.

[81] *J. L.*, xi, 555-7; cf. *J.C.*, ix, 16. One of the few charges common to the attacks of

religious articles were also partly true: Clarendon had, for example, been the chief negotiator with the French over the sale of Dunkirk.

Even if there was some truth in these charges, however, the motives attributed to the chancellor by Bristol were so ludicrous that the impeachment was never likely to succeed. The upper house, with its solid wedge of episcopal votes, referred the charges to the judges, and on their advice refused to accept them. Moreover the king intervened hastily to prevent further enquiry into the court's secret contacts with Rome, and to discount certain statements—offered by Bristol as evidence of Clarendon's perfidy—which were in fact embarrassingly close to the truth.[82] In his haste to help the Catholic cause, Bristol had put the king in a very difficult position, and had to spend the next few years in exile from the court. One should not read too much into Charles's intervention on Clarendon's behalf: it was inspired more by the desire to prevent further disclosures than by a revival of the chancellor's credit with his royal master. In one sense, the events of July 1663 weakened Clarendon's position further, in that another sphere of influence was closed to him. Just as he was no longer employed to negotiate with Protestant dissenters, so he was never used again as a mediator between the king and his Catholic subjects. If Charles needed such a person in future, he had to look no further than the Catholics or crypto-Catholics who remained at court after Bristol's flight, above all Bennet and Clifford.

Never again did Clarendon appear as the king's spokesman on matters of religion. His one public statement on this subject, in 1665, occurred in a speech on a much wider theme—the war against the Dutch.[83] Otherwise his voice was conspicuous only by its absence. He did not attend the early weeks of the session of 1664 in which the first Conventicle Act passed through its early stages. It is also noteworthy that when he had recovered sufficiently to attend the Lords he was not appointed to confer with the Commons on the details of the

1663 and 1667 was that Clarendon had publicly stated that Charles 'was in his heart a Papist'.

[82] *J.L.*, xi, 559.

[83] *J.L.*, xi, 685-9.

bill, though in the first years of the Restoration he had often dominated the conferences between the houses on religious legislation.[84] The leading figure in the conferences on the Conventicle Act seems to have been the earl of Anglesey, the former 'Reconciler' who had already pre-empted Clarendon's role as mediator between court and Puritans.[85] The only known comment of the chancellor on the Conventicle Act is that in his autobiography; the act was regarded as 'the greatest Discountenance the Parliament had yet given to all the Factions in Religion, and if it had been vigorously executed would no Doubt have produced a thorough Reformation'.[86] The chancellor was again indisposed when the Five Mile Act was being discussed in the session of 1665, though he was able to attend the opening of the session and deliver a speech before retiring to his bed. The purpose of this speech was to describe the progress of the Dutch war and pave the way for an appeal for more supply, but at the end he turned from the enemy abroad to the enemy at home, those 'unquiet and restless Spirits in your own Bowels' on whom the Dutch relied to win the war. By implication, he equated these restless souls with the 'horrid Murderers of our late Royal Master'; some of them had actually gone over to fight in the Dutch navy, while others had been plotting to raise a rebellion on 3 September (Cromwell's day of victories). 'Let not those scorpions be kept warm in our bosoms till they sting us to death', he exhorted Parliament.[87] This speech, with its echoes of the 'firebrand' speech of May 1661, set the mood for the rest of the session. Within three days of this speech, the Commons had drafted and given a first reading to the Five Mile Act. This measure forbade any ejected minister or unlicensed preacher to come within five miles of the parish where he had worked or of any city or town; and it also imposed an oath on suspected conventiclers that they would not attempt 'any alteration of government in either Church or State'. A second bill to impose the same oath on all office holders and M.P.s was introduced, but aroused protests even from such orthodox figures as

[84] Ibid., xi, 604–20; cf. *J.C.*, viii, 164, and *J.L.*, xi, 426.
[85] *Hist. MSS. Comm. Ormonde*, new ser. (8 vols., 1902–12), iii, 71.
[86] Clarendon, *Life*, ii, 421.
[87] *J.L.*, xi, 688.

Southampton and was narrowly defeated.[88] Charles may have felt that in his opening speech Clarendon had exceeded his brief, for at a meeting held at Clarendon's bedside shortly afterwards the king snubbed him in the presence of leading ministers and officers of the crown.[89]

Clarendon's tenure of power was nearing its close. Charles was tiring of the chancellor's passive resistance to his schemes for greater toleration. He must also have resented Clarendon's repeated strictures on his private life and the attacks he made on the probity of the other advisers to whom he chose to listen.[90] On a series of occasions in the mid 1660s, the chancellor openly disagreed with the king in council—over the wisdom of fighting the Dutch, the dismissal of Admiral Sandwich, the supervision of the Treasury, the decision to accept Parliamentary appropriation of supply, the importing of Irish cattle, the calling of Parliament in 1666, and other matters.[91] On some occasions, Clarendon was proved right, but his positive achievements were too few to offset the growing irritation felt by the king at the chancellor's pedagogical behaviour. It was perhaps not Clarendon's fault that the court had gained hardly any advantages from the various concessions it had made to Parliament; arguably it was the king's, for tolerating the existence of two court factions which tended to pull in opposite directions.[92] But when the second Dutch war began to go badly, and Charles was faced by an incensed House of Commons, Clarendon was the obvious sacrifice for the king to offer. Charles supported the attacks on Clarendon with a vigour which not only was unusual for one of his languid disposition, but also did him little credit in view of Clarendon's eminent services over the previous quarter of a century. Many seem to have felt that the attack was being pushed home with indecent haste, and that disgrace and exile were too severe a price for such a loyal servant to pay. One of the most remarkable features of the whole distasteful episode

[88] D. T. Witcombe, op. cit., pp. 36-7; Burnet, i, 401; *Rel. Baxt.*, Lib. III, Pt. III, para. 7.

[89] Clarendon, *Life*, iii, 603-9.

[90] E.g. ibid., iii, 681-7, 609-12.

[91] Ibid., ii, 377-83; iii, 580-2; 613-18, 790-4; 700-1; 801-7; D. T. Witcombe, op. cit., pp. 37-9, 43-4, 50-1, 55-7.

[92] Ibid., chapters 2 to 6.

was the way in which nineteen out of twenty-two bishops who attended this session defended the chancellor, despite specific instructions from the king not to offer any obstruction to the impeachment.[93] Not even the bishops could save him, however, for Charles had decided that Clarendon should leave the country before the process of impeachment began, and virtually ordered him out of England. Charles may have suspected that it would be difficult to prove charges against Clarendon, or feared that in his defence he might make some damaging remarks. He may also have guessed that if Clarendon had been allowed to stay in the country he would have become a focus of opposition to the court's religious policy for many of the church party. The subsequent behaviour of the bishops and the emergence of a group of diehard Anglicans known in 1668 as the 'Clarendonians' serve to reinforce this point.[94] Even in disgrace or in prison in England, Clarendon would have continued to be a thorn in the king's flesh, and Charles rejected all pleas for clemency or a royal pardon.

At the start of his second exile, Clarendon was still a man of considerable energy and ability, and these he channelled completely into his writings. At first he revised his *History of the Rebellion,* and wrote some polemical and devotional works in defence of the ideals of the Tew Circle. But at the same time he must have been brooding over his treatment as chancellor, seeking explanations for his fall from favour, and formulating a defence of his conduct when in office. Time and time again he must have returned to his attitude towards the king's religious policy. In his lonely exile, he may have wished to convince himself as well as posterity that he had not done the episcopal Church of England any real harm on those occasions when he had implemented royal policy. Rather the contrary, by his persistent stand on Anglican principles in a court filled with crypto-Catholics, Presbyterians, and unbelievers, he had fought the good fight and now deserved to glory with the saints in heaven. From this there stemmed the misrepresentations in the *Continuation,* the suppression or apologetic accounts of episodes in which he had acted against the church's interests

[93] W. G. Simon, *Restoration Episcopate* (1965), pp. 77–8.

[94] D. T. Witcombe, op. cit., p. 78; cf. p. 36, and chapters 7, 8 and 13.

under instructions from the king. From this there also stemmed the tendency to simplify issues into starkly contrasting shades of black and white. There had been two occasions during his period as chancellor when Clarendon had hesitated to recommend the firm line towards Puritanism which was a cornerstone of his convictions, the first being in the unsettled circumstances of the spring of 1660, the second during a bout of depression in the summer of 1662.[95] But such shades of grey had no place in his thinking a decade later. 'It is an unhappy Policy, and always unhappily applied, to imagine that that *Classis* of men can be . . . reconciled by partial Concessions'; 'Their faction is their religion'; 'Nothing but a severe Execution of the Law can ever prevail upon that Classis of men to conform to Government'.[96]

The uncompromising churchmanship of the *Continuation* should be seen as the culmination of a process by which Clarendon brought his own religious views to the fore. The execution of Charles I had sanctified the Church of England in the hearts of many men, not least Hyde; after 1649 he could never have reverted to the more liberal attitudes of his early years. At the Restoration, however, he had been forced to conceal his hostility to the Puritans, first by the necessity of gaining admittance for Charles and himself, and then by the discovery that the king really did mean to implement the promise of liberty for tender consciences made in the declaration from Breda. Occasionally during the 1660s, he revealed his innermost thoughts, but never for long, and rarely in public. Not until he was in exile was he freed from the need to temporize; only then could he express his true feelings about the Presbyterians—'*They are a pack of knaves*', he told his son in July 1671.[97]

Clarendon's chief difficulty when in office was that he was attempting to serve several masters, and as a result gave none of them his full attention or support. He was a very loyal servant of the crown: he supported the repeal of the Triennial Act and the other 'encroachments' on the prerogative passed in 1641; he resisted Parliament's attempts to supervise royal

[95] See above pp. 208–9, 216–19.

[96] Clarendon, *Life*, ii, 280, 143.

[97] T. H. Lister, *Life . . . of Clarendon*, op. cit., iii, 483.

finances; and he gave theoretical support to the royal prerogative in ecclesiastical affairs.[98] But when the prerogative was going to be used to suspend statutes or to weaken the episcopal church, then Clarendon was one of those who held back. The same is true of his second 'master', Parliament. He always professed himself a champion of that institution, and it is probably true that he understood the Cavalier Parliament, especially its religious enthusiasm, better than any of Charles's other ministers.[99] But when it sought to invade the preserves of royal government, such as foreign policy, or wasted time through being over-jealous of its privileges, the chancellor rebuked it sternly.[100] In his last years of power Clarendon tended to exalt the role of the privy council, that 'most sacred' body which next to the king had 'the greatest Authority in the Government of the State'; [101] yet again he was occasionally reluctant to accept its collective decisions when they contradicted his own views. In one sense, Clarendon was also his own 'master': he could have resigned as a matter of principle over Charles's religious policy, or he could have submerged his own ideas into those of the king. But he would do neither. He talked of resigning, but never came near to doing so, perhaps from a sense of duty to Charles I, perhaps from a sense of innate superiority to Charles II's other ministers. He told Ormonde that he could never oppose royal policy, but his religious principles were so deeply ingrained that he betrayed his dislike of royal policy in some of his speeches and politic absences from Parliament. Grimly he hung on to office, compromising his views, but hating the necessity of doing so. Even when power was prised from his grasp, he would not admit that he had been wrong; it was always the others who were in the wrong—the other politicians, the other religious groups, the other countries.

It is perhaps true, as Feiling has suggested, that Clarendon was frozen in the attitudes of 1641, and that his views were completely out of date by the Restoration. By then Parliament had become so self-confident and so well-informed that it

[98] Clarendon, *Life*, iii, 727-8; Abernathy, 'English Presbyterians', p. 90.
[99] D. T. Witcombe, op. cit., pp. 9, 22, and chapters 1 to 6 generally.
[100] Clarendon, *Life*, iii, 728-32.
[101] Ibid., iii, 676-7.

would not tolerate the chancellor's condescending airs.[102] But Clarendon may also be said to anticipate the attitudes of 1688. Not only Parliament, but also the Stuart monarchy had changed by the 1660s; for whereas the first two Stuarts had adopted an essentially conservative approach to matters of English church government, the next two did not. During the first half of the reign of Charles II and the second half of that of James II, these monarchs tried to modify the basically traditional church settlement of 1660–2 by various schemes for comprehension or indulgence. It may be suggested that in his career as chancellor and in the *Continuation,* Clarendon anticipates those puzzled Tories of 1688 who had preached passive obedience and defended the royal prerogative, only to discover that the prerogative was being used to undermine their church and their liberties. Clarendon's dilemma was visited on his sons when they held office under James II and on the church party at large. Late in 1686, the second earl of Clarendon wrote to his brother that they must do nothing that would 'hurt the best Church in the world' but must 'tread the steps' their father had trod before them.[103] When the Hyde brothers were dismissed from office for their stubborn adherence to the Anglican church, their fall reverberated through every Tory house in England, and subsequent events simply increased the sense of shock and betrayal. It was not for this that the Cavaliers had fought during the 1640s and toiled during the 1660s; nor was it for this that the Tories had supported Charles and James during the Exclusion Crisis. It was to defend the existing forms of government in church and state, and in particular the episcopal Church of England which the Cavalier Parliament had re-established as a guarantee of political and social stability.

The clergy were equally perplexed by the events of 1687–8. By the 1680s a new generation of ministers, trained in the High-Church attitudes of Restoration Oxford and Cambridge, was replacing the moderate parish clergy of the 1660s. Tutors taught them that the doctrine of passive obedience was 'in a manner . . . the badge and character of the Church of

[102] K. Feiling, *A History of the Tory Party 1640–1714* (Oxford, 1924), pp. 117–19, 121.

[103] Ibid., p. 216.

England'.[104] It was this tenet of Anglicanism which so impressed the limited imagination of James II that he expected the clergy to co-operate in the diminution of their own church. His demands placed a severe and, for some, intolerable strain upon their loyalty to the crown.

For the church party, the events of 1688–9 were a disaster. Their cherished ideals of uniformity of Anglican worship and passive obedience were destroyed almost overnight. But not all was lost. The established church retained much of its prestige and influence. Indeed, its influence was so pervasive that once the Whigs had secured limited toleration, their support for the Church of England was almost as strong as that of the Tories. This fact alone ensured that the main features of the Restoration settlement—the reintroduction of a hierarchical state church and the imposition of civil disabilities upon dissenters—would survive for many generations to come.

[104] C. E. Mallet, *A History of the University of Oxford*, op. cit., ii, 448.

APPENDICES

APPENDIX 1

PETITIONS HANDLED BY THE SHELDON-EARLE-MORLEY 'COMMITTEE', JUNE-SEPTEMBER 1660

Petitions for parish livings

Source[1] *S.P.* 29/	Name of petitioner	Living sought	Customary patron[2]	Date and signature on first endorsement[3]	Date and signature on 'committee's' report[4]	Order for appointment to be made[5]
1 ff. 136/7	Alex. Burnett	R. Ivychurch, Kent.	Abp. of Cant.	—	? E	(26.6.60)
4 ff.94* and 94.1	Abraham Allen	R. West Meon, Hants.	Bp. of Winch.	19.6.60 Mason	? S and E	22.6.60 Signet
4 f.116*	Thos Buttolph	R. Northop, Flints.	Bp. of St. Asaph	22.6 Mason	24.7.60 S and E	(1.8.60)
4 f.124*	Thos. Dale	R. Tarring, Sussex	Abp. of Cant.	22.6 Mason	? SE and M	4.7.60 Presentations
4 f.125	Robt. Say	R. Orpington, Kent	Abp. of Cant.	—	22.6 S	(6.7.60)
4 ff.129* and 129.1	J. Anthill	R. Hitcham, Suffolk.	The king	22.6 Mason	27.6 S and E	27.6 Signet
5 f.22*	Thos. Tirwhitte	R. Gt. Munden, Herts.	The king	27.6 Mason	? S and E	4.7 Presentations
5 f.25*	Thos. Fawcett	R. Sudbourne Suffolk	The king	27.6 Mason	3.7 S + E	(None made)
5 f.28*	Thos. Blevin	R. Sudbourne, Suffolk	The king	27.6 Mason	? S and M	11.7 Signet

6 ff.57/8	Robt. Davenant	R. Crawley, Hants.	Bp. of Winch.	—	? S E M and Henchman	(None made)
7 f.54	Thos. White	V. Newark-on-Trent, Notts.	The king	6.7.60 Nicholas	7.7.60 S and E	(30.7.60)
7 f.56*	J. Gilman	R. Withington, Glouc.	Dean of Hereford	6.7 Nicholas	? E and M	(19.7.60)
7 f.58*	Thos. Mallory	R. Houghton, Durham	Bp. of Durham	6.7 Nicholas	? S and M	(None made)
7 f.64*	Thos. Blanchard	R. Worplesdon, Surrey	Eton College	9.7 Nicholas	? E and M	(19.7.60)
7 f.65	Chas. Appleford	R. Chilbolton, Hants.	Bp. of Winch.	—	9.7 S E and M	(24.7.60)
7 ff.84/5*	Wm. Carr	V. Bexhill, Sussex	Bp. of Chich.	11.7 Nicholas	12.7 S and E	25.7 Signet
7 f.86*	Philip Lewis	V. Presteigne, Radnor	(Layman)	11.7 Freeman	13.7 S E and M	(24.7.60)
7 f.87*	Robt. Johnson	R. Welton, Yorks.	The king	11.7 Freeman	? E and M	23.7 Signet
7 f.88*	Bryan Smith	R. Rendlesham, Suffolk	The king	11.7 Freeman	14.7 S and E	(25.7.60)
7 f.90	Edm. Boldero	R. Hadleigh, Suffolk	Abp. of Cant.	—	11.7 S and E	(None made)
7 f.91*	Fran. Drayton	V. Appledore, Kent	Abp. of Cant.	11.7 Freeman	16.7 S and E	(30.7.60)
7 f.92*	Giles Thornborough	R. Worplesdon, Surrey	Eton College	11.7 Freeman	? E and M	(None made: see f.64 above)
7 f.94*	J. Newton	V. Ross, Hereford	Bp. of Hereford	11.7 Freeman	13.7 E and M	(25.7.60)
7 f.95*	Robt. Newlin	R. Wroughton, Wilts.	Bp. of Winch.	11.7 Freeman	14.7 S E and M	(24.7.60)

7 f.100*	Wm. Griffith	R. Polebrook, Northants.	Bp. of Peterboro'	12.7 Nicholas	19.7 S and M	(25.7.60)
7 f.101	Thos. Price	R. Llanyfidd, Flints.	Chancellor of St. Asaph.	—	12.7 Note by Sheldon	(25.7.60)
7 f.105*	Ant. Robinson	R. Oddington, Glouc.	Precentor of York	13.7 Nicholas	14.7 S and M	(21.8.60)
7 f.147	Robt. Matthew	R. Meonstoke, Hants.	Bp. of Winch.	18.7 Nicholas	19.7 S and M	(25.7.60)
8 f.23*	Wm. Sclater	R. Barton, Bedfords.	The king	20.7 Nicholas	21.7 M and S	(26.7.60)
8 f.33*	Peter Ingram	R. Longworth, Berks.	Jesus Coll. Oxford	23.7 Freeman	28.7 S and E	Signet (17.8.60)
8 f.48*	Clem. Thurston	R. Toppesfield, Essex	The king	24.7 Freeman	—	(1.8.60)
8 f.51*	Barnaby Love	R. Wonston, Hants.	Bp. of Winch.	25.7 Nicholas	27.7 S and E	(31.7.60)
8 f.74*	Thos. Sutton	V. Puckle-church, Glouc.	Dean and chapter of Wells	27.7 Nicholas	1.8 S and E	(None made)
8 f.76	Thos. Holyoke	R. Tattenhall, Staffs.	Dean of Coventry & Lichfield	27.7 (Nicholas?)	?	(None made)
8 f.95*	Ant. Clifford	R. Newton Ferrers, Devon	(Layman)	28.7 Nicholas	30.7 S and E	(20.2.61)
8 f.109	Thos. Potter	R. Chidding-stone, Kent	Abp. of Cant.	—	30.7 S and E	(None made)
10 f.4*	Dan. Getsius	R. Bigbury, Devon	(Layman)	1.8 Nicholas	2.8 S	(13.8.60)
10 f.18*	Jas. Wealsh	V. Hilmarton, Wilts.	The king	2.8 Nicholas	—	(None made)

10 f.59*	J. Studdert	V. Crosthwaite, Cumberland	Alt. the king and Bp. of Carlisle	6.8 Nicholas	8.8 S and M	(15.8.60)
10 f.132*	J. Butt	R. Warnford, Hants.	(Layman)	14.8 Holles	? S and E	(None made)
10 f.139*	Henry Warren	V. Loddiswell, Devon	(Layman)	15.8 Nicholas	? S and M	(28.8.60)
11 f.90*	Jeremiah Holled	R. Walgrave, Northants.	Bp. of Lincoln	30.8 Nicholas	? M	(6.9.60)
12 ff.69 and 69.1	Edm. Tracy	V. Bradford, Wilts.	Dean & Chapter of Bristol	—	? E	(None made)
12 ff.70 and 70.1	Wm. Pindar	R. Brasted, Kent	Abp. of Cant.	—	15.8 S	(20.8.60)
12 ff.72/3	Gilb. Coles	R. Chilbolton or R. Easton, Hants.	Both Bp. of Winch.	—	? S E M and Henchman	(Easton 24.7.60)
12 f.74	Sam. Bird	V. Claybrooke, Leics.	The king	—	4.7 E and M	(30.7.60)
12 f.75	Henry Brunsell	R. Clayworth, Notts.	Dean of Lincoln	—	14.8 S	(20.8.60)
12 f.82	Rd. Pearson	R. Epworth, Lincs.	Queen Mother	—	22.8 S	(12.8.60)
12 ff.87 and 87.1	Robt. Bonner	R. Hartburn, Northumberland	Bp. of Durham	—	27.7 S	(3.8.60)
12 f.88	Wm. Goulston	R. Havant, Hants.	Bp. of Winch.	—	? E and M	(30.7.60)
12 f.91	Jas. Scott	R. Kirklington, Yorks.	(Layman)	—	? S E and M	(None made)
12 f.104	Roger Wilford	R. North Berkhamstead, Herts.	The king	—	? E and M	(29.6.60)

12 ff.105 and 105.1 and 2	Sam. Pancke	R. North Creake, Norfolk	Bp. of Norwich	—	? M	(9.7.60)
12 ff.111 and 111.1	Rd. Peacock	R. Shepperton, Middlesex	(Layman)	—	? S	(27.7.60)
12 f.117	J. Doughtie	R. Shere, Surrey	(Layman)	—	? S E and M	(30.7.60)
12 f.123	Ant. Huish	R. Tempsford, Beds.	The king	—	? S E and M	(25.7.60)
12 ff.134/5	Wm. Marketman	V. West Ham, Essex	The king	—	6.8 S	(22.8.60)
14 f.4*	Jonathan Holled	R. Cottingham, Northants.	(Layman)	1.9 Nicholas	1.9 S	(6.9.60)
Petitions for cathedral livings and archdeaconries						
6 f.4 and f.5	Edw. Cotton	Archdeaconry of Cornwall; and Exeter canonry	Bp. of Exeter — both	—	? S E M and henchman; S and M	(25.7.60; 20.7.60)
6 f.6	Francis Fulwood	Archdeaconry of Totnes	Bp. of Exeter	— —	? S and M	(13.8.60)
6 f.7	Rd. Meredith	Archdeaconry of Dorset	Bp. of Bristol	—	? S M and E	(25.7.60)
6 f.8	Rd. Mervyn	Chancellorship of Exeter cath.	Bp. of Exeter	—	? S M and Henchman	(26.7.60)
6 ff.14 and 14.1	J. Castilion	Canterbury canonry	Abp. of Cant.	—	24.6 S M and E	(9.7.60)
6 f.15	Wm. Barker	Canterbury canonry	The king	—	? S and M	(9.7.60)
6 ff.32 and 32.1	Geo. Hall	Windsor canonry	The king	—	? E and M	19.7.60)

7 f.37	J. Neale	York prebend	Abp. of York	—	4.7 S	(13.8.60)
7 f.44	Humphrey Lloyd	Deanery of Bangor	Bp. of Bangor	4.7 Nicholas	4.7 S	(None made)
7 f.47	Geo. Welsted	Winchester prebend.	Bp. of Winch.	—	5.7 S and M	(None made)
7 f.48	J. Middleton	Archdeaconry of Gloucester	Bp. of Gloucester	—	5.7 S and M	(19.7.60)
7 f.49	Ant. Sparrow	Archdeaconry of Sudbury	Bp. of Norwich	5.7 Nicholas	? S	(None made)
7 ff.66 and 66.1	Giles Thorne	Archdeaconry of Bucks.	Bp. of Lincoln	—	9.7 S E and M	(19.7.60)
7 f.69	Jas. Smith	Archdeaconry of Barnstaple	Bp. of Exeter	—	? E and M	(30.7.60)
7 f.89*	Geo. Roberts	Archdeaconry of Winchester	Bp. of Winch.	11.7 Freeman	12.7 S E and M	23.7 Signet
7 f.104	Thos. Mallory	York prebend	Abp. of York	13.7 ?	—	(None made)
7 f.137*	Wm. Thorn-borough	Worcester canonry	The king	17.7 Nicholas	20.7 S and E	(8.9.60)
8 ff.9/10*	J. Coope	Lincoln prebend	Bp. of Lincoln	19.7 Nicholas	22.7 S E and M	(1.8.60)
8 f.106 and f.107	Thos. Potter	2 Lincoln prebends	Bp. of Lincoln	—	30.7 S; ? E	— (9.8.60)
10 ff.19* and 19.1	Kenelm Manwaring	Winchester prebend	Bp. of Winch.	2.8 Freeman	6.8 S and E	(18.9.60)
10 f.48*	Thos. Weston	Manchester Coll. Fellowship	The king	4.8 Nicholas	? S and E	(None made)
10 f.70*	Rd. Beresford	Lincoln prebend	Bp. of Lincoln	7.8 Nicholas	8.8 S E and M	(None made)

10 f.84*	Francis Moseley	Manchester Coll. Fellowship	The king	9.8 Nicholas	9.8 S and E	(None made)
11 ff.67* and 67.1	Daniel Vivian	Southwell prebend	Abp. of York	28.8 Nicholas	? M	(12.9.60)
12 f.4	David Lloyd	Deanery of St. Asaph	The king	—	? E and M	(30.7.60)
12 f.5	Geo. Benson	Archdeaconry of Hereford	Bp. of Hereford	—	? S E M and Henchman	(19.7.60)
12 f.6	Francis Davis	Archdeaconry of Llandaff	Bp. of Llandaff	—	24.7 S	(6.8.60)
12 f.12	Thos. Hyde	Precentorship of Sarum cath.	Bp. of Sarum	—	12.7 S	(14.11.60)
12 f.13	Wm. Owen	Treasurership of St. David's	Bp. of St. David's	—	? S and E	(9.8.60)
12 f.26	Rd. Towgood	Bristol prebend	Lord Chancellor	—	? S and M	(25.8.60)
12 f.27	Rd. Standfast	Bristol prebend	Lord Chancellor	—	? S and M	(25.8.60)
12 f.28	Wm. Kempe	Bristol prebend	Lord Chancellor	—	? M	(5.10.60)
12 f.33	Chas. Gibbs	Canterbury canonry	The king	—	? E and M	(None made)
12 f.34	J. Gough	Canterbury canonry	Either the king or archbishop	—	? S	(None made)
12 f.40	Nath. Ward	Lincoln prebend	Bp. of Lincoln	—	? M	(28.9.60)
12 f.51	Nath. Ward	Worcester canonry	The king	—	? E	(None made)

14 f.5	Wm. Coke	Worcester canonry	The king	1.9 Nicholas	1.9 S and M	(None made)
14 ff.12, 12.1 and 13	J. Breton	Worcester canonry	The king	—	21.8 S	(7.9.60)

[1] Those marked with an asterisk were definitely referred to the 'committee', those not so marked may have been handled by it (see above p. 53, and p. 53, n. 68).

[2] Patrons are taken from *Lib. Inst.* or J. Ecton, *Thesaurus Rerum Ecclesiasticarum* (3rd ed., London, 1743). To save space, lay patrons other than the king have been designated as 'Layman'.

[3] See above pp. 53, n. 68, and 54, n. 71. Edward Nicholas was secretary of state; Ralph Freeman, Robert Mason, and Gervase Holles held lesser posts at court.

[4] A question mark indicates that the report is not dated. Sheldon, Earle, and Morley are here abbreviated to S, E, and M.

[5] 'Signet' or 'Presentations' denotes an endorsement ordering a presentation to be made by the clerk of presentations or the clerk of the signet then attending. Where there is no such reference but an appointment has been recorded on the Patent Roll, the date of presentation, as printed in *46th Report*, is given in brackets.

APPENDIX 2

PRESENTATIONS TO PARISH LIVINGS IN THE DIOCESES OF CANTERBURY AND WINCHESTER ON THE PATENT ROLLS FROM 1.6.60 TO 9.9.60

(Full references to the Patent Roll entries may be found in *46th Report.*)

Part 1—Incumbents confirmed in their livings by royal presentations. (Those who were subsequently ejected in 1662 are marked by an asterisk.)

(a) Diocese of Canterbury.

Minister	Living	Date of original appointment	Date of presentation by king
Robt. Beake	Hackington, V. Kent.	1645[1]	20.8.60
J. Browne	Hope All Sts. R. Kent.	1652[2]	29.6
Thos. Browne	Farningham, V. Kent.	1647[3]	1.9
Edw. Clarke	Chevening, R. Kent.	*c.* 1650[4]	13.8
Isaac Harrison*	Hadleigh, R. Suffolk.	1643[5]	6.8
George May, jun.	Mersham, R. Kent.	1658[6]	9.7
Francis Porter	Eynsford, R. Kent.	1650[7]	18.6
J. Spencer	Newchurch, R. Kent.	1657[8]	29.8

(b) Diocese of Winchester.

Minister	Living	Date of original appointment	Date of presentation by king
J. Barnes	Whippingham, R. I.O.W.	*c.* 1650[9]	6.8
Edw. Buckler*	Calbourne, R. I.O.W.	1653[10]	30.7
Ben. Burnand	Warnford, R. Hants.	1648[11]	31.8
Henry Complin	Avington, R. Hants.	1658[12]	4.9
Wm. Cooper*	St. Olave's R. Southwark Surrey	1654[13]	30.7.60
Rd. Downes	East Meon V. Hants.	1649[14]	13.8
Francis Goodwin	Hinton Ampner R. Hants.	1648[15]	29.7
Wm. Harby	Hambledon V. Hants.	1658[16]	18.8
J. Holney	Dunsfold R. Surrey	1652[17]	31.8
Barnabas Love	Wonston R. Surrey	1649[18]	31.7
Robt. Matthew	Meonstoke R. Hants.	1657[19]	25.7
Thos. Mulcaster	Nutfield R. Surrey.	1654[20]	22.8
J. Ridge*	Exton R. Hants.	1656[21]	30.8
Henry Savage	Sherborne St. John R. Hants.	1648[22]	12.6

Sam. Tomlyns*	Crawley R. Hants.	1655[23]	16.7
Thos. Warren*	Houghton R. Hants.	1651[24]	19.7
Humphrey Weaver*	Crondall V. Hants.	1656[25]	18.8
Thos. Webb	Hannington R. Hants.	1654[26]	24.7
Gilbert Withers	Waltham, North R. Hants.	1653[27]	3.7

Part 2—Royal presentations for ministers not in possession.

(a) Canterbury

Minister	Living given in 1660	Previous career
Wm. Baker	Monks Eleigh R. Suffk.	—
Edmund Beeston	Teynham V. Kent.	B. A. (Cant.) 1657, M.A. (Cant.) 1660.[28]
James Benskin	Eastry V. Kent.	sequestered from Suffolk rectory.[29]
Alex. Burnett	Ivychurch R. Kent.	probably conformist vicar of Teynham, Kent.[30]
Wm. Clewer	Croydon V. Surrey.	possibly conformist rector in Northants.[31]
Robt. Cole	Shadoxhurst R. Kent.	conformist vicar of Lyminge Kent.[32]
Thos. Dale	Tarring R. Sussex	possibly conformist rector in Kent.[33]
Francis Drayton, Jun.	Appledore V. Kent	B. A. (Cant.) 1655, M.A. (Cant.) 1658.[34]
Ben. Harrison	Sandwich St. Clement V. Kent.	sequestered from this parish in 1650 but then a conformist rector in Devon.[35]
Moses Lee	Biddenden R. Kent.	—
Thos. Nightingale	Wormshill R. Kent.	B.A. (Cant.) 1648, M.A. (Cant.) 1652[36]
Wm. Pindar	Brasted R. Kent	sequestered from two Essex livings though he served one again in the early 1650s.[37]
Gregory Pulford	Lower Hardres R. Kent.	conformist curate of Nackington, Kent.[38]
J. Reading	Chartham R. Kent.	conformist rector of Cheriton, Kent.[39]
Geo. Robertson	Leysdown V. Kent.	—
Sam. Smith	{Monks Horton R. Kent {Eastbridge, R. Kent.	sequestered vicar of Boughton under Blean, Kent.[40]
Robt. Say	Orpington R. Kent.	conformist at Oxford[41]
J. Squire	Barnes R. Surrey.	fought for the king[42]

Wm. Stain	Hollingbourne R. Kent.	? B.A. (Oxon.) 1652, M.A. (Oxon.) 1655.[43]
Nath. Willys	Cliffe R. Kent.	ejected fellow of Trinity Camb.; with Charles I at Oxford.[44]
Edw. Wilsford	Lydd V. Kent.	ejected fellow of Peterhouse; staunch Royalist.[45]
(b) Winchester		
Ab. Allen	West Meon R. Hants.	suffered for supporting the king.[46]
Chas. Appleford	Chilbolton R. Hants.	ejected fellow of Queen's Camb.; Royalist sufferer.[47]
Phil. Baker	Grately R. Hants.	conformist rector of Upper Clatford, Hants.[48]
Wm. Bicknell	Portsea V. Hants.	assistant to Puritan vicar on I.O. Wight 1655–60[49]
Thos Blanchard	Worplesdon R. Surrey.	conformist rector of N. Wraxall, Wilts.[50]
Thos. Clutterbuck	Leckford R. Hants.	ejected fellow, but then conformist rector in 1650s.[51]
Gilb. Coles	Easton R. Hants.	ejected fellow New, Oxon.[52]
J. Doughtie	Shere R. Surrey.	possibly sequestered in Warwicks, but conformed in Sarum living.[53]
Wm. Goulston	Havant R. Hants.	—
Alex. Gregson	Middleton R. Hants.	conformist rector of Brown Candover, Hants. 1658.[54]
Thos. Heather	Fareham V. Hants.	—
J. Morecroft	Itchen Abbas, R. Hants.	—
Thomas (Sydserf) Bp. of Galloway	Overton R. Hants.	Royalist sufferer[55]
Giles Thornborough	St. Nicholas R. Guildford, Surrey.	B.A. (Oxon.) 1656, M.A. (Oxon.) 1658[56]
J. Wade	Winnall R. Hants.	—

[1] *Cal. Rev.*, p. 41; later in 1660 the sequestered vicar was restored.
[2] Addit. MS. 37,692, f.53.
[3] Addit. MS. 15,671, f.210.
[4] Hasted, i, 367.
[5] *Cal. Rev.*, p. 249.
[6] Lamb. Pal. Lib., *Comm. III/7*, p. 126; the new classification of Commonwealth ecclesiastical records is described in J. Houston, *Catalogue of Ecclesiastical Records of the Commonwealth 1643–1660 in the Lambeth Palace Library* (1968).
[7] Addit. MS. 36,792, f.19.

[8] *Comm. III/6*, p. 91.
[9] Brit. Lib., Lansdowne MS. 459, f.237.
[10] *Cal. Rev.*, pp. 84–5.
[11] *Lib. Inst.*
[12] *Comm. III/7*, p. 134.
[13] *Cal. Rev.*, pp. 134–5.
[14] *Lib. Inst.*
[15] Ibid.
[16] *Comm. III/7*, p. 110.
[17] *Lib. Inst.*
[18] *J.L.*, x, 646.
[19] *Comm. III/5*, p. 215.
[20] *Walk. Rev.*, p. 352.
[21] *Cal. Rev.*, pp. 411–12.
[22] *Lib. Inst.*
[23] *Cal. Rev.*, pp. 488–9.
[24] Ibid., pp. 511–12.
[25] Ibid., p. 515.
[26] *Comm. III/3/3*, p. 3.
[27] P.R.O., Composition Books.
[28] *Alum. Cant.*
[29] *Walk. Rev.*, p. 237.
[30] *Alum. Cant.; Dict. Nat. Biog.; Cal. St. Pap. Dom. 1656–1657*, p. 247.
[31] *Cal. Rev.*, p. 556.
[32] *Walk. Rev.*, p. 210.
[33] Possibly rector of Kingsdown and Mapiscombe from 1639 and 1641 (*Alum. Oxon.*), for his petition in 1660 is endorsed by the Bishop of Rochester (*S.P.* 29/4, f.124), but he is not listed among the sufferers in *Walk. Rev.*
[34] *Alum. Cant.*
[35] *Walk. Rev.*, p. 218.
[36] *Alum. Cant.*
[37] *Walk. Rev.*, p. 161.
[38] Hasted, iii, 70.
[39] *Walk. Rev.*, p. 224.
[40] Ibid., p. 225.
[41] Fellow and provost of Oriel—*Alum. Oxon.*
[42] Ibid.
[43] Ibid., *sub* Wm. Stane.
[44] *Walk. Rev.*, p. 41 ('Willis').
[45] Ibid., p. 228 ('Wilford').
[46] See Appendix 1, and *S.P.* 29/4, ff. 94, 94.1.
[47] *Walk. Rev.*, p. 39.
[48] Ibid., p. 190.
[49] *Cal. Rev.*, p. 53.
[50] *Alum. Oxon.*
[51] *Walk. Rev.*, p. 73.
[52] Ibid., p. 30.
[53] Ibid., p. 363, but cf. p. 34.
[54] *Comm. III/7*, p. 129.
[55] *Dict. Nat. Biog.*
[56] *Alum. Oxon.*

APPENDIX 3

THREE TYPES OF MINISTER AFFECTED BY ROYAL PRESENTATIONS TO PARISH LIVINGS IN THE SUMMER OF 1660.

Part 1. Incumbents ejected from 'dead' livings by royal grants to other ministers. Full details in *Cal. Rev.* and *46th Report*.

Incumbents in 'dead' livings	New Nominee	Date of presentation
Wm. Durham	Jos. Crowther	16.6.60
Wm. Eastman	Thos. Earnely	16.6
Robt. Taylor	Thos. Tyrer	18.6
J. St. Nicholas	Thos. Pestell	21.6
Thos. Osmonton	Alex. Burnett	26.6
Hen. Holcroft	Nath. Willys	29.6
Gabriel Price	Matthew Day	3.7
Jos. Hemmings	Edw. Wilsford	4.7
J. Weld	Ralph Blakiston	6.7
Miles Burkit	J. Anthill	6.7
Thos. Gardiner	J. Bassett	13.7
Geo. Farroll	Thos. Blanchard	19.7
Ant. Stephens	Geo. Morley	19.7
Vincent Lawson	Rd. Taylor	21.7
J. Flower	Robt. Hill	23.7
Edw. Rolt	Ant. Huish	25.7
Dan. Latham	J. Michaelson	25.7
J. Manship	Giles Thornborough	25.7
J. Doddridge	Rd. Peacock	27.7
Rd. Lawrence	Robt. Thexton	27.7
Wm. Marshall	Hugh Barrow	30.7
Hen. Pierce	Sam. Bird	30.7
J. James	Thos. White	30.7
Thos. Kentish (Hants.)	Thomas Bp. of Galloway	2.8
Ralph Ward	Robt. Bonner	3.8
Ben. Way	Thos. Cartwright	7.8
Gabriel Sangar	Nath. Hardy	11.8
Paul Frewen	Rd. Wilkinson	13.8
J. Spilsbury	J. Wolley	13.8
J. Stanley	Ant. Harwood	16.8

Thos. Kentish (Co. Durham)	Tim. Tulley	16.8
Tobias Tidcombe	Robt. Basket	20.8
J. Cromwell	Hen. Brunsell	20.8
Jas. Illingsworth	Thos. Mallory	20.8
Wm. Tray	Ant. Robinson	21.8
Wm. Horner	Moses Lee	22.8
Ralph Bote	Wm. Jackson	23.8
Wm. Pearse	Nich. Salter	24.8
Peter Ince	Rd. Osgood	25.8
Thos. Archer	J. Hampson	28.8
J. Gunter	Peter Samwayes	28.8
Leon. Hayne	Hen. Warren	28.8

Part 2. Incumbents confirmed in their livings by the king in 1660 but ejected in 1662. (Full details in *46th Report* and *Cal. Rev.*)

Isaac Ambrose; Samuel Annesley; Nathaniel Baxter; Stephen Baxter; Robert Beake; Thomas Bosse; Joshua Bowden; Edward Buckler; William Cooper; Samuel Cradock; Thomas Crane; Robert Eaton; James Farren; Henry Featly; William Hickocks; John James; John Knightsbridge; Thomas Masters; John Mortimer; John Overed; Clement Ray; John Ridge; Alexander Robinson; Samuel Shaw; James Shirley; Thomas Spademan; John Swan; Samuel Tomlyns; Thomas Trescot; Thomas Warren; Humphrey Weaver; John Weeks; Thomas Whately.

(Incumbents who received a royal presentation *after* 9.9.60 only to be ejected in 1662 included John Noseworthy, Edmund Petit, and Francis Soreton.)

Part 3. Sequestered clergy given a new living by the king in 1660. (Full details in *Walk. Rev.* and *46th Report.*)

Charles Anthony; Charles Appleford; Richard Atkinson; Richard Ball; Clement Barksdale; Robert Basket; Samuel Bird; Robert Bonner; Guy Carleton; Gilbert Coles; Christopher Comyn; Henry Deane; John Doughtie; Richard Dukeson; Peter du Moulin (junior); William Evans (possibly two livings, or two men of the same name); Thomas Fawcett; Edward Greathead; Anthony Harwood; George Lawson; Thomas Mallory; Richard Meredith; John Michaelson; George Morley; Hugh Nash; Robert Newlin; Amos Oxley; Richard Peacock; Thomas Pestell; William Pindar; James Reade; John Reading; Edmund Ryves; Anthony Robinson; Peter Samwayes; Samuel Smith; Thomas Stevens; Thomas Tirwhitte; William

Verney; John Weekes; Henry Wilson; and Edward Wolley.

There are nine cases, in addition to the above, where it is difficult to prove a link between the sufferer and the royal nominee of 1660: Thomas Baker; William Baker; Ralph Blakiston; Matthew Day; Thomas Jackson; John Kind; Edward Lawson; Richard Osgood and Richard Taylor.

APPENDIX 4

PETITIONS TO THE KING FOR CATHEDRAL PREFERMENT AND ARCHDEACONRIES MAY TO SEPTEMBER 1660

The sources are P.R.O., *S.P.* 29/1–29/17. Those marked with an asterisk were successful in obtaining a grant for the post they sought by September 1660 (*46th Report*).

Pet. du Moulin* *S.P.* 29/1, f.133; Thos. Wood* 29/4, f.40; Dan. Brevint* 29/4, f.40; Rd. Marsh* 29/6, f.1; Geo. Hall* ibid. f.2; Wm. Jones* f.3; Edw. Cotton** ff.4,5; Fran. Fulwood* f.6; Rd. Meredith* f.7; Rd. Mervyn* f.8; Thos. Clutterbuck* f.10; Pet. Hardres* f.13; J. Castilion* f.14; Wm. Barker* f.15; J. Aucher* f.16; Sam. Wilkinson f.17; Geo. Buchanan* f.18; Lanc. Lowther f.19; Arthur Savage* f.20; Thos. Wood* f.21; Hen. Langley f.22; Rd. Allestree* f.23; Hen. Wilkinson f.24; J. Dolben* f.25; J. Doughtie* f.27; Geo. Beaumont* f.29; Paul Knell f.30; J. Sudbury* f.28; J. Heaver f.31; Geo. Hall* f.32; Ralph Brideoake* f.33; Wm. Dowdeswell* f.34; Fran. Hall f.35; J. Neale* 29/7, f.37; Math. Griffith ibid. ff. 38–9; Humph. Lloyd f.44; Geo Welsted f.47; J. Middleton* f.48; Ant. Sparrow* f.49; Giles Thorne* f.66; Jas. Smith** ff.68–9; Geo. Roberts* f.89; Thos. Mallory* f.104; Wm. Thornborough* f.137; J. Cope* 29/8, f.9; Byrom Eaton ibid. f.40; J. Fell* f.80; Thos. Potter* f.107; Wm. Thomas* 29/9, f.191; Kenelm Manwaring* 29/10, f.19; Rd. Beresford* ibid. f.70; Math. Griffith f.76; Dan. Vivian* 29/11, f.67; Tob. Womock 29/12, f.1; Edw. Rainbow (**after* Sept.) ibid. f.2; Byrom Eaton f.3; Dav. Lloyd* f.4; Geo. Benson* f.5; Francis Davis* f.6; J. Carter(*) f.7; J. Sherman f.8; Laur. Womock f.9; Humph. Lloyd f.10; Thos. Tirwhitte f.11; Thos. Hyde(*) f.12; Wm. Owen* f.13; J. Pulleyn* f.18; Rd. Towgood* f.26; Rd. Standfast* f.27; Wm. Kempe(*) f.28; Hen. Dutton f.29; Jos. Barker f.30; J. Dashfield* f.31; Edw. Wilsford f.32; Chas. Gibbs f.33; J. Gough f.34; Elias Smith f.35; Jas. Harwood f.36; Sam. Cotton* f.37; J. Allington(*) f.38; Young Dixie f.39; Nath. Ward* f.40; Wm. Geree* f.41; Hen. Newcome(*) f.42; Geo. Davenport f.43; Josh. Stopford* f.44; J. Cooth f.45; Wm. Clarke* f.46; Hen. Sutton f.48; Thos. Twitty f.49; Thos. King f.50; Nath. Ward f.51; Rd. Hill f.52; Hen. Bridgeman* f.53; Marm. Cooke* f.54; Mountjoy Cradock f.55; Sam. Cryer(*) f.56; Humph. Lloyd* f.57; Robt. Mossom* f.58; Tob. Swinden* f.59; Rd. Wright f.60; Jas. Atkin f.61; Wm. Coke 29/14, f.5; J. Breton* ibid. f.12; J. Gurgany f.61; Clem. Breton(*) 29/17, f.2.

APPENDIX 5

THE BACKGROUNDS OF SOME OF THE CATHEDRAL CLERGY APPOINTED BY THE KING IN 1660

Part 1—Those presented to cathedral benefices and archdeaconries who do not appear as sufferers in *Walker Revised*.

Source for presentations, *C.* 66/2916–2919 (printed in *46th Report*).

J. Adamson; Edw. Aldey; Chas. Asfordby; Geo. Beaumont; Gilb. Bennett; Edw. Benson; Robt. Bidwell; Thos. Birch; Walt. Blandford; Robt. Boning; Wm. Brabourne; Hen. Bradshaw; Sam. Brunsell; Hen. Brunsell; Wm. Chamberlain; Marm. Cooke; Edw. Cotton; Ben. Crump; J. Dashfield; Edw. Davies; Fran. Davies; Edw. Dixe; Mich. Evans; Walt. Evans; Thos. Fothergill; Fran. Fulwood; Wm. Geree; Geo. Glen; Hen. Greswold; Mart. Harbery; Vere Harcourt; Thos. Hareward; J. Harris; Robt. Harris; Rd. Heylin; Wm. Holder; Thos. Holland; Walt. Jones; Geo. Kent; Fran. Leake; Ste. Lewies; Edw. Lewis; Dav. Lloyd; Thos. Lloyd; Wm. Lloyd; Tim. Long; J. Lydall; J. Manton; Maur. Matthewes; Rd. Newborough; J. Owen; Thos. Owen; Robt. Pare; Hen. Pight; Robt. Powell; Thos. Powell; Edw. Reynolds; Walt. Rogers; Jas. Smith; Thos. Spratt; Chris. Stone; Josh. Stopford; Tob. Swinden; Rd. Swinglehurst; Tim. Tully; Edw. Thorold; Robt. Townshend; Edw. Vaughan; Nath. Ward; Rd. Waring; Robt. Wickham; J. Wilkins.

(72)

Part 2—Sequestered clergy who had conformed during the Interregnum before being presented to a cathedral benefice by the king in 1660.

Sources: *Walk. Rev.* and *46th Report.*

Parish livings: Wm. Belke; Geo. Buchanan; J. Codd?; Fran. Coke; Ralph Cooke; Wm. Creed; Pet. du Moulin; Ant. Elcock; J. Fairclough; Giles Goldsborough; Thos. Good; Geo. Hall; Pet. Hardres; Rd. Harrison; Robt. Hitch; Thos. Hyde; Edw. Jones; Wm. Kempe; Jas. Lake; Jas. Lamb; Jas. Lister; J. Mainwaring; Thos. Mallory; Jasp. Mayne; Rd. Meredith; Rd. Mervyn; Robt. Morgan; Thos. Newcomen; Barn. Oley; J. Oliver; Wm. Paul; J. Pearson; J. Reading; Laur. Sedon; Raphael Throckmorton; Rd. Towgood; Fran. Walsall; Louis West; Dan. Wicherley; Laur. Womock.
University: Paul Hood; Rd. Love; Edw. Pocock; Dan. Vivian.
Teaching: Rd. Busby; Robt. Mossom; Phil. Tennison.

(47)

APPENDIX 6

THE CHRONOLOGY OF EPISCOPAL APPOINTMENTS 1660.

Bishop	Diocese	Date of Nomination	Date of Election	Date of Confirmation	Date of Consecration
Brian Duppa	Winchester	28 Aug.[1]	10 Sept.[2]	4 Oct.[3]	—
William Juxon	Canterbury	2 Sept.	3/13 Sept.	20 Sept.	—
Accepted Frewen	York	2/10 Sept.	22 Sept.	4 Oct.	—
George Morley	Worcester	20 Sept.	9 Oct.	23 Oct.	28 Oct.[4]
Humfrey Henchman	Salisbury	20 Sept.	4 Oct.	23 Oct.	28 Oct.
Gilbert Sheldon	London	21 Sept.	9 Oct.	23 Oct.	28 Oct.
George Griffith	St. Asaph	22 Sept.	17 Oct.	24 Oct?	28 Oct.
Edward Reynolds	Norwich	30 Sept.	28 Nov.		6 Jan. 1661.
Robert Sanderson	Lincoln	3 Oct.	17 Oct.	23 Oct.	28 Oct. 1660
Brian Walton	Chester	5 Oct.			2 Dec.
John Cosin	Durham	5 Oct.			2 Dec.
Richard Sterne	Carlisle	7 Oct.			2 Dec.
Hugh Lloyd	Llandaff	9 Oct.	16/17 Oct.	17 Nov.	2 Dec.
William Lucy	St. David's	15 Oct.	11 Oct?	17 Nov.	2 Dec.
John Gauden	Exeter	20 Oct.	3 Nov.	17 Nov.	2 Dec.
Benjamin Laney	Peterborough	7 Nov.	20 Nov.		2 Dec.

Gilbert Ironside	Bristol	19 Nov.	14 Dec.	24 Dec.	6 Jan. 1661
William Nicholson	Gloucester	29 Nov.	26 Nov?		6 Jan. 1661
Nicholas Monck	Hereford	29 Nov.	1 Dec.	21/24 Dec.	6 Jan. 1661

[1] All dates of nomination are taken from the letters missive (of which there are two copies for York bearing different dates): P.R.O., *S.O.* 1/4, pp. 117, 125–8, 139, 141, 143.

[2] Respectively: Kennett, *Register*, p. 253; *S.P.* 29/14, f.11, and Kennett, *Register*, p. 252; ibid., pp. 270; 273; 272; *Handbook of British Chronology*, ed. F. M. Powicke and E. B. Fryde (London, 1961), p. 241; Le Neve, *Fasti*, i, 76; *Handbook of British Chronology*, p. 244; Le Neve, *Fasti*, ii, 26; Kennett, *Register*, pp. 315–16 and Le Neve, *Fasti*, ii, 254; Kennett, *Register*, pp. 276 (an error perhaps for 11 November); 304; 306; 328; *Handbook of British Chronology*, p. 228; Kennett, *Register*, p. 322.

[3] Respectively: Kennett, *Register*, pp. 272; 252; 270; 273; 288; 288; Le Neve, *Fasti*, i, 76; Kennett, *Register*, pp. 288; 316; 276; 304; 328; Le Neve, *Fasti*, i, 472 and Kennett, *Register*, p. 322.

[4] W. Stubbs, *Registrum Sacrum Anglicanum* (Oxford, 1897) pp. 121–2.

APPENDIX 7

EPISCOPAL VISITATION ARTICLES OF 1662 AND 1663.

These are the first sets of articles that were printed after the Restoration (see above, pp. 135–8).

Articles of Visitation and Inquiry . . . within the diocese of Bath and Wells (London, 1662)

Articles to be Ministered, Enquired of, and Answered in the first Episcopal Visitation of the Lord Bishop of Bristol (London, 1662)

Articles to be enquired of in the Metropolitical Visitation of the . . . Lord Arch-Bishop of Canterbury (London, 1663)

Articles to be Enquired of in the Diocese of Carlisle in the Visitation of the . . . Lord Bishop of Carlisle (London, 1663)

Articles of Visitation and Enquiry . . . within the Diocess of Chichester (London, 1662)

Articles of Inquiry . . . within the Diocess of Durham (London, 1662)

Articles of Enquiry . . . for the Diocese of Ely (London, 1662)

Articles of Visitation and Enquiry . . . within the Diocese of Exeter (London, 1662)

Articles of Visitation and Enquiry . . . within the Diocesse of Gloucester (London, 1662)

Articles of Visitation and Enquiry . . . within the Diocesse of Hereford (London, 1662)

Articles of Visitation and Enquiry . . . within the Diocesse of Landaffe (London, 1662)

Articles of Inquiry . . . within the Diocesse of Lichfield and Coventry (London, 1662)

Articles of Visitation and Enquiry . . . within the Diocess of Lincoln (London, 1662)

Articles to be Enquired of in the Diocesse of Norwich (London, 1662)

Articles of Visitation and Enquiry . . . within the Diocess of Oxon (London, 1662)

Articles of Visitation and Enquiry . . . within the Diocess of Peterborough (London, 1662)

Articles of Visitation and Enquiry . . . within the Diocese of Saint Asaph (London, 1662)

Articles of Visitation and Enquiry . . . within the Diocese of Saint

David (London, 1662)
Articles to be Enquired of in the Diocese of Salisbury (London, 1662)
Articles of Visitation and Enquiry . . . within the Diocese of Winchester (London, 1662)
Articles of Visitation and Enquiry . . . within the Diocese of Worcester (London, 1662)

INDEX